POPES

Antipopes and doubtful popes are not included.

A bronze medallion showing Pope Julian II (1503-1513).

Pope	Year	Pope	Year
St Peter	42	Donus	676
St Linus	67	St Agatho	678
St Anacletus (Cletus)	76	St Leo II	682
St Clement I	88	St Benedict II	684
St Evaristus	97	John V	685
St Alexander I	105	Conon	686
St Sixtus I	115	St Sergius I	687
St Telesphorus	125	John VI	701
St Hyginus	136	John VII	705
St Pius I	140	Sisinnius	708
St Anicetus	155	Constantine	708
St Soterus	166	St Gregory II	715
St Eleutherius	175	St Gregory III	731
St Victor I	189	St Zachary	741
St Zephyrinus	199	Stephen II (III)*	752
St Callistus I	217	St Paul I	757
St Urban I	222	Stephen III (IV)	768
St Pontian	230	Adrian I	772
St Anterus	235	St Leo III	795
St Fabian	236	Stephen IV (V)	816
St Cornelius	251	St Paschal I	817
St Lucius I	253	Eugene II	824
St Stephen I	254	Valentine	827
St Sixtus II	257	Gregory IV	827
St Dionysius	259	Sergius II	844
St Felix I	269	St Leo IV	847
St Eutychian	275	Benedict III	855
St Caius	283	St Nicholas I	858
St Marcellinus	296	Adrian II	867
St Marcellus I	308	John VIII	872
St Eusebius	309	Marinus I	882
St Melchiades	311	St Adrian III	884
St Sylvester I	314	Stephen V (VI)	885
St Marcus	336	Formosus	891
St Julius	337	Boniface VI	896
Liberius	352	Stephen VI (VII)	896
St Damasus I	366	Romanus	897
St Siricius	384	Theodore II	897
St Anastasius I	399	John IX	898
St Innocent I	401	Benedict IV	900
St Zosimus	417	Leo V	903
St Boniface I	418	Sergius III	904
St Celestine I	422	Anastasius III	911
St Sixtus III	432	Landus	913
St Leo I (the Great)	440	John X	914
St Hilary	461	Leo VI	928
St Simplicius	468	Stephen VII (VIII)	928
St Felix III	483	John XI	931
St Gelasius I	492	Leo VII	936
Anastasius II	496	Stephen VIII (IX)	939
St Symmachus	498	Marinus II	942
St Hormisdas	514	Agapetus II	946
St John I	523	John XII	955
St Felix IV	526	Leo VIII	963
Boniface II	530	Benedict V	964
John II	533	John XIII	965
St Agapetus I	535	Benedict VI	973
St Silverius	536	Benedict VII	974
Vigilius	537	John XIV	983
Pelagius I	556	John XV	985
John III	561	Gregory V	996
Benedict I	575	Sylvester II	999
Pelagius II	579	John XVII	1003
St Gregory I (the Great)	590	John XVIII	1004
Sabinianus	604	Sergius IV	1009
Boniface III	607	Benedict VIII	1012
St Boniface IV	608	John XIX	1024
St Deusdedit (Adeodatus I)	615	Benedict IX	1032
Boniface V	619	Gregory VI	1045
Honorius I	625	Clement II	1046
Severinus	640	Benedict IX†	1047
John IV	640	Damasus II	1048
Theodore I	642	St Leo IX	1049
St Martin I	649	Victor II	1055
St Eugene I	654	Stephen IX (X)	1057
St Vitalian	657	Nicholas II	1059
Adeodatus II	672	Alexander II	1061

Pope	Year	Pope	Year
St Gregory VII	1073	Paul II	1464
Victor III	1086	Sixtus IV	1471
Urban II	1088	Innocent VIII	1484
Paschal II	1099	Alexander VI	1492
Gelasius II	1118	Pius III	1503
Callistus II	1119	Julius II	1503
Honorius II	1124	Leo X	1513
Innocent II	1130	Adrian VI	1522
Celestine II	1143	Clement VII	1523
Lucius II	1144	Paul III	1534
Eugene III	1145	Julius III	1550
Anastasius IV	1153	Marcellus II	1555
Adrian IV	1154	Paul IV	1555
Alexander III	1159	Pius IV	1559
Lucius III	1181	St Pius V	1566
Urban III	1185	Gregory XIII	1572
Gregory VIII	1187	Sixtus V	1585
Clement III	1187	Urban VII	1590
Celestine III	1191	Gregory XIV	1590
Innocent III	1198	Innocent IX	1591
Honorius III	1216	Clement VIII	1592
Gregory IX	1227	Leo XI	1605
Celestine IV	1241	Paul V	1605
Innocent IV	1243	Gregory XV	1621
Alexander IV	1254	Urban VIII	1623
Urban IV	1261	Innocent X	1644
Clement IV	1265	Alexander VII	1655
Gregory X	1271	Clement IX	1667
Innocent V	1276	Clement X	1670
Adrian V	1276	Innocent XI	1676
John XXI	1276	Alexander VIII	1689
Nicholas III	1277	Innocent XII	1691
Martin IV	1281	Clement XI	1700
Honorius IV	1285	Innocent XIII	1721
Nicholas IV	1288	Benedict XIII	1724
St Celestine V	1294	Clement XII	1730
Boniface VIII	1294	Benedict XIV	1740
Benedict XI	1303	Clement XIII	1758
Clement V	1305	Clement XIV	1769
John XXII	1316	Pius VI	1775
Benedict XII	1334	Pius VII	1800
Clement VI	1342	Leo XII	1823
Innocent VI	1352	Pius VIII	1829
Urban V	1362	Gregory XVI	1831
Gregory XI	1370	Pius IX	1846
Urban VI	1378	Leo XIII	1878
Boniface IX	1389	St Pius X	1903
Innocent VII	1404	Benedict XV	1914
Gregory XII	1406	Pius XI	1922
Martin V	1417	Pius XII	1939
Eugene IV	1431	John XXIII	1958
Nicholas V	1447	Paul VI	1963
Callistus III	1455	John Paul I**	1978
Pius II	1458	John Paul II	1978

*The original Stephen II died before consecration, and was dropped from the list of popes in 1961; Stephen III became Stephen II and the numbers of the other popes named Stephen were also moved up.
**John Paul died after only 33 days as Pontiff.

ROMAN EMPERORS

	Reigned		
Augustus (Octavian)	27 BC–AD 14	Claudius II	268–270
Tiberius	14–37	Aurelian	270–275
Caligula (Gaius)	37–41	Tacitus	275–276
Claudius	41–54	Florian	276
Nero	54–68	Probus	276–282
Galba	68–69	Carus	282–283
Otho	69	Numerian	283–284
Vitellius	69	Carinus	283–285
Vespasian	69–79	Diocletian	284–305
Titus	79–81	Maximian	286–305
Domitian	81–96	Constantius I	305–306
Nerva	96–98	Galerius	305–311
Trajan	98–117	Constantine I, the Great	311–337
Hadrian	117–138	Constantine II	337–340
Antoninus Pius	138–161	Constantius II	337–361
Lucius Aurelius Verus	161–169	Constans	337–350
Marcus Aurelius	161–180	Julian, the Apostate	361–363
Commodus	180–192	Jovian	363–364
Pertinax	193	Valentinian I (in the West)	364–375
Didius Julian	193	Valens (in the East)	364–378
Septimius Severus	193–211	Gratian (in the West)	375–383
Caracalla	211–217	Valentinian II (in the West)	375–392
Macrinus	217–218	Theodosius, the Great (in the East, and after 394, in the West)	379–395
Elagabalus	218–222		
Alexander Severus	222–235	Maximus (in the West)	383–388
Maximinus	235–238	Eugenius (in the West)	392–394
Gordian I	238	Arcadius (n the East)	395–408
Gordian II	238	Honorius (in the West)	395–423
Pupienus	238	Constantius III (co-emperor in the West)	421
Balbinus	238		
Gordian III	238–244	Theodosius II (in the East)	408–450
Philip 'the Arab'	244–249	Valentinian III (in the West)	425–455
Decius	249–251	Marcian (in the East)	450–457
Gallus	251–253	Petronius (in the West)	455
Aemilian	253	Avitus (in the West)	455–456
Valerian	253–259	Majorian (in the West)	457–461
Gallienus	259–268	Leo I (in the East)	457–474

A cameo portrait of the first Roman Emperor Augustus Caesar (27BC-AD14).

Severus (in the West)	461–465
Anthemius (in the West)	467–472
Olybrius (in the West)	472
Glycerius (in the West)	473
Julius Nepos (in the West)	473–475
Leo II (in the East)	473–474
Zeno (in the East)	474–491
Romulus Augustulus (in the West)	475–476

HOLY ROMAN EMPERORS

FRANKISH KINGS AND EMPERORS (CAROLINGIAN)

Charlemagne	800–814
Louis I, the Pious	814–840
Lothair I	840–855
Louis II	855–875
Charles II, the Bald	875–877
Throne vacant	877–881
Charles III, the Fat	881–887
Throne vacant	887–891
Guido of Spoleto	891–894

The Holy Roman Emperor Charles V (1519-1558) painted by Titian (1477-1576).

Lambert of Spoleto (co-emperor)	892–898
Arnulf (rival)	896–901
Louis III of Provence	901–905
Berengar	905–924
Conrad I of Franconia (rival)	911–918

SAXON KINGS AND EMPERORS

Henry I, the Fowler	918–936
Otto I, the Great	936–973
Otto II	973–983
Otto III	983–1002
Henry II, the Saint	1002–1024

FRANCONIAN EMPERORS (SALIAN)

Conrad II, the Salian	1024–1039
Henry III, the Black	1039–1056
Henry IV	1056–1106
Rudolf of Swabia (rival)	1077–1080
Hermann of Luxembourg (rival)	1081–1093
Conrad of Franconia (rival)	1093–1101
Henry V	1106–1125
Lothair II	1125–1137

HOHENSTAUFEN KINGS AND EMPERORS

Conrad III	1138–1152
Frederick Barbarossa	1152–1190
Henry VI	1190–1197
Otto IV	1198–1215
Philip of Swabia (rival)	1198–1208
Frederick II	1215–1250
Henry Raspe (rival)	1246–1247
William of Holland (rival)	1247–1256
Conrad IV	1250–1254
The Great Interregnum	1254–1273

RULERS FROM DIFFERENT HOUSES

Richard of Cornwall (rival)	1257–1272
Alfonso X of Castile (rival)	1257–1273
Rudolf I, Habsburg	1273–1291
Adolf I of Nassau	1292–1298
Albert I, Habsburg	1298–1308
Henry VII, Luxembourg	1308–1313
Louis IV of Bavaria	1314–1347
Frederick of Habsburg (co-regent)	1314–1325
Charles IV, Luxembourg	1347–1378
Wenceslas of Bohemia	1378–1400
Frederick III of Brunswick	1400
Rupert of the Palatinate	1400–1410
Sigismund, Luxembourg	1410–1437

HABSBURG EMPERORS

Albert II	1438–1439
Frederick III	1440–1493
Maximilian I	1493–1519
Charles V	1519–1558
Ferdinand I	1558–1564
Maximilian II	1564–1576
Rudolf II	1576–1612
Matthias	1612–1619
Ferdinand II	1619–1637
Ferdinand III	1637–1657
Leopold I	1658–1705
Joseph I	1705–1711
Charles VI	1711–1740
Charles VII of Bavaria	1742–1745

HABSBURG-LORRAINE EMPERORS

Francis I of Lorraine	1745–1765
Joseph II	1765–1790
Leopold II	1790–1792
Francis II	1792–1806

This leaping winged ibex, made from partly gilded silver, originally
formed the handle of a bowl. Persian 4th century BC.

DATELINES
OF
WORLD HISTORY

WARWICK PRESS

Above: Staircase leading up to the great columned audience hall, or *adapana*, of King Darius I of Persia (558-486 BC) at Persepolis. The sculptured reliefs show the famous 'immortals', the supreme royal guard of 10,000 foot soldiers.

Far right, top: One of the first flights in a hot air balloon over the court of Versailles, France in 1783. By the middle of the 19th century, balloons were becoming widely used in battle. They helped to direct the fire of artillery, to spot enemy troop movements, and to organize the positioning of troops.

Far right, bottom: Leonardo da Vinci's self-portrait of 1512. It is the only known authentic likeness of the artist. Leonardo was known as 'the complete man' of the Renaissance because of his skill in the fields of science, architecture, engineering, mathematics and, of course, painting.

Editorial

Author
Guy Arnold

Consultant
Geoffrey Trease, FRSL

Editor
Adrian Sington

Designer
Ben White

ACKNOWLEDGEMENTS
Front cover top left French Government Tourist Office, top right M. Holford, bottom left Picturepoint Ltd, bottom centre Science Museum, bottom right United Nations; title page Louvre, Paris; 6 ZEFA; 7 top Mansell Collection, bottom SCALA, Florence; 8 M. Holford; 9 top left Science Museum, top right Mansell Collection, bottom Press Association; 13 top J. Vertut, bottom British Museum; 14 top R. Harding, bottom left R. Sheridan; 15 top Louvre, Paris, bottom W. MacQuitty; 16 left British Museum, right National Palace Museum, Taiwan; 17 top R. Harding, bottom S. Halliday; 18 top ZEFA; 19 bottom M. Holford; 21 British Museum; 22 British Museum; 23 bottom London Museum; 25 top S. Halliday, bottom SCALA, Florence; 26 top S. Halliday; 28 left M. Holford, right R. Sheridan; 29 top Giraudon, Paris, bottom S. Halliday; 30 Mansell Collection; 31 S. Halliday; 32 top Interfoto MTI, Budapest, bottom Universitets Oldsaksamling; 35 top Society for Anglo-Chinese Understanding, centre Mary Evans Picture Library, bottom Mansell Collection; 36 ZEFA; 37 D. Williamson; 38 M. Holford; 39 top SCALA, Florence, bottom British Museum; 40 A. Hutchison; 41 top Mansell Collection, bottom S. Halliday; 42 SCALA, Florence; 43 BBC Hulton Picture Library; 44 left Mary Evans Picture Library, right Bibliotheque Nationale; 45 bottom R. Harding; 46 top Science Museum, bottom Mary Evans Picture Library; 51 M. Holford; 52 British Museum; 53 Mansell Collection; 54 Musée de la Ville de Strasbourg; 58 top CFL-Giraudon, bottom Colour Library International; 59 National Portrait Gallery; 60 Nationalmuseum, Stockholm; 61 top Mary Evans Picture Library, bottom Giraudon, Paris; 63 National Portrait Gallery; 64 top Mansell Collection, bottom R. Hunt Library; 65 Stanley Gibbons; 68 top BBC Hulton Picture Library, bottom India Office Library/R. B. Fleming; 70 top Mansell Collection; 71 SCALA, Florence; 73 BBC Hulton Picture Library; 74 Mansell Collection; 75 R. Hunt Library; 77 Keystone Press Agency; 78 top R. Harding, bottom Atomic Energy Authority; 81 Ferranti Ltd; 82 bottom Syndication International; 83 top B.P., bottom Keystone Press Agency; 86 top S. Halliday, centre S. Halliday, bottom Mansell Collection; 87 left India Office Library, top right National Portrait Gallery, bottom right Mansell Collection; 88 Mansell Collection; 89 top BBC Hulton Picture Library, bottom left Mansell Collection, bottom right National Portrait Gallery; 90 BBC Hulton Picture Library; 91 top left E.E.C., top right United Nations; endpapers (front) left British Museum, top right British Museum, bottom SCALA, Florence; endpapers (back) top left Mansell Collection, top right National Portrait Gallery, centre National Portrait Gallery, bottom left Mary Evans Picture Library, bottom centre National Portrait Gallery, bottom right Giraudon Paris.

Published 1983 by Warwick Press,
387 Park Avenue South, New York, New York 10016

First published in Great Britain by
Kingfisher Books Limited 1983

Copyright © 1983 Kingfisher Books Ltd.

LIBRARY OF CONGRESS CATALOGING IN PUBLICATION DATA

Arnold, Guy
    Datelines of world history.

    Includes index.
    Summary: Presents a history of the world from
40,000 B.C. to the present.
    1. World history — Juvenile literature. (1. World
history) I. Trease, Geoffrey. II. Title.
D21.A76 1983   909   83–1085
ISBN 0–531–09212–7

Printed in Italy by Vallardi Industrie Grafiche, Milan

Contents

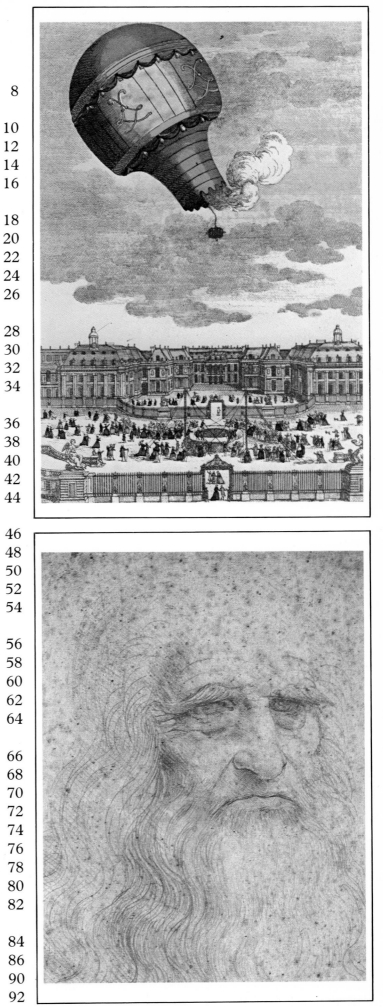

Looking at the Past

English students learn that Dr Johnson produced the first English dictionary in 1755. Not many are also taught that the Chinese produced their first dictionary 1100 years before Christ. What was seen as a great achievement by Dr Johnson's contemporaries had been done nearly three thousand years earlier in another very different civilization. History helps us make comparisons like these.

In part history is a record of facts. Too often, unfortunately, these are wars and conquests. But they are also man's advances – the beginning of agriculture, the first machines, new developments in science.

There are different theories about what aspects of history are most important. Some historians emphasize the rôle played by people and suggest that history is especially about great men such as Alexander or Lenin or Churchill. Others suggest that the really important events in history are new ideas and what the ordinary people – the masses – do. It is important to find a balance between these views.

History poses many questions for students. Why was there a revolution in France in the 18th century but not in Britain? Europe, including Britain, was horrified in 1793 when the French guillotined Louis XVI – yet 150 years earlier the English beheaded Charles I. What was the difference? History provides us with a record of changing attitudes.

Biased History
Much of history is written not impartially but from the point of view of a particular country. All accounts of the past, therefore, have to be examined with care. The question must be asked: who was writing and whose side did the historian favour, because historians like anyone else can be prejudiced by the attitude of their country.

Monks in medieval Europe were almost the only people educated enough to record history. They nearly always described the Roman Emperor Nero as a monster. This was because he had persecuted Christians during his reign. As a result they never found anything good to say about him. They were biased writers. Any enemy of the Church was unlikely to receive an impartial report.

In 1982 there was a war between Britain and Argentina over the Falkland Islands. The British won the war. The British gave their reasons for defending the islands and the Argentinians gave theirs for invading them. In time each country will write its own historical account of the war. These accounts are likely to be very different from each other and in 500 years,time when perhaps a Nigerian reads them he may find it very difficult to be sure which account is the right one or even if they are both accounts of the same event.

The perspectives of history change. At the end of the 19th century there occurred what we call the 'Scramble for Africa' when the European powers carved up the African continent into colonies. The colonists adopted superior attitudes (what we now describe as racist) and assumed they *were* superior. One result was that they wrote histories of Africa as though little of importance had occurred on the continent before their arrival. In the 1950s and 1960s the African colonies became independent and since then their own historians have begun to rewrite their histories. This is not a matter of changing facts but rather of altering emphasis. What may have seemed important to a British colonial official is not of much interest to an African in the 1980s.

Sources
Another problem of history concerns sources. Where does the historian look to find his information? If an historian is writing in Britain or France most of the material available to him is likely also to be British or French and this will

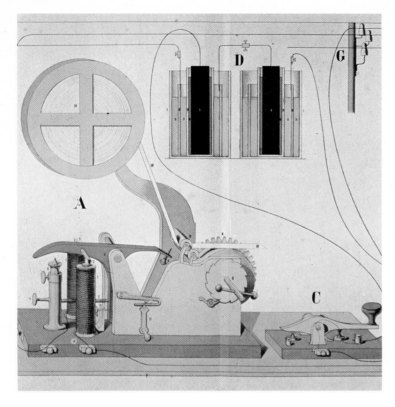

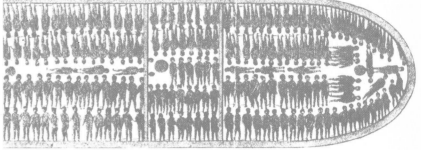

Far left: Stonehenge, standing on a lonely plain in Wiltshire, England, is one of the world's finest prehistoric monuments. It can be dated by a process known as radiocarbon dating. The process shows that the oldest part was built in about 2200 BC. But the age of a pick made from a deer antler, found buried in the ruins, shows that the high arches were erected about 400 years later.

Left: Diagram of an electric telegraph first used in 1838. In the 60 years following its invention, communication developed until news and information could be sent around the world in seconds.

Below: Plan of a slave ship that travelled from Africa to America in the early 19th century.

unbalance the events of that time. There will be a great deal of information about 10th century Europe but not very much about 10th century Japan. If, on the other hand, an historian is Chinese then he will start by assuming that China is the most important country in the world and he will probably not write very much about medieval England. So the way history is written will depend upon where the historian lives.

1500 or 1980?
Time is of great importance when analysing history. In the last 50 years momentous changes have occurred – the Second World War, the Cold War, the end of empires, the emergence of nearly 100 new states and the first man on the moon. It is an exciting period in which to live but is it more

exciting than living in 1500? In 1500, men would have said changes then taking place were just as momentous. In Europe a flood of new ideas in what we call the Renaissance made men alter their concepts about the world in which they lived. In turn this led to the religious upheavals in Europe which we call the Reformation. A few years later two mighty empires in South America – those of the Aztecs and Incas – were to collapse before the European intruders. In Africa the great Songhay empire was at the height of its power. In Asia, Babar was on his throne and about to conquer vast areas in northern India to establish the Mughal empire.

Changing History
It goes without saying that changes in the world's development have been a matter of chance. The Romans were magnificent engineers. They were capable of building aqueducts with an incline so gradual that they could maintain a uniform level of drop over many miles. With their expertise they came very close to discovering the secret of making steel. If they had, an industrial revolution would have occurred 1700 years before it in fact took place. Had that happened our world would have developed in a totally different way.

History, then, is a record not just of events, but more important, of ideas and changing attitudes. The ancient world took slavery as a matter of course – it existed everywhere. Today we regard slavery as an infringement of man's rights and it has been almost completely eradicated. So, if we can understand how people thought in the past and why they acted in the way they did, then perhaps we can learn from them. That will help us to see more clearly what we are doing today – and why.

Three great men: President Roosevelt of the USA met prime minister Winston Churchill of Britain and the Russian dictator Joseph Stalin at Yalta to discuss Allied plans for ending World War II.

9

40,000
BC

MOVEMENT

40,000–29,000 Cro-Magnon people move into Europe from Asia.
30,000–20,000 Humans appear in Australia.
30,000–10,000 Early (Neanderthal) humans replaced by hunters in Africa.
28,000 *Homo sapiens* cross land bridge from Asia to North America.
16,000–10,000 Hunters roam southern Europe.
10,000 Hunters reach tip of South America and south Africa.

6000 First settlements in Crete.

Cro-Magnon man, 40,000 BC.

2300 Semites from Arabia migrate to Mesopotamia to found Assyrian and Babylonian empires.
2200 Greeks arrive in Crete.
2150 Aryans invade Indus Valley.
2100 Abraham migrates from Ur.
2000 Beginnings of great migrations east and south from west Africa. Hittites move into Anatolia (modern Turkey).
1300 Medes and Persians move into Iran.
1200 Devastation through Asia Minor, Near East, Greek world by Sea People.
1100–1050 Dorian invasions of Greece.

500
BC

500 Bantu peoples spreading in east Africa.

TECHNOLOGY

Two Stone Age hunting weapons, 25,000 BC.

10,000 Development of hunting weapons at the end of the Ice Age.
8000 Development of agriculture– farming and settled villages in eastern Anatolia.
7000 Metal working in Anatolia. Walled settlement at Jericho.
6000 Cattle raising in Anatolia. Early trade in obsidian and flint. Çatal Hüyük – one of first towns.
6000–5000 Neolithic period begins.
5000 Village farm communities along Hwang-ho River in China.
5000–2000 Farming spreads south in Africa.
4500 Real metal work begins – heating and pouring metal.
4000 Wheel in Mesopotamia. Use of potter's wheel.
Yang-shao rice farming culture in China.

3500 Copper tools in Thailand.

3100 Early use of bronze in Egypt and Sumer.

3000 Cities and temples in Sumer and Egypt – use of bricks for building. Windmill culture in Britain. Agriculture in Téhuacan Valley, Mexico.
3000–2000 Bronze Age in Anatolia. Stone villages in Crete.
2500 Bronze tools in Thailand. Metal working reaches Indus Valley.
2000 Bronze age begins in Europe.
1600 Mycenaeans trade through Mediterranean.
1500 Bronze worked in Anyang region of China.
1400 Iron Age reaches western Asia/India.
1200 Horses and chariots used on Sahara trade routes.
1000 Iron tools in Ganges Valley.

Model of an oxcart. Indus Valley, 2000 BC.

CULTURE

25,000 Hunters make clay models.
20,000 Early cave paintings in France and Spain.

6000–5000 African rock paintings.

Death mask of Tutankhamun, c 1350 BC.

4236 First date in Egyptian calendar.
3760 First date in Jewish calendar.
3372 First date in Mayan calendar.

3100 Sumerians devise first known system of writing.
3000 First pottery in Mexico.
2780 First pyramid in Egypt.
2200 Linear (A) Minoan writing. Linear (B) Greek writing.

1379 Amenhotep inaugurates sun worship in Egypt.
1300 Construction of temples at Abu Simbel.
1200–1028 Twelve tribes adopt Yahweh worship in Israel.
1100 First Chinese dictionary.
1000 Phoenicians in Tyre employ full alphabet.
Rig Vega (religious text) compiled in India.
800 Homeric poems, *Iliad* and *Odyssey*, take their final shape.
776 First Olympic Games.
621 Dracon – laws for Athens.
594 Solon – new laws for Athens.
580 Nebuchadnezzar constructs the Hanging Gardens of Babylon.
563 Birth of Siddhartha Gautama (The Buddha).
551 Birth of Kung Fu-tzu (Confucius).
508 Cleisthenes introduces democracy in Athens.

CIVILIZATIONS   the coloured bands represent the time span and rise and fall of each empire where appropriate

	3000 BC
EGYPT 3000-500	
SUMER and AKKAD 2850-1900	
CHINA 2697-500 +	2500 BC
INDIA 2500-500 +	
CRETE (MINOAN) 2500-1400	
HITTITE EMPIRE 2000-1200	2000 BC
ASSYRIA 1920-612	
BABYLONIA 1900-538	
MYCENAE 1900-1100	1500 BC
PHOENICIA 1500-500	
GREECE 1100-500 +	
MEDES 835-550	1000 BC
CARTHAGE 814-500 +	
ROME 753-500 +	
PERSIA 559-500 +	500 BC

11

THE FERTILE CRESCENT	NORTH & EAST	AFRICA & AMERICA

40,000 BC

25,000 Hunters make clay models.

The Fertile Crescent – where farming first developed.

8000 Eastern Anatolia (Turkey): Farming and settled villages. Domestication of sheep and cattle.
7000 Anatolia: Metal working in copper, silver, gold. Jericho (Israel): Walled settlements.
6000 Anatolia: Cattle raising; trade in obsidian and flint with Sicily and Greece.
6000–5000 Çatal Hüyük (Anatolia): one of the world's first towns – perhaps 5000 population.
5000 Sumer: First agricultural settlements in river valleys of Tigris and Euphrates.
4500 Egypt and Sumer: Real metal work begins – heating and pouring metal.
4000–3500 Mesopotamia: Potter's wheel first used. Disastrous floods.
Sumer: First towns – Ur, Eridu.
Egypt: White painted pottery. Ships in Mediterranean.
3100 Egypt: First Egyptian dynasty. First harps and flutes.
Sumer: First known system of writing using 2000 pictographic signs – on clay tablets. Early use of bronze.
3000 Elamite civilization in Iran.
Sumer and Egypt: Cities and temples built. Bricks used for building.
Sumerians grow barley – make bread and beer. Invention of wheel.
Phoenicians settle eastern Mediterranean (Levant).
3000–2400 Troy – the first city state.
3000–2000 Bronze Age in Fertile Crescent (did not begin in Europe until later).
First iron objects made in Mesopotamia 3000–2500.
2850–2450 First dynasty of Ur.
2800–2400 City states of Sumer at their zenith – Sumer the world's richest market. Metal coins replace barley as legal tender.
2800–2175 Old Kingdom in Egypt.
2780 First pyramid in Egypt at Saqqara. Designed by Imhotep.
2772 Egypt introduces a 365-day calendar.
2750 Gilgamesh, legendary king of Uruk, Sumeria.
2700 Cheops rules Egypt and builds the Great Pyramid at Giza.
2500 First Egyptian mummies.
2450–2270 Akkadian empire – the largest to date.
2350 Sargon, the Akkadian emperor, conquers Sumer.
2300 Semites from Arabia migrate to Mesopotamia to found the Assyrian and Babylonian empires.
2230 Fall of Akkadian empire.
2140–2030 Empire of Ur reaches to Persian Gulf – a thriving commerce.
2133 Middle Kingdom in Egypt: the 7th dynasty.
2100 Abraham migrates from Ur.
2030 Decline of Sumer.

2000 BC

16,000–10,000 Hunters roam southern Europe – animal paintings at Lascaux in France and Altamira in Spain.
10,000 End of Ice Age. Hunting weapons develop – disappearance of large mammals.

6000 New Stone Age.
6000–5000 Earliest settlements in Crete.
5000 Sea separates Britain from Europe.
China: Village farming communities along the Yellow River.
4000 China: Yang-shao rice farming culture.
4000–3000 Coloured pottery from Russia reaches China. Cretan ships in Mediterranean.
3500 Thailand: Copper tools.
3100 Early use of bronze.
3000 Wild horses domesticated in the Ukraine.
3000–2000 Stone villages in Crete. Crete trades with Egypt, Levant, Anatolia. Weaving loom in Europe. Lake dwellings in central Europe.

2697 Huang-ti, emperor of China.
Chinese court musician, Linglun, cuts the first bamboo pipe.
Bronze tools in Thailand.
Metal working reaches the Indus Valley – start of major civilization there.
Yak tamed in Tibet.
2500 Early Minoan civilization – the foundation of Knossos, Crete.
First picture of skiing – rock carving, Rodoy, S. Norway.
Metal working spreads through Europe – reaches Britain 2300.
2350 China: Yao dynasty.
2250 Yu-shun, emperor of China.
China: Hsia dynasty.
Japan: Jomon culture.
2200 Greek speakers arrive in Crete: Linear (A) – Minoan writing (still undeciphered); Linear (B) – early Greek writing (deciphered in 1952).
2150 Aryans first invade Indus Valley.
2000 Bronze Age.

30,000 Neanderthal humans still exist in Cyrenaica, N. Africa.
30,000–10,000 Human hunters in Africa.

15,000–10,000 Africa cooler than today – last rainy period in north.
12,000–5000 Formation of main ethnic types in Africa.

8400 First domesticated dog – Idaho (North America).

6000–5000 African rock paintings.
5000 Neolithic Africa: working of polished stone; development of civilizations at Fayoum and Nubia in Nile Valley.
5000–2000 Agriculture spreads southwards in Africa.

3372 First date in Mayan calendar.
3000 Development of agriculture in Tehuacan Valley, Mexico – maize, beans, squash.
Villages and towns on the coast of Peru.
First pottery in Mexico.
3000–2000 Spread of farming in Ethiopia, Chad, Niger.

The Japanese Jomon people in about 2200 BC lived in pit dwellings like these. Villages of 15 or more are found. The huts are sometimes floored with stone.

2000 Beginnings of Bantu migrations from west Africa eastwards and southwards. Cotton is cultivated in Peru.

Sowing the Seeds of Empire

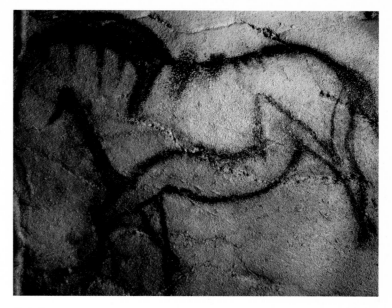

When our early ancestors made the switch from hunting to settled farming they made civilization possible. A hunting family requires many square kilometres of land to sustain it. A farming family needs only a few hectares which can be used again and again. Hunters were always on the move; their settlements lasted until the prey had been exhausted – usually only a few months. The little we know of ancient hunters has been learned from tools or remains of food left at their camps.

There are two kinds of farming – growing crops and keeping animals or *animal husbandry*. While some of our ancestors were discovering how to grow the same crop in the same place each year others, possibly in quite different areas, were learning to domesticate cattle, sheep and goats to become herdsmen instead of hunters. They were often nomads, moving about to fresh pastures and water.

People first learnt to harvest *wild* grains. Then they began to keep some of the grain so that they could replant their seeds the following year. The next stage came when early farmers developed tools – flint sickles to cut grain, primitive millstones to separate the grain from their husks to make flour, the first wooden ploughs to sow the seeds.

Farming became possible when the last Ice Age ended and temperatures all over the world changed. The earliest agriculture probably began in about 10,000 BC, with the growing of millet and rice in south-east Asia. Wild grasses were harvested in Asia Minor as early as 9500 BC. We know

This horse, outlined in black paint at Le Portel in France, skilfully gives an impression of movement. Many of the paintings are difficult to see because they are found deep inside caves. It was thought that a pre-hunt ritual of drawing the animal and then stabbing it after a dangerous climb would bring luck in the hunt.

most about early agriculture along the great rivers of the Near East – known as the 'Fertile Crescent' (see map). By 9000 BC food-growing and sheep-herding were taking place in northern Iraq and both agriculture and pastoralism (herding) had developed around Jericho by 8000 BC. Later it spread north-west, and south to Egypt. By then sheep and cattle had been domesticated. From 8000 BC onwards farming in Mesopotamia (the land between the rivers Tigris and Euphrates) led to the rise of villages, towns and cities.

Perhaps as early as 6000 BC planting and husbandry spread to Europe. Certainly, by 5000 BC the Sumerians had developed an agricultural economy and the beginnings of city life. At Fayoum in the Nile Delta the growing of wheat and flax (used for making linen clothes) made possible the early rise of Egyptian civilization. In Asia, on the other side of the world, the Yang-shao culture, based on rice and millet farming, had emerged in China by 4000 BC.

The development of agriculture meant the pattern of human behaviour altered. People stayed in one place, populations became larger and, most important, they produced more food than their daily needs, something hunters could not do. Only when a community produced a food surplus did it become possible for some people to be specialists – craftsmen, artists, builders or administrators – instead of everyone gathering food or hunting. The next stage was to use food surpluses for barter and so trade developed. Surplus food could be stored against periods of shortage, making communities more secure.

Agriculture made possible the accumulation of possessions, leisure for at least some people, the development of arts and crafts, the building of cities and so the need for governments and laws. It also led to a division of labour and the emergence of different classes. The wealth of settled people then tempted nomads to attack them. This led to the creation of armies for protection. Single cities joined to form states and in turn this led to the birth of empires.

One of the earliest decipherable documents (above) is in cuneiform script from Sumer in about 3100 BC. It is so called (from the Latin for wedge – *cuneus*) because of its wedge-shaped symbols impressed on clay tablets. Cuneiform signs developed from pictograms – pictures of the objects they stood for. As the script developed, the pictograms came to be used as the sound of the word they represented. For example, if used in English the pictogram for pen could be used for pen – writing implement; pen – enclosure; Penn – surname and the syllable pen – hap*pen*. One of the reasons writing developed in this area was the need to record the very complicated trading of goods around the empire at that time.

A sculptured relief of an Egyptian woman of the 18th dynasty showing how Egyptians made themselves up. She has long hair in many plaits or ringlets. Her eyes are outlined with black and her brows are painted. Both sexes outlined their eyes with *kohl* (green or dark grey paste). Scent was also popular. Egyptians made cones of perfumed grease to place on the head. As the grease melted it ran down the face. It was fragrant and cooling.

Egypt – The Great Empire

By 2000 BC a single state of Egypt had already existed for 1100 years. In 3100 BC Menes, king of Upper or southern Egypt, conquered Lower or northern Egypt and founded the 1st dynasty. From the time of Menes until 332 BC when Alexander the Great conquered Egypt there were 30 dynasties and for most of these 3000 years Egypt was either the greatest or one of the greatest powers in the world.

Egyptian history may be conveniently divided into four periods: The Old Kingdom (2800–2175 BC), the period when the pyramids and sphinx were built; The Middle Kingdom (2133–1633 BC), a time of great splendour and achievement; 1633–1567 BC when Egypt fell under foreign rulers and was ruled by the Hyksos (Semites and Hurrians from Palestine, Syria and farther north), they introduced the horse to Egypt; and then the New Kingdom (The Empire) from 1567 to 1085 BC, the period of the 18th to 20th dynasties after the Hyksos had been driven out. At this time the Egyptian empire reached to the River Euphrates in Mesopotamia.

Egyptian kings (pharaohs) were immensely powerful. They established officials and scribes to run their empire,

EGYPTIAN POWER

2133–1633 Middle Kingdom. Egyptian power extends southwards. Trade with Aegean and Levant.

Anubis – god of embalming.

1786–1567 Dynasties 13 to 17: period of the Hyksos invaders who found the 15th dynasty.
1570 Hyksos driven from Egypt. Temple of Amun at Karnak begun.
1567–1087 New Kingdom.
1504–1450 Period of expansion under Thutmosis III – controls Palestine, Syria, and south to Nubia.
1500 Egypt is the world's greatest power.
1479 Battle of Megiddo – Thutmosis III conquers Palestine.
1420–1379 Amenhotep III – the Golden Age of Egypt.
1400 Temples at Luxor under construction.

AEGEAN WORLD

2000 Bronze Age begins in Europe.
Earliest Minoan palace at Knossos.
2000–1450 Minoan Crete dominates Aegean.
1900–1600 Development of Mycenaean culture.

1650–1450 Growth of Mycenaean power centred on Mycenae and Pylos.

A gold jug in the shape of a lion's head, 1500 BC. It was used at Mycenae for pouring offerings of wine to the gods.

1600 Mycenaeans trade throughout the Mediterranean.

THE NEAR EAST

2000 Hittites move into Anatolia. Hittites monopolize the secret of working iron.
2000–1225 Patriarchs of Genesis (Bible).
1950 End of Ur empire.
1925 Hittites conquer Babylon.
1920–1850 Assyrian merchants establish a colony at Cappadocia in Anatolia.
1900–1600 Amorites at Babylon.
1830 Founding of first Babylonian dynasty.
1830–1810 Assyria under Babylonian rule.
1810 King Shamshi-Adad makes Assyria independent.
1800 Accession of Hammurabi of Babylon, author of great Code of Laws.
1800–1750 Babylon conquers the city states of northern and southern Mesopotamia – Hammurabi the Great is 'King of the Four Quarters of the World'.
1750–1500 Old Kingdom of the Hittites.
1700 Expansion of Hittites across Anatolia into Syria.
1600 Hittites take Aleppo.
1590–1245 Kassites from Persia rule Babylon.
1500 Hittite royal succession becomes hereditary, Hittites control all Anatolia.
1430–1200 New Kingdom of Hittites.
1400 Iron Age reaches western Asia.
1390–1350 Suppiluliumas, greatest Hittite king, reconquers Anatolia, subjects northern Syria and makes the Mitanni tribes into Hittite subjects.
1366 Assurubalit I of Assyria – period of expansion.
1300 Medes and Persians move into Iran.
1232 Zenith of Assyrian power.
1232–1116 Decline then new growth of Assyria.
1200 Sea People invade Anatolia – Hittites disappear from history except in Syria.
Period of Judges in Israel.
1170 Growing power of Phoenicians in Levant – Tyre is main city.
1146–1123 Nebuchadnezzar I defeats Elamites but is routed by Assyrians.
1140 Phoenicians found Utica, their first N. African colony.

2000 BC

1500 BC

collect taxes and manage the huge programmes of public works. The period to 1788 was one of classical literature (with the first known fiction), superb architecture and art. Later, under Thutmosis III (1504–1450 BC) Egypt's power reached its greatest extent and included Palestine and Syria. Egyptian traders went as far as Crete in the Mediterranean or south in Africa to Nubia and Punt. Egypt exported gold, grain, building stone, papyrus and manufactured (finished) products. She imported slaves, wood, resins, oils, wine, silver and copper. Egyptian power and wealth were always based upon her rich agriculture. This depended upon the Nile whose floods left behind immensely rich alluvial black soil deposits every year along more than 960 km of the river between Aswan in the far south and the river's delta or estuary. The main crops were wheat, barley, grapes, fruit, vegetables and flax. Cattle, sheep, goats, pigs and poultry as well as donkeys were the main livestock. Most of these were raised in the Delta region.

Ancient Egypt had many gods. At one time each city had its own, Amun of Thebes becoming the most important. Egyptians believed in everlasting life. Pharaohs built immense tombs and pyramids. The records of their lives on earth were left inside these burial chambers. Osiris was the god of death. Perhaps no other empire in history has left behind such awe-inspiring monuments as Egypt.

The Hittites

The Hittites, like the Minoans, came from across the Balkans in about 2000 BC. They settled in Anatolia. For centuries they were the only people in the area who knew the secret of how to make iron, which gave them their great military strength. For a brief period (about 1700 BC) they ruled all the territory from Syria to the Black Sea. In 1590 BC they invaded and conquered Babylon.

The Hittites then went into decline but rose again to even greater power in the 14th century BC, the period of the second Hittite empire. At the battle of Qadesh in 1290 they challenged Egypt, though the battle was a draw. In 1283 BC after fighting on and off for years, Egypt and the Hittites made peace. The Egyptians recognized the Hittites as the only other great power of the time. For a while during this second empire the Hittites ruled the whole of the Fertile Crescent from the Mediterranean to the Persian Gulf. But by then others had discovered the secret of iron and when the great wave of invasions by the Sea People (see Date Chart: 1179) came in about 1200 BC the Hittites disappeared from history.

EGYPTIAN POWER

1379 Amenhotep IV starts sun worship and takes name Akhenaton – other gods abolished.
1361 Pharaoh Tutankhamun – idea of single god abandoned – return to old gods.
1320 Rameses I founds 19th dynasty.
1292–1225 Rameses II (the Great) – restoration of Egypt's Asiatic empire.
1290 Battle of Qadesh against Hittites – both sides claim victory.
1283 Peace between Egypt and the Hittites.
1280 Construction of temples at Abu Simbel.
1250 Moses leads Israelites out of Egypt.
1232 Israelites in Canaan are defeated by Egyptians under Merneptah, son of Rameses II.

1200–1167 Rameses III.
1200–1087 20th dynasty.
1179 Egypt invaded by the Confederation of Sea Peoples – Philistines, Greeks, Sardinians, Sicilians; defeated by Rameses III.
1087–751 High priests of Amun become rulers of Egypt.

AEGEAN WORLD

1500 Minoans still the predominant power but growing competition from Mycenae.
1450–1400 Collapse of Minoan power.

1400 Knossos, the Minoan capital, is destroyed by fire. Mycenaeans occupy Crete.

1300 Arcadians settling in central Peloponnese.

1200 Aegean devastated by Sea People.
1193 Destruction of Troy by Greeks.
1150–1100 Collapse of Mycenaean power.
1100 Dorians invade Greece from north, destroying the Mycenaean citadels.
1050 Dorians reach Peloponnese.
1045 Death of Codron – last king of Athens.
1000 Greeks establish colonies in Aegean.

THE NEAR EAST

Hammurabi, the law maker of Babylon, before Shamash, god of justice. This relief is on top of a stone slab, or *stele*, on which are inscribed 282 laws, c 1800 BC.

1125 Nebuchadnezzar beats back Assyrian invasion of Babylon.
1116 Tiglath-pileser I of Assyria conquers Babylon and controls Asian trade.
1100–900 Aramaic tribes invade Babylonia.
1093–939 Assyria just survives as a power.
1050 Philistines conquer Israel.
1020 Samuel, last of Judges, anoints Saul king of the Israelites. They rebel against Philistines.
1000 Death of Saul at Gilboa. David, king of Judah, and then Israel – makes Jerusalem his capital.

THE FAR EAST

1500 Indus Valley civilization falls to Aryan invasion: destruction of Mohenjo-Daro.
China: First historical period begins under the Shang dynasty; Anyang becomes capital. Bronze is worked in Anyang region.
1500–1000 India: Early period in Ganges Valley.
1400 India: Iron Age.

Chinese bronze chariot mounting, c 400 BC.

1100 First Chinese dictionary.
1027 China: Emperor Wu Wang founds Chou dynasty and establishes feudal system by overthrowing Shang dynasty.
1000 India: Iron tools are made in Ganges Valley. Rig Vega (sacred hymns) compiled.

1500
BC

1000
BC

MEDITERRANEAN

1000–700 Etruscans in upper Italy – race with a unique language and religion.
814 Phoenicians found Carthage.
800 Homer composes the *Iliad* and *Odyssey* at about this time.
776 First Olympic Games in Greece.
760 Greeks found colonies in the Bay of Naples, southern Italy and Sicily.
753 Foundation of Rome.
700–500 Formation of Greek city states.
683 Athens replaces hereditary kings with nine archons chosen annually from the nobles.
650–630 Sparta subjugates Messenia.
650–500 Self-made, one man rule (tyranny) in Greek cities.
621 Dracon provides Athens with its first written laws which are severe.

A Greek soldier, *hoplite*, in his armour, 500 BC.

600–480 Growth and expansion of Carthage.
594 Solon made sole archon of Athens. New laws replace those of Dracon.
539 Greeks defeat the Carthagians in battle.
510 Rebellion at Rome – Tarquinius Superbus, the last king of Rome overthrown.
509 Foundation of Roman republic.
508 Cleisthenes introduces democracy in Athens. Rome survives attack by Lars Porsena of Clusium – Horatio holds the bridge! Treaty between Rome and Carthage gives Latium to Rome and Africa to Carthage.
507 Sparta attempts to restore the aristocracy in Athens – the beginning of a century of rivalry.

GREAT EMPIRES

1000–774 Great period of Tyre under Phoenicians.
935–782 First phase of the Assyrian empire.
900–625 Assyria and Babylon constantly at war – Babylon the weaker power.
782–745 Assyria in decline; growth of Urartu.
748–625 Revival of Assyrian empire.
748–727 Tiglath-pileser III – huge Assyrian expansion to include Israel, Damascus, Babylon.
722 Sargon of Assyria captures Samaria and brings an end to the kingdom of Israel.
722–682 Ethiopian kings rule Egypt.
710 Assyrians destroy Chaldea.
701 Nineveh is made Assyrian capital.
689 After revolt the Assyrians destroy Babylon.
663 Assyrians sack Thebes in Egypt.
626 Nabopolassar (a Chaldean general) seizes throne of Babylon – breaks away from Assyria.
625–593 Cyaxares founds the Median empire.
625–538 Neo-Babylonian empire.
612 Babylonians, Medes and Scythians destroy Nineveh.
609 End of Assyrian empire.

605–561 Nebuchadnezzar II of Babylon defeats Egyptians at Carchemish – brings Judah under Babylon.
586 Nebuchadnezzar retakes Jerusalem, sacks it – people of Judah taken captive to Babylon.
580 Nebuchadnezzar builds the Hanging Gardens of Babylon.
559–530 Cyrus the Great founds the Persian empire.
550 Media incorporated into the Persian empire.
546 Battle of Sardis – Cyrus defeats Croesus of Lydia.
539 Babylon, Phoenicia and Judah come under Persia.
530 Death of Cyrus – the Persian empire includes all Asia Minor, Babylonia, Syria and Palestine.
530–521 Cambyses rules Persian empire.
525 Egypt brought under Persia (until 404BC).
521–486 Darius rules Persian empire.

THE HEBREWS

973–933 Solomon – development of trade, laws, taxes; great buildings – temple, palace and walls at Jerusalem; a magnificent reign.
933 Solomon's kingdom is divided between his sons – Israel (the north) under Jeroboam; and Judah (the south) under Rehoboam.
933–586 Judah.
933–722 Israel.
843 Jehu founds a new dynasty in Israel.
783–748 Jeroboam II – period of prosperity for Israel.
722 Assyria absorbs Israel into its empire.
682 Judah submits to Assyria.

A typical Jewish home in Jerusalem, c 700 BC.

608 Battle of Megiddo – King Josiah of Judah defeated and killed by Necko of Egypt.
597 and 586 Nebuchadnezzar of Babylon (605–561) twice takes Jerusalem.
586 Judah ceases to exist with the destruction of Jerusalem.

520–515 Completion of the rebuilding of the temple at Jerusalem under the prophets Haggai and Zechariah.

DEVELOPMENTS

1200–800 India: Aryans worship nature gods.
1000–950 China: Western Chou dynasty establishes its capital at Hao in Wei Valley.

800–550 India: Aryan expansion. Gradual development of caste system.
770–256 China: Eastern Chou dynasty.
722–481 China: Period of loose confederations under the Eastern Chou dynasty.

600 India: Early cities in Ganges Valley.

Confucius, Chinese philosopher, b 551 BC.

563 India: Birth of Siddhartha Gautama who became the Buddha (the Enlightened One).
551 China: Birth of Kung Fu-tzu (Confucius), died 497BC.
500 Bantu peoples spreading in east Africa.

Assyrian Domination

The Assyrians dominated the Near East for 600 years. Their heartland was on the upper Tigris River between the cities of Nineveh and Asshur. Assyrian expansion began after the collapse of the Hittites in 1200 BC. Their empire reached its first great period in the second half of the 10th century. There was a decline in the 8th century before what is known as the second phase of their empire (748–625 BC). Tiglath-pileser III (748–727 BC), one of the greatest Assyrian monarchs, made his army into a full-time trained force, and was able to conquer more territory.

Beginning with his reign the Assyrian empire grew to include most of Syria, Palestine, Phoenicia and northern Egypt. Babylon fell to Assyria in 729 BC; Cyprus and Cilicia were also brought under Assyrian rule. Nineveh then replaced Asshur as the capital of Assyria. In 646 BC Elam was conquered.

The impact of Assyria over these centuries was profound. The Assyrians were great builders and levied heavy taxes, which made the provinces poor, to pay for the building. Mass deportation was used to crush the resulting revolts. Above all Assyria was a military power. It developed the best armed, trained and disciplined forces yet seen in ancient times. All males were liable to be conscripted. The army included cavalry and its siege equipment was highly developed.

Much Assyrian culture was derived from that of the Hittites, Babylonians and Hurrians; their own greatest contributions were in architecture and sculpture. The palace at Khorsabad, built by Sargon II (721–705 BC) was a vast monument to Assyrian power. Asshurbanipal

The carved reliefs at Behistun, Persia. Above King Darius hovers the winged symbol of Ahura Mazda. Behind him are two attendants, and grovelling before him are nine rebel kings. At the end of the row of figures is a strange being called *Skuna*, wearing a conical hat. Beneath the relief is a cuneiform inscription.

(669–627 BC) made a great collection of tablets for his library. These consisted of copies of records and the literature of ancient Mesopotamia. Subsequently these became a prime source for modern knowledge. Aramaic was to spread over the empire to become a universal language but the harsh side of Assyria is best seen in the sculptures and stone reliefs which show kings as warrior-hunters defeating enemies and sacking cities. The empire was finally destroyed when the combined forces of Medes, Babylonians and Scythians sacked Nineveh in 612 BC.

The Hebrews

Hebrews were a Semitic people traditionally descended from Abraham who, with his father, had led them out of Ur. They wished to establish a kingdom where they could worship their God. Under King David who died in 973 BC the Hebrews defeated the Philistines and for a short while established a united Hebrew kingdom with its capital at Jerusalem. David's son, Solomon, renowned for his magnificence and wisdom, built the temple, palace and walls of Jerusalem. Under his sons the kingdom was split into two – Israel and Judah. For most of the next two hundred years these states were at war with each other when not defending themselves against the attacks of the great neighbouring empires – Babylon, Assyria and Egypt.

Israel disappeared into the Assyrian empire in 722 BC and Judah, which existed precariously for another 150 years, then fell to Babylon. After the subsequent exile in Babylon, the Hebrews returned and rebuilt their temple at Jerusalem under the protection of Persia. In about 750 BC Amos declared that Yahweh was an international god of justice and by doing so he paved the way for the recognition of one god. The Hebrew religion of *Judaism* was the first to succeed permanently in establishing this idea.

Mosaic of the seven-branched candlestick or *menorah*. A golden *menorah* stood in the Tabernacle, the Jew's first Holy Temple. The seven branches are supposed to represent the Sun, Moon and five planets known to them.

THE WEST

The Parthenon in Athens, built between 447 and 432 BC.

500 Etruscan empire at its most powerful.
480 Greek naval victory at Salamis.
477–405 Golden Age of Athens.
450–400 Etruscan empire in decline.
356–338 Philip II of Macedon unites Greek states.
336–323 Alexander the Great conquers Persian empire.
264–241 Rome wins the First Punic War against Carthage.

218–201 Second Punic War – Hannibal crosses the Alps. Scipio annihilates Carthagian army. Rome at war with Macedon – Rome gains Greece.

149–146 Third Punic War – destruction of Carthage.

60 Triumvirate of Caesar, Pompey and Crassus to rule Rome.

44 Assassination of Caesar.
31 Battle of Actium – Octavian (later Augustus) defeats Antony.
23BC–AD14 Augustus (Princeps) makes himself first emperor of Rome.
AD43 Romans invade Britain.
AD68 Death of Nero. Year of the Four Emperors.
AD70 Titus captures Jerusalem. *Diaspora* (dispersal) of Jews.
AD98–117 Trajan – last period of Roman expansion.
180 Death of Marcus Aurelius. End of Golden Age of Rome.

268 Goths sack Athens, Sparta, Corinth.
286 Diocletian divides the Roman empire into west and east.
313 Emperor Constantine the Great issues Edict of Toleration (for Christianity) at Milan.
330 Constantine founds Constantinople.

379–395 Theodosius the Great, emperor of the east.

385?–407 Legions leave Britain.

410 Alaric and the Goths sack Rome.
451 Attila and the Huns invade Gaul.
476 Romulus Augustus the last emperor of Rome deposed – end of western empire.

THE EAST & AFRICA

550–530 Achaemenid empire in Persia.

500 Nok culture in N. Nigeria.

500BC–AD320 Kushite kingdom centred on Meröe, Sudan.

458–424 Partition of China by Han, Chao and Wei.
403–221 Period of warring states in China.

321–184 Mauryan dynasty. Capital at Pataliputra, N.E. India.

221–207 Chin dynasty unites China.
214 Building of the Great Wall.
202BC–AD9 Han dynasty in China.
184–72BC Sunga dynasty in Ganges Valley, India.
140–87BC Wu Ti – 'The Martial Emperor'. Expansion of China.
100BC–AD225 Munda kings rule the Deccan, central India.
AD43 China conquers Tonkin and Assam.
AD74–94 China brings the states of Turkestan under its control – opens silk trade to west.
78–96 Kamishka founds 2nd Kushana dynasty. Capital at Peshawar, Pakistan.
166 Presents from Roman Emperor Marcus Aurelius to Chinese Emperor Huang-ti – one of the few known direct contacts between the two empires.
200 Iron Age in central Africa.
220–264 China divided into three kingdoms.
226 Ardashir founds Sassanid empire in Persia.
313 Collapse of Chinese colonies in Korea.
317–589 Southern and Northern dynasties again divide China.
320 Axum brings Kushite empire to an end.
320–525 Gupta dynasty in north India.
361 Empress Jingo of Japan invades Korea.

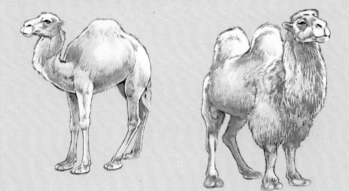

The camel becomes the prime beast of burden throughout north Africa by 100 BC.

407–553 First Mongol empire of Avars.

PHILOSOPHY & ART

460–429 Pericles strives to make Athens the most beautiful city in the world.

450 12 Tables of Roman Law.
Herodotus in Egypt.

429 Acropolis of Athens completed.
Birth of Plato.
399 Socrates put to death for heretical teaching.

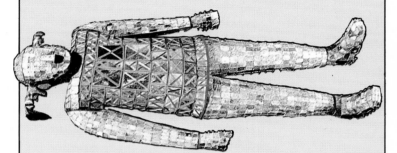

Jade funeral suit of Chinese princess Tou Wan, d 113 BC.

213 Banning of books in China. Roll silk used for new writing.
191 Ban on old literature in China withdrawn; scholars transcribe into new scripts.
180 Early Meroitic writing in Africa.
155–130 Liu Teh collects archaic scripts in China; compilation of early writing, especially Taoism.
124 Philosophical teachings of Confucius become official in China.
100–1 BC Period of great literary importance in China.
50 BC Golden Age of Latin literature – Caesar, Virgil, Horace, Catullus and Cicero.
45 BC Caesar establishes the Julian calendar.

AD18 Death of Ovid.
65 Death of Seneca.
80 Colosseum and Baths of Titus completed in Rome.
124 Pantheon completed in Rome.
150 *Geographia* of Claudius Ptolemy.

Roman arch at Djemill, Algeria, AD 216.

RELIGION

Marble top of a pillar, c 250 BC, which stood in Benares, N.E. India on the spot where the Buddha preached his first sermon.

300 First Hindu philosophical schools start.
250 Hebrew scriptures translated into Greek – the *Septuagint*.

4? BC Birth of Christ.

AD30? Crucifixion of Christ.
33–156 Taosim flourishes under the tutelage of Chang Tao-ling in China.
45 Paul begins missionary journeys.
58 Buddhism introduced to China.
65 St Mark's Gospel.
70 First *diaspora* (dispersal) of Jews.
St Matthew's Gospel.
75 St Luke's Gospel.
95 St John's Gospel; Revelations.
135 Final *diaspora* of Jews.
226 Zoroastrianism becomes official Persian religion under Sassanian rule.
246 Mani founds Manichaeism in Persia. Crucified by Zoroastrians in 276.

313 Edict of Toleration at Milan – Christianity allowed in Roman empire.
350 Christianity reaches Ethiopia.
354 Birth of Augustine in Numidia, N. Africa.
372 Korea receives Buddhism from China.
396 St Augustine made bishop of Hippo, N. Africa.
401–417 Pope Innocent I claims universal authority over Roman Church.
432 Mission of St Patrick to Ireland.
478 First Shinto shrines appear in Japan.

Democracy and Tyranny

Western civilization derives its basic concepts of politics, philosophy and science from the ideas which came out of Greece in the early 5th century BC.

By 500 BC the Greek city state was highly developed both socially and politically. Yet most of these cities had populations far smaller than 20,000. The leading states were Athens, Sparta, Corinth and Thebes.

For a brief period at the beginning of the 5th century there was a degree of unity as all the Greek states banded together to fight off the Persian threat under Darius and then Xerxes. But without a common cause, the rivalry of Athens and Sparta tore the Greek world apart. Geography compelled Athens to be a naval power, Sparta a land power, and for most of the 5th century Athens was victorious at sea, Sparta on land, both fighting for control of Greece. The war between these two cities and their allies (known as the Peloponnesian Wars – 431 to 404) ended in victory for Sparta. The Greek world was permanently weakened as a result.

During the 5th century, Athens pioneered the concept of democracy – one man one vote. This was only for adult male citizens, not slaves or foreigners. Sparta was a military power ruled by kings – two at a time. All male citizens were soldiers. Other activities depended on slaves (known as Helots).

The statesman, Pericles, dominated political life in Athens from 460 until 429 BC when he died of the plague. During his reign he used Athens' enormous wealth – derived from sea power – to create a city of art and culture. This was Athens' 'Golden Age' when the city became perhaps the most beautiful in the world. Under Pericles the Athenian assembly of commoners took power from the council of aristocrats and opened up offices of state to all citizens. The great dramatic tradition of Greece was led by Aeschylus (525–456), Sophocles (495–405) and Euripides (480–406) who wrote tragedies, and Aristophanes (448–385) who was the master of comedy. At the same time new styles of architecture were employed in the buildings of the Acropolis while the sculptures of Myron, Polycleitus and Pheidias have arguably never been surpassed. The historian, Herodotus, is known as the 'Father of History', while Thucydides' *History of the Peloponnesian War* is the earliest example of contemporary and scientific history.

The ideas of the great Greek thinkers or philosophers from this period have dominated western thought to the present day: Socrates argued that truth *existed* and that moral right was essential. His ideas were written down by Plato. One of Plato's pupils was Aristotle, who, as well as studying biology, developed the science of logic. Greek philosophers discussed *how* a state should be run, *what* the laws should do and *why*.

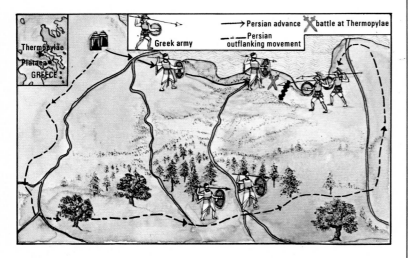

In 480 BC, the Persian king Xerxes set out with his army of 150,000 men to conquer Greece. The Greek army was not powerful enough to defeat the Persians in a pitched battle so they decided to prevent the Persian advance by holding the narrow pass at Thermopylae. Here the Spartan king, Leonidas, took his stand with 7300 soldiers. Xerxes' problem was how to get round it. With the aid of a Greek traitor, Xerxes sent part of his army by a route through the mountains to attack the Greeks from the rear. Leonidas was surrounded but he and his army fought to the end.

Alexander the Great

Alexander's father, Philip II of Macedon (a state in the north east of Greece), united all the Greek city-states under his own control. He was assassinated in 336 BC and his son then aged 20 became Alexander III of Macedon to be known through the ages as 'The Great'. After putting down a revolt at Thebes with great brutality, Alexander crossed into Asia (modern Turkey) in 334 BC with an army of 24,000. In the succeeding ten years of brilliant military campaigns he conquered the Persian empire of Darius. By the time Alexander died he ruled from Greece to Kashmir (he might have conquered all India and beyond had not his troops refused to go any farther) and south as far as Egypt. His was the first European-based empire. Alexander became 'universal', rather than Greek in his habits, and adopted Persian dress and customs. The most famous monument he left behind was the city of Alexandria in Egypt. Alexander died in 323 BC (perhaps poisoned) and his generals then fought over his empire.

334 Alexander begins campaign against Persia; defeats Darius III at River Granicus in Asia Minor.
333 Alexander defeats Darius again at the battle of Issus, capturing the Persian queen and her children – Alexander refuses Darius's offer of ransom and part of his empire. Alexander captures Tyre – end of Phoenician empire.
332 Alexander invades and conquers Egypt – foundation of city of Alexandria.
331 Renewal of the Persian campaign – Alexander defeats Darius at Arbela; end of the Persian empire.
330 Darius is murdered; Alexander in control of Persia.
327 Alexander begins invasion of India.
326 Alexander wins battle of the Hydaspes – his soldiers refuse to go any farther east, and he has to retreat.
323 Alexander dies at Babylon. His generals divide his empire among themselves.

GREEK WARS

499–494 Ionians of Anatolia, with help from Athens, rebel against Persian rule under Darius. Bad organization allows Darius to win – destroys Miletus, the Ionian capital, ending the revolt.
492 Persians send fleet against Athens – wrecked by storm.
490 Defeat of Darius at battle of Marathon.
480 Xerxes of Persia invades Greece after battle of Thermopylae. Persian fleet defeated at Salamis, necessitating retreat of Persian army.
479 Defeat of Persian army at Plataea. Their fleet destroyed.
477–405 Greek navy dominates the Aegean.
460 First Peloponnesian War between Athens and Sparta.
431–404 Second Peloponnesian War.
421–415 Nicias of Athens negotiates 50-year truce between Athens and Sparta – lasts for six.
411 Revolution in Athens – dictatorship of Five Thousand, but democracy soon restored.
406 Athenian fleet defeats Spartans at Arginusae.
405 Spartan fleet under Lysander destroys Athenian fleet at Aegospotami.
404 Lysander captures Athens and sets up government of Thirty Tyrants.
403 Pausanias restores democracy in Athens.
400 Greek army under Xenophon is defeated at Cunaxa in revolt against Artaxerxes II of Persia.
395 Athens, Thebes, Argos in coalition against Sparta. Death of Lysander.
394 Battle of Coronae – Sparta defeats coalition.
370–362 Thebes forms Arcadian League against Sparta, ending Spartan power.
356–336 Philip II of Macedon – controls all of Greece.
336 Assassination of Philip of Macedon.
336–323 Alexander III of Macedon, 'The Great' maintains order in Greece and creates his empire.
323 Death of Alexander. End of great age of Greece.

ROMAN WARS

496 Romans take over Latium by defeating Latins at Lake Regillus.
494 Revolt of the debt-ridden 'plebeians' (peasant masses) – they win independence and increased rights from Roman patricians.
493 Roman-Latin alliance – the Latin League – fight the Etruscans.
451 Three Roman senators go to Athens to study the laws of Solon.
450 Twelve Tables of Roman Laws – wooden tablets on which the laws of Rome are written.
440 Plebeians can now marry patricians.
391 Romans under Camillus defeat Etruscans.
390 Gauls sack Rome.
366 First plebeian council elected in Rome.
343–275 Rome comes to dominate Italy.
338 Battle of Trifanum – tribes and cities of Latin League revolt against Rome. Roman victory ends years of tension and League is dissolved.
312 Appius Claudius builds the Appian Way from Rome to Capua, near Naples.
310 Rome defeats an Etruscan-Samnite coalition (or alliance) at Lake Vadimo.
306 Trade treaty between Rome and Carthage.
304 Rome makes peace with the Samnites (tribes around Naples) – takes Naples and surrounding area.
300 Treaty between Rome and Carthage.
298–290 Rome-Samnite war – Rome victorious.
287 Full equality between patricians and plebeians in Rome.
264–241 First Punic War between Rome and Carthage – the beginning of a century of struggle for mastery of the Mediterranean world.
254 In Sicily, Rome takes Palermo from Carthage.

WORLD CULTURE

500 Africa: Appearance of iron-using. Nok culture in northern Nigeria.
497 Death of Pythagoras, Greek philosopher and scientist (b 581).
477–405 Golden Age of Athens.
470 Carthaginian explorer, Hanno, maps west African coast by sailing down it as far as Cameroun.
460 Hippocrates, Greek physician – 'The Father of Medicine'.
460–429 Pericles, leader of Athens.
450 Herodotus, the Greek historian, in Egypt. Celtic La Tène culture develops in central and northern Europe.
447 Construction of Parthenon at Athens.
445 Nehemiah rebuilds walls of Jerusalem.
430 Plague in Athens.
429 Completion of Acropolis in Athens.
400 Africa: Use of iron spreads south of the Sahara.
384–322 Aristotle, Greek philosopher.
343 Aristotle becomes teacher of Alexander the Great.
323 Birth of Euclid, the Greek philosopher.

A Roman clay lamp, c 250 BC showing two men crushing grapes for wine.

288 Birth of Archimedes, Greek mathematician and inventor.
265 First Roman contact with Greek medicine, through prisoners of war.
250 Hebrew scriptures translated into Greek – the *Septuagint*.

OTHER EMPIRES

770–256 China: Eastern Chou dynasty reigns powerless at Loyang. No authority over warring princes of surrounding states.
550–221 India: Aryan parts divided into many states. Maghada empire established in north-east India. Development of great cities in northern India.
500–250 Africa: Kushite kingdom centred on Meröe.
480–400 Carthage develops sea power and controls the western Mediterranean and western Sicily.
465–424 Artaxerxes I rules Persia.
424–404 Darius II of Persia.
404–359 Artaxerxes II – Egypt breaks free of Persian rule.
387 Artaxerxes takes Greek cities in Asia Minor.
380–343 30th Egyptian dynasty – last native house to rule the country.
367–268 Century of war between Carthage and Sicily.
359–338 Artaxerxes III.
343 Persia retakes Egypt.
338–330 Darius III.
323 Alexander's generals divide up empire. General Ptolemy becomes satrap (ruler) of Egypt.
323–319 Alexander's generals dispute his empire.
321–184 India: Chandragupta founds the Mauryan dynasty.
320 Ptolemy takes Jerusalem. Libya becomes an Egyptian province.
312 General Seleucus takes Syria.
305 Foundation of Seleucid empire and dynasty based at Babylon. Ptolemy takes title of pharaoh in Egypt.
300 Central America: Mayan civilization in Yucatan – begins to spread south. N. Korea: State of Choson.
273–232 India: Asoka – greatest of Mauryan emperors.

THE CLASSICAL WORLD 250 BC–1 BC

CHINA

221–207 Ch'in dynasty established by Shih Huang Ti. Empire is organized into 36 provinces each under civil, military and supervisory officials. Standardization of laws and regulations.
214 Convict labour starts construction of Great Wall to keep out the Hsiung-nu (Huns).
213 Ban on books with exception of scientific works and those kept by officials. Roll silk used for writing – standardization and simplification of script.
202–AD9 Han dynasty.
200 Emperor's palace surrounded for 7 days by Hsiung-nu but his gift of an imperial princess secures peace.
191 The ban on old literature withdrawn – scholars begin to transcribe them into the new script.

155–130 Liu An directs a compilation of early philosophies, especially Taoist.
140–87 Emperor Wu Ti expands the empire. Establishment of Confucian scholarship as qualification for government administrator.
121–119 Hsiung-nu driven north of Gobi desert.
111–110 Subjugation of eastern and southern Yueh and the south west (China then covered about the same area as it does now). Chinese traders travel Indian Ocean during following century.
108 Wu Ti conquers Choson, Korea.
102 Further conquests on borders of China.
100–1 Period of great literary importance – Shih Chi (Historical Memoirs) – first general history of China. Compilation of standard religious texts. First classical inventory of extant literature.
87 Death of Wu Ti. Disorder follows.

JUDEA

250–198 Judea part of Ptolemaic empire based in Egypt.
198–166 Judea part of Seleucid empire under Antiochus III and IV.
167 Antiochus IV persecutes Jews.
Jewish revolt under Judas Maccabeus lasts until 164BC when Jewish worship restored.
160 Maccabeus dies fighting Syrians – his younger brother Jonathan becomes leader of Jews.
157 Judea becomes independent principality.
143–134 Simon Maccabeus, elder brother of Judas and Jonathan, succeeds the latter.
141 Jews liberate Jerusalem. Judea proclaimed an independent kingdom.
134–104 John Hyrcanus rules Judea.
104–103 Aristobulus I, king of Judea.

Gladiator's bronze helmet.

103–76 Alexander Janneus, king of Judea.
90 Revolt of Pharisees.
76–67 Salome Alexandra rules Judea.
67 Civil war in Judea between Hyrcanus II and his brother Aristobulus II.
65 Pompey invades Syria – Palestine falls to Rome.
63 Jerusalem falls to Pompey. Judea annexed to Rome.
Mithridates VI of Syria commits suicide. Syria made Roman province.
37–4 Herod the Great, king of Judea.
c4 Birth of Jesus Christ.
4 Death of Herod the Great – Judea split between his three sons.

ROMAN REPUBLIC

241 Peace between Rome and Carthage. Carthage gives up Sicily – Sicily the first Roman province.
238 Carthage begins conquest of Spain.
225 Rome defeats Celts at Telamon in Italy.
218–201 Second Punic War – Hannibal (247–183) crosses Alps and defeats Romans at Ticinus and Trebia.
217 Hannibal defeats Romans at Trasimene.
216 Hannibal wins battle of Cannae.
215 Hannibal defeated by Marcellus at Nola.
215–205 First Macedonian War – Macedonia, in Greece, supports Carthage against Rome.
Peace of Phoenice between Rome and Macedonia.
206 Scipio Africanus (237–183) defeats Carthaginians, under Hannibal, in Spain.
200–196 Second Macedonian War – Rome gains Greece.
183 Hannibal commits suicide while in exile on Crete, to avoid being handed over to the Romans.
171–167 Third Macedonian War, Macedonians led by Perseus.
170 First stone bridges and paved streets appear in Rome.
168 Perseus defeated at Pydna – Macedonia becomes a Roman province.
149–148 Fourth Macedonian War – Macedonia again conquered.
149–146 Third Punic War – Romans destroy Carthage under Scipio the Younger (185–129).
Rome consists of 7 provinces: Sicily, Sardinia and Corsica, Spain, Morocco, Gallia Transalpina (Gaul), Africa and Macedonia.
133 Asia Minor becomes eighth province.
91 Civil war between Rome and the Italian cities.
89 General Sulla regains control of rebelling Italian cities.
All Italians granted Roman citizenship.
87 Sulla defeats Mithridates and takes Athens.
82 Sulla, dictator of Rome.
78 Death of Sulla – revolt of Lepidus defeated by Pompey.
73–71 Spartacus leads slave revolt – crushed by Pompey and Crassus.
61 Gaius Julius Caesar, governor of Spain.
60 Triumvirate of Caesar, Pompey and Crassus rules Rome.
58 Caesar, governor of Gaul.
55 Caesar conquers northern Gaul.
54 Caesar invades Britain. He leaves again but forces British chief, Cassivellaunus, to pay tribute to Rome.
52 Pompey sole consul at Rome, Caesar defeats Vercingetorix of Gaul.
51 Caesar completes conquest of Gaul and writes *De Bello Gallico*.
50 Rivalry between Caesar and Pompey comes to a head.
49 Senate orders Caesar to relinquish the command of Gaul. Caesar crosses River Rubicon into Italy to start civil war – Pompey flees.
48 Caesar defeats Pompey at Pharsala in Greece. Pompey flees to Egypt, where he is murdered on Cleopatra's orders in 47.
45 Caesar virtual dictator at Rome. Establishes Julian calendar of 365.25 days. Adopts Octavian (63BC–AD14) as his heir.
44 Assassination of Caesar – Mark Antony (83–30) seizes power.
43 Triumvirate of Octavian, Antony and Lepidus.
42 Caesar declared a god. His murderers, Brutus and Cassius, defeated at battle of Philippi.
32 Antony falls in love with Cleopatra.
Octavian declares war on Antony and Cleopatra.
31 Octavian defeats Antony's fleet at Actium.
30 Suicide of Antony and Cleopatra.
Egypt becomes a Roman province.
27 Octavian given supreme power in Rome and title of Augustus.
23 Augustus resigns consulship and takes title *Princeps* – Chief of the Republic.
15 Rome extends frontier to upper Danube River.
8 Death of poets, Virgil and Horace.

China – The Isolated Empire

Shih Huang Ti, who founded the short-lived Ch'in dynasty (221–207 BC), 'civilized' China and helped provide a framework for government that was to last for more than 2000 years. He ruthlessly unified six squabbling Chinese states into an empire. He established the seat of government in one place. He divided the empire into provinces. He created uniform standards throughout the empire – weights and measures, writing and laws.

Shih Huang Ti's greatest monument is the Wall built to keep out and control the barbarian Huns to the north – a fierce warlike people who for centuries had fought and raided Chinese settlements. Many local walled defences already existed but the concept of a continuous wall, 2400 km long, was that of Shih Huang Ti. The wall, which defended China's north and north-west frontiers, was built in less than 20 years at immense cost in lives through cold, exhaustion and skirmishes with the Huns. The wall was constantly added to in the centuries that followed and it dominated Chinese war strategy for more than 1000 years.

Shi Huang Ti's successor was very weak and a power struggle followed. In 202 the Han dynasty emerged to rule China, until AD 9. During these two centuries a network of officials was established to run the huge empire. All officials received the same training according to the teachings of Confucius. They were then posted throughout the empire, and as a result government policies were the same all over China. People were expected to follow them without question. The aristocracy provided the administrators and soldiers. Ancestor worship became the principal religion. Most of the population consisted of peasants. But little is known of their lives or customs.

China has always had a sense of isolation. To the north lies the bleak Manchurian plain or the Gobi desert, to the west the mountains of Tibet and though the Silk Road linked ancient China with the West there was little other contact. The Great Wall strengthened this sense of being cut off from the rest of the world and, in this way, Chinese civilization is unique. While empires in the west were to rise and fall, always battling against each other, the Chinese empire created by the Ch'in dynasty was to continue in an unbroken line of centralized authority and single culture to the time of Mao-tse Tung and communism in 1949.

Making paper from wood ash and cloth pulp was one of the great technical achievements of the Han dynasty. The pulp was added to water and spread onto frames which were dried in the sun. The result was a sheet of dried paper. The Chinese also knew how to melt iron as well as forge it (Europe first melted it 1600 years later), how to mine salt, and how to cure diseases using the system of *acupuncture* (it is still used today).

The Romans saw divine power in everything around them, so they had an enormous number of gods. They also tended to see in other religions something their own lacked, so they would take it over. As a result many Roman gods are the equivalents of Greek gods. Jupiter, the Roman king of gods – corresponded to the Greek Zeus, Neptune with the Greek Poseidon. Apollo, the Greek god, was, also important in Rome.

Rise of Rome

While the foundations of the Chinese empire were being laid in the east the Romans were striving to master the Mediterranean world. The old Roman republic embarked on a century of bitter wars with Carthage, over trade and occupation. Only after three Punic Wars – 264 to 241, 218 to 201 and 149 to 146 (when Carthage was destroyed) did Rome finally emerge totally victorious. But while Rome was fighting against Carthage in the west she was also fighting another series of wars against a hostile Macedonia in the eastern Mediterranean.

In the first century BC, Pompey the Great was to conquer Syria and Palestine and, in the north, Julius Caesar was to conquer all Gaul and make two attempts to invade Britain. Bitter rivalry between these two powerful men brought the old republic to an end. And in the unrest that followed, Julius Caesar was assassinated in 44 BC. Rome was then ruled by a triumvirate of Octavian, Antony and Lepidus but they soon fell out and civil war again erupted. Finally Octavian defeated Antony at the sea-battle of Actium off Greece and a year later made Egypt a Roman province. Octavian took the title of Augustus and ruled Rome as its first real Emperor until AD 14. Roman power then and for another four centuries rested upon the strength of the standing army whose legions were recruited on a voluntary basis from Roman citizens.

1 AD

100 AD

ROME	CHINA	CHRISTIANITY
2 Rome deposes Herod – procurator to rule Judea. **5** Rome acknowledges Cymbeline king of Britain. **14** Death of Augustus. Tiberius Caesar succeeds. **18** Death of poet, Ovid. **26** Tiberius retires to Capri and rules from there. **37** Death of Tiberius. Gaius 'Caligula' succeeds. **41** Assassination of Caligula; Claudius emperor. **43** Romans under Aulus Plautius invade Britain. Foundation of London. **54** Claudius murdered. Nero becomes emperor. **59** Nero murders his mother, Agrippina. **61** Boadicea of the Iceni leads a revolt in Britain. Put down with great severity by Suetonius Paulinus. Boadicea dies. **62** Nero divorces his wife, Octavia, and has her killed – marries Poppaea Sabina, wife of Otho. **64** Fire destroys Rome – Christians blamed. Nero has new public buildings erected. **65** Philosopher Seneca commits suicide on Nero's orders. **68** Rebellion at Rome. Nero commits suicide – Year of the Four Emperors with Galba, Otho, Vitellius. **69–79** Vespasian defeats Vitellius to become emperor. **70** Titus (Vespasian's son) captures and destroys Jerusalem and suppresses Jewish revolt. First *diaspora* (expulsion of Jews). **73** Jewish stronghold at Masada falls to Romans. **77–84** Agricola governor of Britain – completes conquest. **79–81** Emperor Titus. **79** Vesuvius destroys Pompeii, Herculaneum and Stabiae. **81** Death of Titus – Domitian succeeds; constructs defensive lines on the German frontier. **96** Assassination of Domitian. Nerva emperor to 98, adopts Trajan as his heir. **98–117** Trajan – the last period of Roman expansion.	**9–23** Wang Mang establishes the short Hsia dynasty. **25–220** Later Han dynasty. **58** Emperor Ming-ti introduces Buddhism to China. **74–94** Pan Ch'ao brings petty states of Turkestan into submission and so opens silk trade to the Roman empire. **82–132** Empire is dominated and ruled by women.  Chinese Emperor Kwang-wu, ruled AD. 25-56.	**26–36** Pontius Pilate procurator of Judea. **27** Baptism of Jesus by John the Baptist. **28** John the Baptist executed on the orders of Herod. **30** Christ crucified. **31** Martyrdom of St Stephen. **32** Saul converted to Christianity – becomes 'Paul'. **34** Paul visits Jerusalem. **37–44** Herod Agrippa is king of northern Palestine. **40** One of earliest Christian churches erected at Corinth. **45** Paul on missionary journeys. **58** Paul imprisoned in Caesarea. **60** Paul on trial before the Roman procurator, Festus – he appeals to Rome. **64** St Peter executed. **65** St Mark's Gospel. **67** Martyrdom of St Paul. **70** Titus captures and destroys Jerusalem. St Matthew's Gospel. **73** Fall of Masada, last stronghold of the Jewish Zealots in Palestine. **75** St Luke's Gospel.

The Roman World

By the beginning of the Christian era when Augustus presided over Rome the empire already included most of the Mediterranean world – Spain and Gaul, most of north Africa and Egypt, the southern Balkans and Greece, and Syria. The Mediterranean was a Roman sea. More conquests were to come but the pattern of the empire had been established and for most of the succeeding 250 years Rome's wars were to be fought far away on the borders of this vast empire. During the 1st century AD England (but not Ireland or Scotland) was brought under Roman rule. Under the great Trajan (98–117) the empire reached its greatest extent. Its western borders were the Atlantic coasts of Britain, Gaul and Spain, its eastern border the River Tigris (in modern Iraq).

The Romans were soldiers, traders, lawgivers and builders and during this period their system was extended to the remotest corners of this vast empire. Roman laws become the foundation upon which Europe was to build for centuries. Roman architecture was magnificent. It was more massive and functional than Greek architecture but Roman roads, viaducts and aqueducts remain standing to the present day and are monuments to their thoroughness.

The emperors' courts became noted for their magnificence and luxury. Some emperors were bywords for cruelty and corruption.

The second century was the 'golden age' of Rome when for 80 years only four emperors were to rule the Roman world: Trajan (98–117) the soldier who expanded it to its greatest limits; Hadrian (117–138) the consolidator, the emperor who built the wall in Britain; Antoninus Pius (138–161) who encouraged literature and trade; and Marcus Aurelius (161–180) the 'philosopher' emperor. But the pressures upon this great empire were constant. Domitian built a series of defences along the Rhine to keep out the Franks and the Alemanni. Hadrian's Wall was to preserve Britain from the Picts and Scots. Hadrian was always on the move reviewing his legions, building, lawgiving, while Marcus Aurelius spent nearly half his 19 years as emperor with his legions facing the Barbarians (Goths) across the Danube. Yet, except on the frontiers of the empire, this great area enjoyed peace and prosperity for most of this period.

The latter years, however, saw the beginnings of decline. Commodus (180–192) had none of the greatness of character of his predecessors and actually appeared in the arena to fight animals and gladiators. Following the death of Septimius Severus (another great emperor) in 211 a succession of weak and corrupt men ruled Rome so that the army became the real controller of the fortunes of the empire, a fact of immense importance in the centuries which followed.

ROME

101–107 Dacian Wars – empire at its greatest extent.

116 Tigris becomes the eastern frontier of the empire. Mesopotamia and Syria become new provinces.
117–138 Emperor Hadrian.
122 Hadrian, in Britain, commences building of the wall.
130 Hadrian founds Antinopolis in Egypt.
132 Jewish revolt establishes an independent state in Israel. Jerusalem captured.
133–135 Julius Severus, governor of Britain sent to Palestine, crushes revolt.
135 Final *diaspora* of Jews.
138 Death of Hadrian. Antoninus Pius succeeds.
161 Death of Antoninus Pius. Marcus Aurelius succeeds.
180 Death of Marcus Aurelius, the 'philosopher' emperor who recorded his *Meditations.*
180–192 Emperor Commodus.
193 Pertinax emperor for a few months, murdered by Praetorian Guard.
193–211 African-born Septimius Severus seizes Rome.
212–217 Emperor Caracalla – extended citizenship to all free inhabitants of the empire.
217–218 Emperor Macrinus.
218–222 Emperor Elagabulus – introduces a form of sun worship; real ruler – his mother Julia Maesa.
222–235 Emperor Alexander Severus.
235–238 Emperor Maximinius – great soldier not recognised by the senate.
238–244 Empeor Gordian.
244–249 Emperor Philip the Arab.
249–251 Emperor Decius.
250 Emperor worship made compulsory.

CHINA

105–121 Dowager Empress Teng rules.
144–150 Empress Liang rules on behalf of three boy emperors.
150 Korea independent from China.
166 Emperor Huang-ti receives gifts from the Roman Emperor Marcus Aurelius.
184 Rebellion of 'Yellow Turbans' against power and rapacity of the Eunuchs.
189 Massacre of the Eunuchs by Yüan Shao.
189–220 Hsien-ti, weak last emperor of the Han dynasty.
220–264 Empire divided into three kingdoms. Loyang the capital. Eunuchs excluded from government.
221–264 Shu-Han dynasty.
222–264 Wu dynasty founded by Sun Ch'uan in the lower Long River Valley: capital at Chien-K'ang (Nanking).
230 Accession of Sujin, 10th Emperor of Japan. The beginning of historical records in Japan.

CHRISTIANITY

95 St John's Gospel and Book of Revelation.
132 Jewish revolt led by independent state of Israel against Roman rule. Jews capture Jerusalem.
133 Julius Severus is sent to Palestine from Britain to crush the revolt.
135 Revolt is crushed; death of leaders – final *diaspora* of Jews.
180 Martyrdom of Christians at Scillium in Africa.
200 Bishop of Rome, as pope, recognised as head of western Christendom.

St Vitalis, an early Christian saint.

Early Christianity

Our knowledge of Jesus Christ comes from the four gospels. The first of these, that of St Mark, was written in about AD 65, more than thirty years after Christ's death. The gospels were based upon stories that had been passed down over the years so that to some extent the details of Christ's life are as much hearsay as a matter of strict historical record. After his conversion in AD 32, Paul spent nearly thirty years travelling and spreading Christ's teachings. For the next two hundred and fifty years the great majority of Christians were drawn from the lower classes of the Roman world, including huge numbers of slaves. Christian teaching had a special appeal for women because of the rôle of the Virgin Mary and for those who had no power and little hope. However, Christians were persecuted in the Roman world until the Emperor Constantine the Great was himself converted to Christianity in the 4th century.

At first the centre of Christianity remained at Jerusalem, but by the 2nd century, the two main centres were Alexandria and Rome. Gradually Rome, as the place where Peter and Paul were martyred, became the heart of Christendom.

The spread of Christianity in the 200 years after the death of Christ was astonishingly fast. By AD 250 there were probably churches in Asia Minor, Greece, Italy, Egypt, Gaul, Carthage, Britain, Spain, Germany, Mesopotamia, Persia and India.

25

The Decline of the Roman Empire

In the end the Roman empire was the victim of its own success. Its sheer size, the fact that all the civilized Mediterranean world was a part of it, and still more the dangers from the Barbarians pressing in from the north made it too unwieldy to be run as a single state. Moreover, from the death of Septimius Severus in 211, to 284 when Diocletian became emperor, there were constant revolts and many claimants to the imperial throne. The army always made the final decision. Rome urgently needed a strong ruler. She found one in Diocletian (284–305).

Diocletian was a first class administrator who re-organized the structure of the empire. He recognized that the power was increasingly concentrated in the eastern half where the larger populations and richer provinces lay. So he divided the empire to be ruled in two parts. The senior, more powerful of the two emperors usually ruled the east, the junior partner the west. Sometimes attempts were made to reunite the empire – Constantine and Theodosius for example – but Diocletian's division remained. The strength of this arrangement lay in the recognition of how to administer such a vast area. Its weakness was that it encouraged rivalry. In the next two centuries emperors of east and west struggled for mastery of the Roman world.

Unlike so many of his predecessors who had been murdered, Diocletian abdicated. A power struggle followed and after a war another strong man, Constantine the Great (306–337), emerged as emperor. His reforms as well as the length of his reign gave Rome a new lease of life. He will be remembered above all for two things – he became a Christian (he was baptized on his deathbed at Nicomedia) and he founded Constantinople (modern Istanbul) on the site of ancient Byzantium and made it the capital of the eastern empire.

Although the empire was still to last for centuries its great days were past. Its emperors spent more and more of their time on its widespread frontiers trying to hold back the barbarians – the Franks, the Alemanni, the Goths, the Vandals, the Huns and the Visigoths. By the end of the 4th century the Romans began to withdraw their legions from Britain to defend the empire nearer home. In 410 Alaric and the Goths managed to sack Rome. The city recovered and lasted as the centre of a disintegrating western empire for another 60 years until its last emperor was deposed in 476 and the Visigoths overran and ruled all Italy. The Eastern empire with its capital at Constantinople was to last for another 1000 years.

A coin of Constantine (306-337), the first Christian emperor. Constantine the Great became emperor of Rome when he defeated Emperor Maxentius at the battle of Milvian Bridge. Legend has it that before the battle he saw the outline of a cross superimposed on a cloud and this converted him to Christianity. At once he set about ending persecution of the Christians. In 325 he called the first world council of the Christian church to meet at Nicaea in Turkey. In 330 he moved the empire's capital from pagan Rome to a new city, Constantinople.

The Barbarians

Who were the barbarians? No one really knows. However, it is probable that one group – Goths, Vandals, Saxons, Angles, Jutes – came from Scandinavia and the other – the *hsiung-nu* or Huns – from Asia. Each group was made up of many tribes.

The Romans scorned the barbarians as rustic simpletons. But, although they did not live in cities, they could write, were superb metalworkers and craftsmen and, above all, great warriors.

In 476 under Odovacar, the Goths swept into Italy and deposed the last western emperor of Rome, Romulus Augustulus. The Vandals, Suevi and Alemanni broke through the Rhine frontier, scoured Gaul before settling in Spain and Africa. In Britain, the Angles, Saxons and Jutes drove the Romanized Britons into Cornwall and Wales. While the Huns, under the leadership of the great warrior Attila, attacked all before them until they occupied half of Europe and Asia. In 451 Attila invaded Gaul, but the Romans, Franks and Alemanni held him off and he retreated to Hungary where he died in 453.

476: Europe at the time of the fall of Rome.

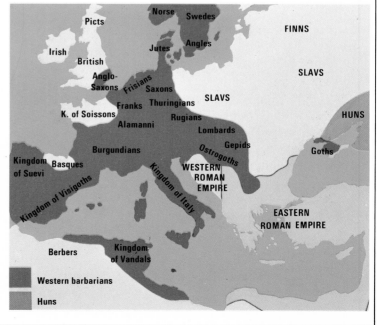

ROME IN DECLINE

251–253 Emperor Gallus succeeds Emperor Decius – killed fighting in Dacius (Romania).
253–259 Emperor Valerian – his son Gallienus is co-emperor.
259 Gallienus rules but there are rivals for his 'throne' throughout this period.
268–270 Emperor Claudius II – capable.
270–275 Emperor Aurelian – fortifies Rome.
275–276 Emperor Tacitus – reluctant emperor killed by his troops.
276–282 Emperor Probus brings peace but when he orders his troops to carry out works of peace they kill him.
282–283 Emperor Carus – campaigns against Persia.
284–305 Emperor Diocletian.
286 Diocletian divides the empire for ease of government. Diocletian rules the eastern half, Maximian the west.
287 Carausius, commander of the Roman British fleet, revolts in Britain and rules independently to 293. He is murdered by co-rebel Allectus.
303 Diocletian orders a general persecution of Christians.
305 Diocletian and Maximian abdicate.
Power struggle follows.
306–337 Constantine the Great, emperor in the east.
308–312 Maxentius, emperor in the west.
312 Battle of Milvian Bridge – Constantine defeats Maxentius. Constantine is converted to Christianity.
313 Edict of Toleration proclaimed at Milan – Christianity allowed by Constantine.
324 Constantine reunites the empire.
330 Constantine founds Constantinople, at Byzantium, to be capital of the empire.
Basilican church of St Peter erected in Rome.
337 Constantine baptized on his deathbed. His three sons are joint rulers of the empire.
360 Scrolls begin to be replaced by books.
361–363 Emperor Julian reverts to paganism.
363–364 Emperor Jovianus surrenders Mesopotamia to Persia.
364–375 Valentine, emperor in the west.
364–378 Valens, emperor in the east.
369 General Theodosius drives the Picts and Scots out of Roman Britain.
375–383 Emperor Gratian (west).
378 Defeat and death of Valens at Adrianople (W. Turkey) at hands of Goths.
379–395 Theodosius the Great (east).
Constantinople is now the real centre of imperial power.
383–388 Magnus Maximus (west). His legions begin to leave Britain to conquer Gaul and Spain, but is executed by Theodosius.
394 Theodosius briefly reunites the empire.
He forbids the Olympic Games.
395–397 Stilicho, Vandal leader of Roman forces, drives Visigoths from Roman Greece.
395–408 Emperor Arcadius – brother of Honorius (east).
395–423 Emperor Honorius (west).
401–417 Pope Innocent I claims universal jurisdiction over Roman Church.
407 Last Roman troops leave Britain and Romano-Britains are left to fend for themselves.
408–450 Theodosius II, emperor of the east.
425 Founding of Constantinople University.
425–455 Emperor Valentinian III (west).
440–461 Pope Leo the Great.
450–457 Emperor Marcian (east).
457–475 Emperor Leo I (east).
475–476 Romulus Augustulus last emperor in the west.
476 He is deposed by the Goths under Odovacar – end of the western empire.
Eastern empire continues under Teno and Anastarius and lasts for 1000 more years.

PERSIA AND INDIA

240–271 Shapur I founds the powerful neo-Persian empire of the Sassanids – crushes opposition in Armenia and Hatra. Repeatedly invades Roman Mesopotamia and Syria, but does not hold the territory.

271–301 Persia ruled by Shapur's descendants.
296–297 Persia at war with Rome. At the peace Rome gives Mesopotamia to Persia. River Tigris becomes boundary between two empires.
309–379 Shapur II of Persia.
320–330 Chandragupta I founds Gupta dynasty in India which lasts to 525.
330–375 Samudragupta, emperor of India – patron of poetry and music; extends empire to the north west.
337–350 Shapur II at war with eastern Roman strongholds – fails to capture them.
339 Persecution of Persian Christians.
350 Persians take Armenia from Romans.
359–361 Shapur II again goes to war against Rome. But repulsed by Emperor Julian in 363.
371–376 Third war with Rome under Shapur II – indecisive, but Persian power reaches its zenith.
379 Death of Shapur II followed by a series of weak rulers.

409–416 Persian Christians allowed to worship openly.
420–440 Varaharan V of Persia declares war on Rome when Persian Christians cross border seeking Theodosius' protection.
440–457 Yezdigird II of Persia, forcibly converts Armenia to Zoroastrianism.
477–496 Buddhagupta – last emperor of the Indian Gupta dynasty.
483–485 Volagases of Persia grants Edict of Toleration to Christians of Armenia and its regions.

THE BARBARIANS AND ELSEWHERE

250 Barbarians from north established in south-west Korea. Chinese colonies in Korea extinguished.
265–317 Nominal reunion of China under Western Chin dynasty.
268 Major Goth invasion – Athens, Corinth and Sparta sacked.

317–589 Six dynasties, including the Eastern Chin dynasty (317–420), rule China.
360–390 Period of Japanese influence in Korea.
370 Mongol Huns invade Europe.
372 Korea receives Buddhism from China.
400 Incas establish themselves on the South American Pacific coast.
406 Vandals overrun Gaul.
407–553 First Mongol empire under the Avars.
410 Alaric of the Goths sacks Rome.
413–490 King Changsu brings Korea to its greatest power.
425–455 Angles, Saxons and Jutes raid Britain.
429–535 Vandal kingdom in north Africa.
433–453 Attila leads the Huns.
439 Gaiseric of the Vandals captures Carthage.
449 Jutes under Hengist and Horsa invade Kent.
451 Attila invades Gaul – held back at Châlons by Romans, Franks and Alemanni.
452 Attila invades northern Italy.
Venice is founded by refugees from the Huns.
455 Gaiseric of the Vandals attacks Rome.
465 Skandagupta of India repulses the White Huns from the north.
481 Clovis, king of the Franks.
Increasing attacks on Persian empire from the barbarians north of Caspian Sea.
493 Theodoric of the Ostrogoths becomes king of all Italy.

The Middle Ages AD 500–AD 1100

EUROPE

503 Battle of Mount Badon – Arthur the Briton defeats Saxons from Germany.

584 Anglo-Saxon kingdom of Mercia is founded in England.
664 Synod of Whitby – Oswy of Northumbria accepts Rome's form of Christianity.

710–711 Roderic, the last Visigoth king of Spain. Moors invade Spain.

1066: Scene from the Bayeux tapestry. Harold pulls an arrow from his eye during the battle of Hastings.

732 Charles Martel, ruler of the Franks, holds Moors at Tours because Martel's cavalry is equipped with stirrups allowing more effective use of sword and spear.
751 Pepin the Short, ruler of the Franks founds the Carolingian dynasty.
771–814 Charlemagne, king of the Franks.
787 First Danish invasion of Britain.
796 Death of Offa ends Mercian supremacy in England.
800 Pope Leo III crowns Charlemagne first Holy Roman emperor.
800–850 Feudalism – the granting of land by a powerful person to a less powerful man in return for service – established by the Franks mainly for military purposes. Horses bred as big as possible for war.
843 Treaty of Verdun – division of Frankish (Holy Roman) empire. Louis the German rules east of the Rhine, Charles the Bald rules France, Lothair rules Italy, Provence, Burgundy, Lorraine.
851 Crossbow used in France.
871–899 Alfred the Great, king of Wessex.
900 Alfonso III of Castille begins to reconquer Spain from the Moors.
Castles become seats of the European nobility.
911 Hrolf the Ganger is granted Normandy.
936–973 Otto I, the Great, king of Germany revives Holy Roman empire and in 962 has himself crowned Emperor Augustus, founding a line of emperors which endure until Napoleon I abolishes the empire in 1806.
982 Eric the Red settles Greenland.
1016 Danes rule England.
1066 Norman conquest of England.
1075 Dispute between pope and emperor over which ruler should appoint bishops.
1096–1122 First Crusade follows an appeal by Pope Urban to free the Holy Places.

ELSEWHERE

527–565 Justinian, emperor of Byzantium (eastern Roman empire).
570 Birth of Muhammad at Mecca.
585 Reconstruction of Great Wall of China.
618 T'ai Tsu founds the Tang dynasty in China.
625 Muhammad begins dictating the Koran.
632 Death of Muhammad.
635 Muslims begin conquest of Syria and Persia.
642 Fall of Persia and Egypt to Muslims.

661–750 Omayyad dynasty in Islam founded by Caliph Muawiya.
668 Korea united under Silla.
674 Arab conquest reaches River Indus in India.
675 First Bulgar empire south of the River Danube.

700 Arabs capture Tunis – virtual end of Christianity in north Africa.

A bust of Charlemagne (800-814) made to hold parts of his skull.

751 Arabs defeat Chinese at Samarkand.
786–809 Harun al-Raschid, caliph of Baghdad.
850 Citadel built in Zimbabwe.
880 Basil, emperor of Byzantium, drives Arabs from mainland Italy.
922 Fatimids seize Morocco.
960 Sung dynasty in China (to 1275).
976–997 T'ai Tsung completes re-union of China.
980 Arabs settle the east coast of Africa.
999 Bagauda, first king of Kano in northern Nigeria.

1061 Establishment of the Almoravid dynasty in north Africa – the conquest of Spain follows.
1071 Battle of Manzikert – Seljuk Turk leader, Alp Arslan, defeats Byzantine army and conquers Asia Minor.
1090 Foundation of the Assassin sect in Persia.
1099 Crusaders capture Jerusalem.

500 AD

1100 AD

TRAVEL & TRADE

500 Stirrup starting to be used – at first for greater comfort when riding, later used in battle.

The invention of the padded horse collar in about 950 allowed horses to pull heavier weights, such as wagons and carriages.

800 onwards. Lateen (triangular) sail used in the Mediterranean. Made it possible for boats to beat into the wind.
800–900 Growth of trans-Sahara trade in Africa.
890 Nailed horseshoes first used allowing long journeys – cheap enough to be afforded by peasants for agricultural use.
900 Mayas emigrate into Yucatan.
Vikings develop the art of shipbuilding and discover Greenland.
907 Commercial treaties between Kiev and Constantinople.
950 Padded horsecollar means horses can pull heavier loads and wagons. Previously harnessed with a breast-band which choked the horse when pulling heavy loads.
Kupe, the great Polynesian navigator, discovers New Zealand on canoe voyage.
982 Viking, Eric the Red settles Greenland.
983 Venice and Genoa trade with Asia.
1000 Viking, Biarni Heriulfsson is blown off course and sights North America.
1002 Leif Ericsson (son of Eric the Red) journeys down the American coast possibly as far as Maryland.

The Prophet Muhammad before the battle of Uheed in 625. By Muslim convention Muhammad's face is veiled.

CULTURE & RELIGION

529 Monastery of Monte Cassino, Italy, founded by St Benedict of Nursia. Although they lead a life of prayer and manual labour, the monks provide almost all medical skill and preserve much classical learning that would otherwise be lost.
529–565 Codification of Byzantine laws under Justinian. Byzantine empire has own form of Christianity, preserved as the Eastern Orthodox Church.
550 St David brings Christianity to Wales.
552 Buddhism reaches Japan.
563 St Columba converts the Picts from Scotland to Christianity and founds monastery on the island of Iona off the west coast of Scotland.

597 St Augustine converts the kingdom of Kent to Christianity.
610 Vision of Muhammad when Angel Gabriel commands him to proclaim the one true God, Allah.
622 The *Hegira* – Muhammad flees to Medina from persecution in Mecca.
624 Buddhism becomes the official religion of China.
669 Theodoric of Tarsus becomes Archbishop of Canterbury and reorganizes the English Church.
700 Translation of the psalms into Anglo-Saxon – the Lindisfarne Gospels.

731 Bede's *Ecclesiastical history of the church in England*.

782 onwards. Revival of learning in Europe under Charlemagne.

841–846 Wu Tsung persecutes all religions in China except Buddhism.
867 Photian Schism – Byzantine Church challenges the authority of Rome.
891 Alfred begins the *Anglo-Saxon Chronicle* – a history of England.
910 Foundation of Cluny Abbey in France – epitomizes the Romanesque style of architecture.
932 Wood block printing is adopted in China allowing mass production of books.
978 Chinese begin the compilation of 1000 volume history.
988 Vladimir of Kiev introduces Eastern Orthodox religion to his lands.
993 Olaf Skutkonnung – the first Christian king of Sweden.
995–1028 Golden Age of the arts in Japan.
1000 Widespread fear of the 'End of the World' and the 'Last Judgement'.

1052 Edward the Confessor founds new Westminster Abbey.
1054 Final break between Roman and Byzantine churches.
1076 Synod of Worms – bishops depose Pope Gregory; beginning of a power struggle between popes and Holy Roman emperors.
1086 *Domesday Book.*

WEST EUROPE	AFRICA & EAST	ISLAM	BYZANTIUM
507 Franks conquer Visigoths in southern France. **511** Death of Clovis, the Frankish king – his empire divided between his four sons – the Meroving dynasty starts. **561** Civil war breaks out between the Merovings. Rulers of the Frankish kingdom now known as Mayors of the Palace. **568** Lombards under Alcuin conquer northern Italy. **584** Anglo-Saxon kingdom of Mercia founded in England. **629** Dagobert I re-unites the Frankish kingdom until 639. **639 and 642** Penda and the Mercians defeat North-umbrians. **655** Oswy, king of Northumbria defeats and kills Penda of Mercia. **687** Pepin the Younger re-unites the Frankish kingdom after the battle of Tertry. **710–711** Roderic – last Visigoth king of Spain. Moors invade Spain – Roderic defeated; end of Visigoth monarchy.	**496–534** N. Africa: Vandals rule. **534–550** China: Eastern Wei dynasty. **550–577** China: The Northern Ch'i dynasty. **562** Korea: End of Japanese power. **589** China re-united by Wen Ti who founds Sui dynasty. **593–628** Suiko, empress of Japan. Buddhism takes root and Japan is much influenced by Chinese civilization. **604** Japan gets her first written constitution. **605–610** China: Building of Grand Canal. **613–618** China: Domestic revolts. **618–907** China: T'ang dynasty founded by T'ai Tsung. **627–649** T'ai Tsung, the Great, emperor of China – a period of military conquest, patronage of arts and letters. **700–800** Bantu Africans cross the River Limpopo taking Iron Age to the south.	**570** Birth of Muhammad at Mecca. **610** Vision of Muhammad. **622** The *Hegira* – Muhammad flees from persecution in Mecca to Yathrib (Medina). **625** Muhammad begins dictating the *Koran*. **630** Muhammad captures Mecca – principles of Islam set out. **632** Death of Muhammad. **632–634** Abu Bekr (Muhammad's father-in-law) – the first caliph (deputy to Muhammad). **634–644** Omar I, caliph of Mecca. Holy War against Persians. **635–641** Muslim conquest of Syria. **638** Muslims capture Jerusalem. **639–642** Muslims conquer Egypt. **644–656** Othman caliph, following Omar's assassi-nation. **645** Byzantines recapture Alexandria – people rise against Arabs. **646** Arabs recapture Alexandria. **655** First Arab naval victory – battle of the Masts at	**500–642** Constant fighting between Byzantium and Persia. **527–565** Justinian, emperor of Byzantium. **529–565** Justinian has Byzantine laws codified. **533–534** 'Eternal Peace' between Byzantium and Persia. **534** Belisarius, the Byzantine general conquers Vandals of north Africa. **535–554** Byzantium reconquers Italy. **542–546** Plague spreads in Byzantine empire. **554** Justinian reforms the administration of Egypt. **565–578** Justin II, emperor of Byzantium. **572–628** Persians control Arabia. **589** Arabs, Khazars and Turks invade Persia and are defeated. **626** Emperor Heraclius of Byzantium expels Persians from Egypt. **642** Final defeat of Persians by Arabs at Nehawand. **710** Justinian II confirms papal privileges. **726** Pope Gregory II opposes iconoclasm (violent Byzantine

A monk copies out a manuscript in a *scriptorium* (writing room). In the Middle Ages few people outside the Church could read and write and those who could had usually been educated by monks. The monastery libraries preserved much classical learning but books disapproved of by the Church were kept hidden away or destroyed. Monasteries were often very rich and able to provide relief for the poor and sick, as well as shelter for travellers. They were, in effect, the first modern guest houses.

Muhammad and Islam

When Muhammad was born at Mecca in 570 the Arabs, a pagan Semitic people of the Arabian peninsula, had no influence or power beyond their desert kingdoms and were little known. Not much more than a century later an astonishing series of Arab conquests had taken place and they ruled an empire which stretched from the Atlantic coast of Morocco to India. When Muhammad was about 40 years old he had a vision. He was commanded by the Archangel Gabriel to proclaim the one true God, Allah. Muhammad accepted the Bible's Old Testament and respected Jesus as a prophet, but not as the Son of God. He preached in Mecca until persecution forced him to flee with his followers to Medina in 622. His flight, known as the *Hegira*, begins the Muslim calendar.

In 630 Muhammad captured Mecca. Between the *Hegira* and 630 Muhammad dictated the *Koran*, the Holy Book of the Muslim faith. He forbade the worship of idols and ordered that non-believers should never enter Mecca. To this day only Muslims are allowed to go there.

By the time of Muhammad's death in 632 his followers controlled all Arabia. There then followed one of the most spectacular and rapid periods of conquest in history as the Arabs spread through Egypt and across north Africa to

WEST EUROPE

718 Pelayo, a Visigoth, founds the kingdom of Asturias in the Spanish mountains. Moors hold the rest of peninsula. Battle of Covadonga – Moors defeated by Christians in north-west Spain.
732 Charles Martel, ruler of the Franks, holds the Muslim Moors at the battle of Tours, halting north-west advance.
737 Charles Martel defeats Moors at Narbonne.
741 Pepin the Short succeeds his father, Charles Martel, as Mayor of the Palace.
751 Pepin the Short crowned king of the Franks – founds Carolingian dynasty to replace Merovingian dynasty. Lombards under Aistulf take Ravenna from the Byzantine empire.
756 Pepin leads an army to protect Pope Stephen III from Lombards – formation of papal states.
757 Offa, king of Mercia builds his dyke to keep out the Welsh.

771–814 Charlemagne (Pepin's son), king of the Franks.
772 Charlemagne conquers Saxony in Germany and converts it to Christianity.
773 Charlemagne annexes Lombardy.
778 Battle of Roncesvalles – Moors and Basques ambush the Franks.
779 Offa of Mercia becomes king of all England.
782 Revival of learning in Europe under Charlemagne who summons Alcuin of York (monk and scholar) to head palace school at Charlemagne's capital, Aachen.
787 First Danish invasion of Britain.
788 Charlemagne annexes Bavaria.
796 Death of Offa – end of Mercian supremacy in England.
800 Pope Leo III, in gratitude for protecting and expanding Christian Europe, crowns Charlemagne Holy Roman emperor of the west.

ISLAM

which Byzantines are defeated off Alexandria.
656–661 Ali, caliph following Othman's assassination.
661 Muawiya, caliph to 680, founds the Omayyad dynasty – to 750.
673–678 Arabs besiege Constantinople but without success.
680 Arab civil war.
685–705 Caliph Abdalmalik reorganizes Arab administration.
697 Arabs destroy Carthage.
700 Arabs capture Tunis – virtual end of Christianity in north Africa.
702 Arabic made official language of Egypt.
707 Arabs capture Tangier.
712 Muslim state established in Sind.
716–717 Arabs besiege Constantinople – fail to take.
751 Arabs defeat Chinese at Samarkand.
756 Omayyad dynasty established at Cordoba in Spain by Ad-al-Rahman ibn Mu'awiya.
767–772 Christian Coptic revolt in Egypt.
786–809 Haroun-al-Raschid, caliph of Baghdad.

BYZANTIUM

movement against sacred images started by Emperor Leo III).
730 Pope Gregory II excommunicates Leo III.
733 Emperor Leo III withdraws Byzantine provinces from papal jurisdiction.
787 Council of Nicaea – restoration of images in churches.
791 Constantine VI imprisons his cruel mother.
797 Empress Irene has her son Constantine blinded and rules to 802 when deposed.

Byzantine emperor, Justinian (527–565).

700 AD

800 AD

invade Spain at the beginning of the 8th century, taking their Islamic faith with them. At the same time they expanded eastwards. They invaded Syria and Iraq in 633 and by 642 they had brought the Persian empire of the Sassanids to an end. In 712 they crossed the Indian mountains of the Hindu Kush where briefly they established an Arab state in Sind (Pakistan). In 732, having conquered all Spain, they were finally turned back by Charles Martel, the Frankish ruler, after penetrating deep into France. The Byzantine empire based upon Constantinople managed to survive this Arab onslaught – but, as a result, was greatly reduced in size.

It was not just a question of conquest. The Islamic faith had enormous appeal and people were converted to it wherever the Arabs conquered and settled. Converts were encouraged by the promises which Allah made about Paradise, where Muslims hoped to go when they died.

The chief cities of the Arab empire which flourished in the centuries following Muhammad – Damascus, Baghdad and then Cordoba in Spain – were centres of wealth and learning. But above all they led in the science of mathematics, chemistry, pharmacy and medicine. Haroun al-Raschid, the caliph of Baghdad from 786 to 809, presided over one of the most magnificent courts in the world. The influence of the Arabs and Islam was to reach its zenith over the next three centuries. Today Islam is one of the world's great religions and the countries where it is chiefly found were the main areas of Arab conquest in the 7th and 8th centuries.

Emperor Justinian

Emperor Justinian (527–565) was a Christian and one of the most influential men of the early Middle Ages. Because of what he did, the eastern half of the old Roman empire centred upon Constantinople lasted to 1453 as the Byzantine empire centred on Byzantium. Justinian was a great diplomat. He struggled throughout his reign to re-unite the eastern empire with the old empire of the west. He was almost always at war – the greatest threat came from the pagan Persians to the east. His general Belisarius defeated the Vandals in north Africa. He went on to defeat the Ostrogoths in Italy driving them from Rome in 554. Justinian's fleets controlled the western Mediterranean and were to do so for another 100 years.

Splendid architecture was a feature of his reign, its greatest monument being the church of Saint Sophia – completed in 537. Justinian's political and economic reforms laid the foundations for the Byzantine empire which survived until the 15th century when it was overthrown by the Muslim Turks.

The Empire of Ghana

Ghana's foundations go back to the 4th century AD when Romans still ruled north Africa. At its greatest extent between 920 and 1076 the empire of Ghana stretched from the Atlantic coast in the west to Timbuktu in the east and was bounded on the north side by the Sahara. It was a federation of tribes with a highly developed central government under a powerful king and an advanced culture.

The Soninke people of the savannahs or grasslands of western Africa were responsible for the rise of Ghana. By the 10th century the empire was strong enough to control the trade routes across the Sahara to the north and the ports on the Atlantic (west) coast.

Ghana was known as the 'Land of Gold', but it also had a large trade in salt and Saharan copper. Other manufactured goods were bought in exchange. Ghana made enough money from this trade to allow its king to keep large armies. Iron was used to shoe the horses for their mounted troops and to make spears and lances.

The kings of Ghana became famous for their wealth and lavish feasts. All gold was the property of the king, although trade in gold dust was left in private hands. On every donkey load of salt entering or leaving Ghana a tax was paid to the king.

Kumbi Saleh was the principal capital of the empire. In the 10th century it probably had 20,000 inhabitants, making it one of the largest cities anywhere at that time. Kumbi Saleh was really two towns: one was a great suburb for the Muslim traders who came across the Sahara – here there were mosques and stone storehouses for their merchandise; the other was that of the king. The empire was finally extinguished around 1240 when a new west African empire, that of Mali, emerged to dominate that part of the continent.

The crown of St Stephen (997-1038), part of the Hungarian royal regalia. According to tradition, it was given to Stephen by the pope in recognition of his work converting pagans to Christianity. Taken by the Nazis in the Second World War, it came into American hands, and was returned to Hungary only in 1978. In the 9th century AD the Magyars, a tribe from central Asia, settled in the Hungarian plains. The Magyars were expert horsemen and raided as far west as central France and Italy. But in the mid-10th century they were defeated by the Germans in two great battles and then settled down in the Hungarian plains, with many Slav subjects. Not long after, they became Christian, largely due to King Stephen.

A major reason for the Vikings' success lay in the speed and seaworthiness of their ships. Vikings believed that the spirits of important people were buried in their ships, so many of them were buried and have been preserved in the mud. This ship was found at Oseberg and was made for a queen.

The Vikings

Scandinavia was a bleak land which could not support many people. Whenever the population grew too large for the land to support it, its fierce warriors would take to the sea to colonize other places.

The Vikings were ruthless raiders and greatly feared. During their raids, they set up camps. It is from the Scandinavian word for 'camp' that the Vikings got their name. Early in the 800s they began to expand into what is now Russia. (The name Russia comes from a tribe – the Russ – led by the Viking, Rurik.) Vikings seized parts of northern Russia in the 860s. They founded the city of Novgorod.

Other Vikings attacked England during a period of almost continuous raids between 856 and 875 when they conquered the kingdoms of Mercia and Northumbria as well as East Anglia.

Yet other Vikings were to discover Iceland (861) which they settled in 874. Towards the end of this period great Viking explorers like Eric the Red and Leif Ericsson took their followers as far as Greenland and North America (1002).

EUROPE

801 Charlemagne prohibits prostitution.
802–839 Egbert, king of Wessex.
814–840 Political importance of western empire in decline after Charlemagne's death.
Louis the Pious, son of Charlemagne, emperor and king of the Franks.
828 Egbert of Wessex becomes the overall ruler of England.
838 Louis the Pious divides the Frankish empire between his three sons – Lothair, Louis the German, Charles the Bald.
839–858 Ethelwulf, son of Egbert, king of Wessex.
843 Treaty of Verdun – Frankish empire is re-divided. Three Carolingian dynasties – Louis the German rules east of the Rhine, Charles the Bald rules France, Lothair rules Italy, Provence, Burgundy and Lorraine.
844 Kenneth MacAlpine, king of the Scots, defeats the Picts and founds a united Scotland.
850 Jews settle in Germany and begin to develop their own language – Yiddish.
855–875 Emperor Louis II (son of Lothair) – lands again divided.
856–875 Continuous Viking assaults on England.
858–860 Ethelbald, eldest son of Ethelwulf, king of Wessex.
860–865 Ethelbert, second son of Ethelwulf, king of Wessex.
861 Vikings discover Iceland.
865 Vikings invade England – conquer Northumbria, East Anglia, Mercia.
865–871 Ethelred I, third son of Ethelwulf, king of Wessex.
870 Calibrated candles used in England to measure time.
871 Danes attack Wessex – they are defeated by Ethelred at Ashdown.
871–899 Alfred the Great, last son of Ethelwulf, king of Wessex.
874 Vikings settle in Iceland.
875–877 Emperor Charles the Bald – anarchy follows his death.
878 Battle of Edington – Alfred inflicts a decisive defeat on the Danes.
Treaty of Wedmore divides England – Wessex in the south and the Danes in the north – beginning of Danelaw.
881 Charles III, the Fat, emperor and king of Germany, becomes also king of the Franks and re-unites the empire of Charlemagne.
886 Alfred takes London from the Danes.
889 Magyars under Arpad invade Hungarian plain.
899 Alfred's death – Edward the Elder becomes king of Wessex. Magyars invade Moravia (modern Czechoslovakia).
900 Alfonso III, the Great, of Castille begins to reconquer Spain from the Moors.
901 Edward the Elder takes title king of the Angles and Saxons.
906 Magyars begin to invade Germany.
911 Viking Rollo (Hrolf the Ganger) is granted Normandy by the Franks since they are unable to dislodge him from France.
912 Rollo is baptized and takes the name Robert.
913 Edward the Elder recaptures Essex from the Danes.
924–939 Athelstan, king of Wessex, comes to rule most of England.
926 Athelstan annexes Northumbria – the kings of Wales, Strathclyde, the Picts and Scots submit to him.
929 Murder of Wenceslas of Bohemia by his younger brother after attempting to convert his people to Christianity.
936–973 Otto I (the Great), king of Germany.
937 Ba[ttle of] Brunanburh – Athelstan defeats an alliance of Scot[s, D]anes, Vikings. He takes the title 'King of all Brita[in'.]
939–[..]mund, brother of Athelstan, king of England.
942–9[..] [M]alcolm I, king of Scots.
945 Du[n]stan becomes abbot of Glastonbury. Scots annex Cumberland and Westmorland from the English.
946–955 Edred, younger brother of Edmund, king of England. Dunstan his chief minister.
950 Otto I conquers Bohemia.

ELSEWHERE

740–1036 North India: Gurjaru-Prathi-Nara dynasty.
800 Africa: Ghana already known as the 'Land of Gold'.
800–900 Africa: Growth of trans-Sahara trade between west and north Africa – development of cities such as Gao.
800–950 North India: Many petty states exist.
803 Islam: Harun al-Raschid ends the power of the Barmecide family in Baghdad.
813–833 Islam: Mamun the Great, caliph of Baghdad – liberal religious attitudes, a great artistic period.
841–846 China: Wu Tsung initiates persecutions of all religions except Buddhism which is allowed to survive.
862 Russia: Rurik, with the Viking tribe of Russ, seizes power in northern Russia and founds Novgorod.
865 Russia: Russian Vikings attack Constantinople.
867 Byzantium: Photian Schism – the Byzantine Church under Photius, the patriarch of Constantinople, challenges the authority of the pope. In 879 they excommunicate each other.
869 Islam: Arabs conquer Malta.
880 Byzantium: Emperor Basil drives Arabs from mainland Italy.

900 Africa: Hausa kingdom of Daura founded in northern Nigeria.
Zimbabwe in southern Africa a major power.
Byzantium: Bulgars accept the Eastern Orthodox religion.
Islam: The beginnings of the famous Arabian tales: 'A Thousand and One Nights'.
907 China: End of T'ang dynasty is followed by civil wars which last to 960.
907–1123 China: Mongol expansion in Inner Mongolia and northern China.
908–932 Islam: Caliph Muqtadir – the Fatimids conquer north Africa.
916 Africa: Al-Masudi, the Arab scholar, travels from the Gulf down the African coast as far as Mozambique.
920 Africa: Golden Age of Ghana begins.
922 Africa: Fatimids seize Morocco.
930 Islam: Cordoba in Spain becomes the seat of Arab learning.
932 China: Wood block printing adopted to mass-produce classical books – a cheap substitute for stone engraving. Nine Classics are printed.
939 Japan: Civil war.

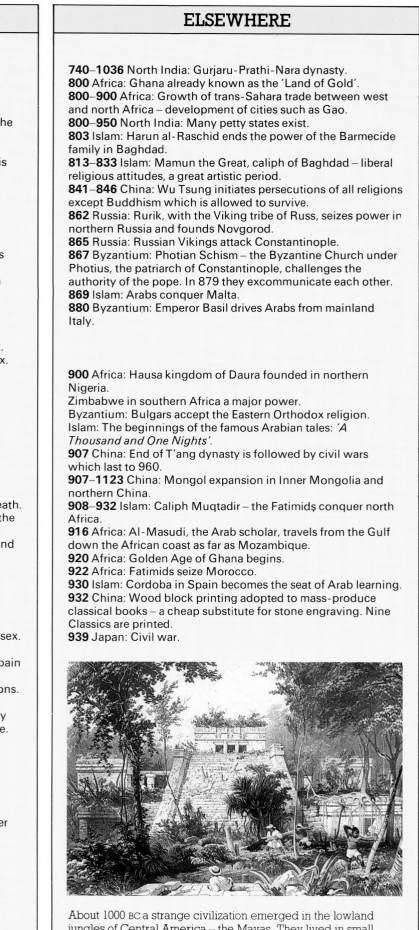

About 1000 BC a strange civilization emerged in the lowland jungles of Central America – the Mayas. They lived in small farming villages, but by 850 they were building great complexes of pyramids, temples and palaces which were the focal points of their religion and their social life. This is a drawing of the ruin of a temple at Tulum in Mexico.

THE MIDDLE AGES AD 950–AD 1100

ENGLAND AND SCOTLAND

955–959 Edwy, son of Edmund, king of England.
956 Edwy exiles Dunstan, King Edward's chief minister.
957 Mercia and Northumbria rebel against Edwy.
959–975 Edgar, brother of Edwy, king of England. Dunstan returns – made Archbishop of Canterbury.
971–995 Kenneth II, king of Scots.
975–978 Edward the Martyr, king of England.
978–1016 Ethelred II succeeds Edward the Martyr who is murdered at Corfe Castle.
980 Danes raid England.
991 Battle of Maldon – Byrhtnoth of Essex defeated by Danes. Ethelred II buys off the Danes with 10,000 pounds of silver (Danegeld).
992 Ethelred concludes a truce with Duke Richard I of Normandy.
994 Sweyn of Denmark and Olaf Trygvesson of Norway sail up the Thames to besiege London – Ethelred buys them off.
995 Olaf returns to Norway, deposes Haaken the Great and makes himself king.
1002 Ethelred marries Emma, sister of Duke Richard of Normandy.
Massacre of St Brice's day – Ethelred orders the slaughter of all Danes in southern England.
1003 Sweyn lands in England to avenge the massacre.
1007 Ethelred buys two years' peace from the Danes.
1012 Danes sack Canterbury – they are bought off.
1013 Sweyn lands in England and is proclaimed king – Ethelred flees to Normandy.
1014 Ethelred II is recalled on the death of Sweyn. Canute retreats to Denmark.
1015 Canute the Dane invades England – war between Danes and Saxons.
1016 Edmund Ironside, king of England, divides it with Canute who holds the north while Edmund holds Wessex, Edmund is assassinated.
1016–1035 Canute, king of England.
1017 Canute divides England into four earldoms.
1019 Canute marries Emma (see 1002), widow of Ethelred II.
1034–1040 Duncan, king of Scots.
1035–1040 Harold I Harefoot, king of England.
1040–1042 Hardicanute, king of England and Denmark (1035–42) – dies of drink.
1040–1057 Macbeth, king of Scots after killing Duncan at the battle of Elgin.
1042–1066 Edward the Confessor, king of England – power in the hands of Earl Godwin of Wessex and his sons.
1051 Godwin exiled – returns with fleet to win back power.
1052 Edward the Confessor founds new Westminster Abbey.
1053 Godwin's son Harold succeeds as earl of Wessex.
1055 Harold's brother, Tostig, becomes earl of Northumbria.
1057 Malcolm, son of Duncan, defeats and kills Macbeth. Lulac, Macbeth's son, is king for a year.
1058–1093 Malcolm Canmore, king of Scots.
1061 Malcolm invades Northumbria.
1063 Harold and Tostig subdue Wales.
1064 Harold is shipwrecked in Normandy and reluctantly swears to support William of Normandy's claim to England.
1065 Northumbria rebels and Tostig is exiled.
1066 Harold, king of England. Tostig and Harold Hardrada king of Norway (1046–66) invade England – they are defeated and killed by Harold at Stamford Bridge.
Battle of Hastings – William defeats and kills Harold to become William I, king of England to 1087.
1066–1069 William completes conquest of England.
1067 Beginning of Tower of London.
1070 Saxons revolt under Hereward the Wake in the Fens.
1071 Hereward the Wake submits.
1072 William invades Scotland.
1087–1100 William II (Rufus), king of England; elder brother Robert is Duke of Normandy.
1093–1097 Donald Bane king of Scots.
1097–1107 Edgar, king of Scotland.

EUROPE

951 Otto I campaigns in Italy.
955 Battle of Lechfeld – Otto I defeats Magyars and stops their westward advance.
960–992 Mieszko I, first ruler of Poland.
961–964 Otto I defends Pope John XII.
962 Pope John XII crowns Otto, emperor in Rome.
987–996 Hugh Capet elected king of France – founds Capetian dynasty.
996–1031 Robert II, son of Hugh Capet, king of France.
998–1038 Stephen I (St Stephen), first king of Hungary.
999 Poles conquer Silesia.
1000 Battle of Svolder – Sweyn kills Olaf of Norway and annexes Norway to Denmark.
1016–1028 Olaf II, king of Norway.
1027–1035 Robert (the Devil), duke of Normandy.
1028 Denmark under Canute conquers Norway and his son Sweyn becomes king.
1031–1060 Henry I, king of France.
1035 William becomes duke of Normandy.
1058–1079 Boleslav II, the Bold, king of Poland, conquers Upper Slovakia.
1060–1108 Philip I, king of France.
1072–1091 Normans invade and conquer Sicily.
1076 Synod of Worms – bishops declare Pope Gregory deposed – Gregory excommunicates Henry IV.
1077 Holy Roman emperor, Henry IV, his throne threatened, does penance to pope at Canossa.
1077–1080 Civil war in the Holy Roman empire.
1080 Pope Gregory again excommunicates Henry and declares him deposed.
1080–1086 Canute IV, king of Denmark.
1083 Henry IV storms Rome.
1084 Robert Guiscard, duke of Apulia, forces Henry to retreat to Germany.
1085 Spain: Alfonso VI captures Toledo from the Moors.
1086 Canute IV of Denmark assassinated – threat to England is lifted.

AFRICA & ASIA

960–1275 China: Sung dynasty.
972 China: Buddhist Canon is printed in Szechuan.
976–997 China: T'ai Tsung completes reunion.

995–1028 Japan: Rule of the Fujiwara Michinaga clan – a literary and artistic golden age.
998–1030 Mahmud, Turkish ruler of Ghazni, founds empire in northern India and eastern Afghanistan.
999 Africa: Bagauda, first king of Kano, in northern Nigeria.
1000 Chinese perfect their invention of gunpowder. Ghana at the height of its power – controls Atlantic ports and trade routes across the Sahara.

1018 India: Mahmud of Ghazni pillages the sacred city of Muttra.
1021 Islam: Caliph al-Hakim declares himself divine – founds the Druse sect.
1028–1050 Zoe, empress of Byzantine empire.
1054 Africa: Abdullah ben Yassim begins the Muslim conquest of west Africa.
1061 Establishment of the Muslim Almoravid dynasty in north Africa – conquest of Spain follows.
1063 Africa: Ghana under Tunka Manin – can field an army of 200,000.
1069–1072 Famine in Egypt.
1071 Turkey: Battle of Manzikert – Alp Arslan, the Seljuk Turk, defeats the Byzantine army and conquers most of Asia Minor.
1075 Seljuk Malik Shah conquers Syria and Palestine.
1081–1118 Alexius I Comnenus, emperor of Byzantium.
1090 Hasan ibn al-Sabbah, first Old Man of the Mountain founds Assassin sect in Persia.
1098 Crusaders defeat the Muslim Saracens at Antioch.
1099 Crusaders capture Jerusalem and Godfrey of Bouillon is elected king of Jerusalem.

The Seljuk Turks

In the 900s Seljuk led a nomadic tribe of Turks from central Asia to the area of Bokhara now in the Soviet Union. After 1000 the Seljuk Turks spread rapidly, creating the first Turkish empire which lasted until the early 13th century. An event of enormous importance was their conversion to Islam in 960.

In 1055 Turghil Beg took Baghdad and was proclaimed Sultan and 'King of the East and the West'. Turghil Beg's nephew, Alp Arslan (the Lion Hero) ruled from 1063 to 1073. He conquered Georgia and Armenia and then in 1071 defeated and captured the emperor of Byzantium, Romanus IV Diogenes, at Manzikert. (Romanus was eventually released for ransom.) The battle was one of the most important of the 11th century for it ended Byzantine power in Asia Minor. From that time the area began to be known as Turkey.

The Seljuks called the sultanate which they established in Asia Minor the sultanate of Rum after the old Roman Empire, for they saw themselves as successors to the Romans. Alp Arslan's son Malik Shah (1073–92) conquered Syria and Palestine. The Seljuks were by now extremely powerful and a great threat to Christian influence in the Middle East, but as new converts to Islam they were less tolerant than the Arabs. When they began to deny Christian pilgrims access to the Holy Places, Pope Urban III called for a crusade to free the Holy Land from the *Saracens* (as the Muslims were known). This led to a growing and bitter conflict between Christian Europe and the Muslim Middle East that was to last for centuries.

The Seljuks made poor imperial rulers however, for they depended largely upon tribute and standing armies to maintain their control rather than creating efficient systems for governing the people.

The Seljuk empire reached its zenith under Malik Shah. When he died in 1092 civil war broke out between his successors which lasted over a century and the Seljuk empire began to break up into separate kingdoms.

Below: Robert II, the Pious, ruler of France (996-1031) – composing church music. The royal family which ruled France for more than 800 years owed its name – Capetian – to the nickname of its founder, Hugh, duke of Francia. Hugh was called Capet from the short cape he wore as lay abbot of St Martin de Tours. As the most powerful vassal of Louis V, king of France, Hugh contrived to have himself elected king on Louis' death in 987. Hugh made sure of keeping the throne in his family by having his son, Robert, crowned in his own lifetime.

Above: This Chinese wine pot was made during the Sung dynasty (960-1279). This dynasty owed its existence to a young officer, Sung T'ai Tsu, who thought he saw a vision. It meant, he said, that a new emperor was about to take over from the young Chou emperor Kung Di. T'ai Tsu and his successors did their best to pull China together after more than 50 years of civil war, but it was not possible. The reforms were not properly carried out and the way was paved for the Mongol take-over by Genghis Khan.

The Norman Conquest

William, duke of Normandy, and his army were slightly out-numbered at Hastings and might have lost the battle, for Harold was an able commander. Only 19 days earlier Harold had decisively defeated Tostig and Harold Hardrada of Norway at Stamford Bridge. But the fortunes of war went against him and at Hastings William was victorious.

Over the next five years William completed the conquest of England. Hereward the Wake, the last to hold out against him, submitted in 1071. The following year William felt strong enough to attack Scotland.

William I was an able administrator who imposed Norman rule and unity over all England. Because of its compact size, England was relatively easy to rule (compared with European lands). For a time, under his successors, England became the most powerful state in Europe.

Hastings was a turning point in English history. Generations were to pass before Normans and English had become sufficiently fused to regard themselves as one people.

Otto III, crowned Holy Roman emperor (983-1002) at the age of 15. He was involved in several disputes with popes. Popes claimed complete spiritual authority over Christian Europe. Emperors claimed control over the Church's activities within their territories, and the right to confirm the election of popes. Matters came to a head in 1075 when Pope Gregory VII forbade the Emperor Henry IV to control the election of bishops in Germany. Henry declared Gregory deposed, whereupon Gregory ex-communicated Henry – that is, banned him from the Church.

The Feudal Age AD 1100–AD 1453

EUROPE & MIDDLE EAST

1100
AD

1104 Crusaders capture Acre.

1154–1189 Henry II of England controls half France.
1164 Constitutions of Clarendon – laws to control trial of rebellious churchmen in England.
1170 Murder of Thomas à Becket (canonized in 1173).
1171 Henry II annexes Ireland.
1174 Saladin, sultan of Egypt, conquers Syria.
1187 Saladin captures Jerusalem.
1189–1192 Third Crusade.
1204 Crusaders sack Constantinople and install Latin Christian ruler.
1212 Children's Crusade – 30,000 children from France and Germany set out for Palestine. Thousands are sold into slavery.
1215 Magna Carta.
1217 Fifth Crusade ends – fails to capture Egypt.
1218 Mongols conquer Persia.
1228–1229 Sixth Crusade – recaptures Jerusalem.

1240 Mongols capture Moscow.
1241 Mongols invade Hungary and then are forced to withdraw from Europe following the death of Ogadai Khan.
1242 Batu sets up Mongol kingdom of 'Golden Horde' on lower Volga River.
1243 Egyptians capture Jerusalem from Christians.
1265 Simon de Montfort's parliament in England – leading citizens from the main towns appointed to take part.
1290–1320 Osman I founds Ottoman dynasty in Turkey.
1291 Saracens capture Acre – last Christian stronghold. End of Crusades.
1295 Edward I holds Model Parliament – de Montfort's principles put into practice.
1301 Osman defeats Byzantines.
1302 Battle of Courtrai – Flemish burghers defeat French knights.
1305–1377 Popes established at Avignon.
1337 Edward III of England claims throne of France – '100 Years' War' begins because of French attacks on Edward's French territories.
1344 Emergence of Hanseatic League.
1345 Ottomans cross into Europe.
1346 English defeat French at Crécy.
1348 Black Death ravages Europe.
1358 Jacquerie revolt of French peasants.
1365 Turks make Adrianople their capital.
1369 Tamerlane becomes king of Samarkand.
1381 Peasants revolt for their rights in England.
1390 Turks complete conquest of Asia Minor.
1401 Tamerlane takes Baghdad and Damascus.
1402 Tamerlane defeats Turks at Angora and overruns most of Ottoman empire.
1405 Death of Tamerlane.
1410 Battle of Tannenberg – Poles defeat Teutonic Knights.
1415 Henry V of England invades France and defeats French at Agincourt.
1420 Treaty of Troyes – Henry V is acknowledged as heir to French throne.
1431 Jeanne d'Arc (Joan of Arc) burnt as a witch at Rouen.
1451–1481 Muhammad II, sultan of Turks.
1453 Fall of Constantinople to Turks. End of Byzantine empire and the Middle Ages.
End of '100 Years' War' – England retains only Calais.

1453
AD

ELSEWHERE

1100 Polynesian islands colonized.

1151 Mexico: End of Toltec empire.
1156 Japan: Civil wars.
1167 Almaric, king of Jerusalem, captures Cairo.
1168 Arabs recapture Cairo.
1190 Temujin (later Genghis Khan) begins to create Mongol empire.
1210 Mongols invade China.
1227 Death of Genghis Khan.
1240 Africa: End of old Ghana empire – rise of Mali.
1260 Kublai has himself elected Khan by his army.
1274 Mongols invade Japan.
1275 Marco Polo enters service of Kublai Khan.
1294 Death of Kublai Khan.
1325 Mexico: Foundation of Tenochtitlan by Aztecs.
1363 Tamerlane begins conquest of Asia.
1368 China: Foundation of Ming dynasty by Chu Yuan-chang.
1398–1399 India: Tamerlane invades kingdom of Delhi.
1421 Chinese transfer capital to Peking.
1438 S. America: Incas establish empire in Peru.

One of the medieval gates of the north German city of Lübeck. Its position on the Baltic, between Scandinavia and mainland Europe meant that it was an important trading centre from 1250 onwards. In the early Middle Ages trade in the Baltic was dominated by Vikings and Friesians. But by the beginning of the 13th century, German settlers had gained control. Cities like Lübeck, Hamburg and Cologne housed families of merchants who travelled far and wide. Often they were attacked by pirates. In 1241 Lübeck and Hamburg made a treaty and pooled their resources to protect each other's merchants. Soon many other towns banded together, they set up trading associations known as *hanse* and together they are known as the Hanseatic League. Until the end of the 15th century, the League dominated the trade of northern Europe.

CULTURE & RELIGION

1100 Chanson de Roland, French heroic poem.
1115 St Bernard founds the abbey of St Clairvaux.
1119 Bologna University founded.
Foundation of Knights Templar. Specially formed to fight in the Crusades. Name came from the fact that the knights' head-quarters on the site of Solomon's Temple.
1122 Concordat of Worms.
1123 Death of Omar Khayyam – Persian poet.
1150 Founding of Paris University.
1170 Beginnings of Oxford University.
1174 'Leaning Tower' of Pisa built.
1176 Roman de Renard (Reynard the Fox) written in French.
1191 Second era of Mayan civilization.
1201 Façade of Notre-Dame in Paris.
1208–1213 Crusade against Albigensian heretics in France.
1209 Beginnings of Cambridge University.
1210 Francis of Assisi founds the Franciscan Order of friars. Friars did not withdraw from the world like the first religious orders but went out to teach and preach.
1212–1311 Rheims Cathedral built.
1215 St Dominic founds the Dominican Order of friars.
1225–1274 Thomas Aquinas, Italian theologian.
1240–1302 Cimabue, Florentine painter.
1245–1270 Choir and cloisters of Westminster Abbey built.
1248 Work begins on Moorish stronghold – the Alhambra in Granada, Spain.
1250–1500 High Gothic period in German art.
1252 Spanish Inquisition begins to use instruments of torture.
1265–1321 Dante Alighieri, Italian poet.
1266–1337 Giotto, Italian painter.
1277 Roger Bacon, English Franciscan philosopher, exiled for heresy (to 1292).
1289 Friar John of Montecorvino, first Archbishop of Peking.
1296 Building of Florence Cathedral under Arnolfo di Cambio.
1304–1374 Birth of Petrarch.
1305–1377 Popes at Avignon – the 'Babylonian Captivity'. Clement V removed the papal court from Rome to southern France, to escape the political turmoil which was raging in Italy. Gregory XI transferred the papal court back to Rome.
1307–1321 Dante composes *Divine Comedy*.
1314 Completion of old St Paul's Cathedral, London.
1325 Development of Nō plays in Japan.
1340–1377 Guillaume de Machaut, (French) the greatest musician of his day.
1340–1400 Geoffrey Chaucer, English poet.
1348–1353 Boccaccio (1313–1375, It) writes the *Decameron*.
1369–1453 John Dunstable, English composer.
1375 Robin Hood appears in English popular literature.
1376 John Wyclif calls for Church reforms in England.
1378–1417 Great Schism – rival popes at Rome and Avignon.
1386–1466 Donatello, Italian sculptor.
1387–1400 Chaucer writes *The Canterbury Tales*.
1399–1474 Guillaume Dufay, Dutch composer.
1400 Modern English develops from Middle English.
1400–1460 Gilles Binchois, Dutch-Burgundian composer.
1403 Compilation of *Yung Lo Ta Tien*, Chinese encyclopaedia in 22,937 volumes (only three copies made).
1414 Medici family of Florence become bankers to the papacy.
1420 Brunelleschi designs dome on Florence Cathedral. Erection of the Great Temple of the Dragon, Peking.
1426 Holland becomes the centre of European music.
1450 Florence under the Medicis becomes centre of Renaissance and humanism.
1452–1519 Italian painter Leonardo da Vinci.
1453 Fall of Constantinople – scholars flee to the west.

DISCOVERIES

The 13th-century castle of Malbork, near Gdansk in Poland. It was the seat of the grand master of the Teutonic Knights from 1309 to 1457. The knights worked under a monastic and military rule and grew rich by exploiting the local peasants.

1100 Decline of Islamic science begins.
1120 Chinese invent playing cards.
1125 Earliest account of a mariner's compass by English scholar, Alexander Neckam.
1161 Explosives used in battle by Chinese. In use in Europe by 1341.
1180 Glass windows appear in English private houses. First windmills with vertical sails in Europe.
1190 Crusaders encounter Saracen warship with centre-line rudder.
1202 Arabic numerals introduced into Europe.
1214–1294 Roger Bacon (English), greatest scientist of his time.
1225 Cotton manufactured in Spain.
1233 Coal mined in Newcastle, England.
1238–1311 Arnold of Villanova, Spanish physician and alchemist, discovers poisonous property of carbon monoxide gas.
1250 Pivotal compass in common use in Mediterranean. Goose quills used for writing.
1252 Golden florins minted at Florence.
1254–1324 Marco Polo, Venetian traveller.
1260–1320 Henri de Mondeville, French surgeon and anatomist.
1280 Death of Albertus Magnus, German scientist and philosopher.
1289 Block printing used at Ravenna.
1290 Invention of spectacles in Italy. First mechanical clock devised by an unknown inventor.
1320 Lace first made in France and Flanders.
1328 Invention of the sawmill.
1337 First scientific weather forecasts by William Merlee of Oxford.
1352 Arab geographer Ibn Battuta explores Sahara desert and visits Mali.
1360 First francs coined in France.
1370 Steel crossbow used as a weapon of war.
1396–1468 Johannes Gutenberg, Swedish inventor of printing from movable type (1440) in Europe.
1405–1433 Cheng Ho, the Chinese explorer makes seven voyages to south-east Asia, India, Persia and Africa.
1415 Oil colours introduced in painting by Flemish artists, Jan and Hubert van Eyck.
1416 Dutch fishermen the first to use drift nets.
1430 'Mad Marjorie', the great cast iron gun, introduced.
1432–1434 Portuguese explorers discover the Azores and round Cape Bojada.
1450 Brandy claimed to have been distilled in the Duchy of Modena, Italy, for the first time.
1451–1506 Christopher Columbus, the 'discoverer of America'.
1452 Metal plates are used for printing.

THE FEUDAL AGE AD 1100–AD 1200

EUROPE	NEAR EAST	ELSEWHERE

EUROPE

1100–1135 Henry I, king of England. Youngest son of William the Conqueror crowned on assassination of William II.
1106 Battle of Tenchebrai – Henry I defeats his brother Robert, duke of Normandy and imprisons him for the rest of his life.
1106–1125 Henry V, Holy Roman emperor.
1108–1137 Louis VI, king of France.
1111 Emperor Henry V forces Pope Paschal II to acknowledge his power.
1114 Matilda (daughter of Henry I) marries Henry V.
1115 St Bernard founds the abbey of Clairvaux in France and becomes the first abbot.
1119 Hugues de Payens founds the Order of Knights Templar in Jerusalem.
1122 Concordat of Worms – German princes end the dispute between pope and emperor over appointment of bishops.
1125–1137 Lothair of Saxony elected Holy Roman emperor.
1128–1143 Alfonso Henriques, count of Portugal, makes Portugal independent of Spain and becomes king.
1129 Empress Matilda, widow of Henry V, marries Geoffrey Plantagenet (1113–1151) Count of Anjou, in France.

1135 Stephen of Boulogne seizes the English throne on the death of Henry I – rival claims of Matilda causes civil war.
1137–1180 Louis VII, king of France.
1138–1152 Conrad III, Holy Roman emperor.
1139 Matilda lands in England.
Second Lateran Council ends schism in Church following illegal election of Anacletus II as a rival to Innocent II.
1141 Battle of Lincoln – Matilda captures Stephen but after a disastrous, short reign is driven out by popular uprising – Stephen is restored.
1148 Matilda leaves England for good.
1152 Annulment of marriage of Louis VII of France and Eleanor of Aquitaine on grounds of blood relationship. Eleanor marries Henry of Anjou allying Aquitaine with Anjou and Normandy.
1152–1190 Frederick I Barbarossa, Holy Roman emperor.
1153 Henry of Anjou, son of Matilda, invades England and forces Stephen to make him his heir.
1154–1159 Pope Adrian IV (Nicholas Breakspear) – only English pope.
1154–1189 Henry II, king of England – also rules more than half of France.
1155 Henry appoints Thomas à Becket chancellor.
Adrian IV grants Henry II the right to rule Ireland.
1159 Henry II levies scutage (money) in place of military service.
1162 Becket is appointed Archbishop of Canterbury – he quarrels with the king over church rights.
1164 Constitutions of Clarendon – set out laws governing the trial of rebellious churchmen in England. Becket flees to France.
1170 Becket, reconciled to Henry II, returns to Canterbury where he is murdered in the cathedral.
1171 Henry II annexes Ireland.
1173 Henry's three eldest sons – Henry, Richard and Geoffrey, supported by Queen Eleanor – rebel.
Canonization of Thomas à Becket.
1179 Grand Assize of Windsor increases the power of the royal courts in England.
1180–1223 Philip II, king of France.
1182 Philip banishes Jews from France.
1185–1211 Sancho I, king of Portugal.
1189–1199 Richard I (Coeur de Lion), king of England.
1190–1197 Henry VI, Holy Roman emperor.
1193 Leopold of Austria who had captured Richard I on his return from the Holy Land hands him to the Emperor Henry who demands ransom.
1194 Henry VI captures Sicily.
Richard is ransomed and returns to England.
1197 Civil war in Germany on death of Henry VI.

NEAR EAST

1104 Crusaders capture Acre.
1118–1143 John II Comnenus, Byzantine emperor – a revival of Byzantine power especially in Asia Minor.
1143–1180 Manuel Comnenus, the greatest of the Comneni, continues the Byzantine revival. Constantinople the acknowledged capital of the world and centre of culture.
1147–1149 Second Crusade follows an appeal by St Bernard of Clairvaux to Conrad III and Louis VII – nothing significant achieved.
1169 Saladin, vizier of Egypt – in 1174 he becomes sultan (to 1193).
1174 Saladin conquers Syria.
1177 Baldwin IV of Jerusalem defeats Saladin at Montgisard.
1179 Saladin besieges Tyre.
1180 Truce between Saladin and Baldwin IV.
1180–1183 Alexius II Comnenus, Byzantine emperor.
1183–1185 Andronicus I Comnenus, Byzantine emperor – a reformer, he is deposed and executed. A period of corruption follows and the empire goes to pieces.
1185–1195 Isaac II, Byzantine emperor.
1186–1188 Peter and John Asen lead insurrection against Byzantium – the formation of new Bulgarian state.
1187 Saladin captures Jerusalem.
1189–1192 Third Crusade led by Richard of England, Philip of France and Frederick Barbarossa (Holy Roman emperor). A lay affair precipitated by the fall of Jerusalem – gave Englishmen their first taste of eastern adventure.
1191 Richard I conquers Cyprus and captures Acre.
1192 Richard captures Jaffa, makes peace with Saladin.
1193 Muslims capture Bihar and Bengal.
1193–1198 Al-Aziz Imad al-Din succeeds Saladin.
1195–1203 Alexius III, Byzantine emperor.

ELSEWHERE

1100 Colonization of the Polynesian islands.

The 12th-century ambulatory at Peterborough Cathedral. Founded in 1119 in eastern England, the Cathedral is typical of the Romanesque style of architecture introduced to England by the Normans. The rounded arches and sturdy pillars became a familiar feature of church design in the years that followed.

1130–1169 Africa: Almohad dynasty (founded by preacher Ibn Tumant) in power in Morocco.
1145–1150 Africa: Almohads conquer Moorish Spain.
1151 Mexico: End of Toltec empire.
1156–1185 Japan: Civil war.
1161 China: Explosives used at the battle of Ts'ai-shih.
1185–1333 Japan: Kamakura period.
1189 America: Last (known) Norse visit to North America.
1190 Mongols: Temujin begins to create the Mongol empire.
1190–1225 Africa: Lalibela, emperor of Ethiopia.
1192 Japan: Minamoto becomes shogun.
1196–1464 Africa: Marimid dynasty in Morocco – foundation of Fez.

Stability and Change

The Lion of St Mark, the symbol of Venice because St Mark's supposed relics were brought to Venice from Alexandria in 829. Venice was founded in the 500s by refugees from the Huns and Lombards. Settling on islands among the lagoons along Italy's north Adriatic coast, they gradually established trade based on salt and fish. Venetian merchants built fleets in which they sailed to the eastern Mediterranean where they traded their own wares for goods from the Far East.

In the 12th century the Byzantine empire challenged the west as Constantinople again became the 'centre of the world'. In China on the other side of the world progress of a different kind – in the arts and sciences – proceeded virtually unknown to western civilization.

The Feudal System

It provided the structure of society in England, France, Germany, Spain and Italy for several centuries. The king or emperor granted land or estates to his greatest followers (barons or lords) in return for military service. In their turn these barons gave land on a smaller scale to vassals, lesser nobles or knights whose loyalty was first to them but eventually to the king. At the lower end of the scale came the freemen and serfs. Freemen had land of their own but still had to work for their lords several days a week. Serfs had few rights of any kind and were tied to their lords' estates. So everyone owed duty to someone above him. This was discharged in the form of service, usually to the lord of the manor and by fighting in time of war. When in 1159 Henry II of England levied scutage – allowing knights or barons to pay money instead of fighting in his wars – he began a process of immense historical significance. The levying of taxes rather than the giving of service finally destroyed the feudal system.

The Third Crusade

The character of Saladin fascinated Christian Europeans. They found it difficult to believe that a man of such chivalry and accomplishments could be a Muslim. The Third Crusade (1189–1192) was sparked off by Saladin's

planta genista

King Richard I of England (1189-1199) on a 13th-century tile. Richard led the Crusades to the Holy Land with great success earning himself the name *Coeur de Lion* or Lionheart. But although a popular hero, he was a poor king of England; he neglected government and sold off crown rights to raise money to pay for his crusade. Richard was the son of Henry II who had founded a new dynasty – the *Angevins* from the family estate of Anjou in France. Its popular name is *Plantagenet* after the nickname applied to Henry's father who wore a sprig of broom (*planta genista*) in his cap as a badge.

capture of Jerusalem. It was led by three of the greatest European kings: Richard Coeur de Lion of England (regarded in his time as the perfect example of knightly chivalry), Philip of France and the Emperor Frederick Barbarossa (he drowned on the way to the Holy Land). Philip and Richard quarrelled, so Philip returned to France after the capture of Acre in 1191. Eventually the Crusade broke up but not before Richard had come within sight of Jerusalem. Although he refused to look upon the Holy City he could not conquer Richard concluded a truce with Saladin which allowed Christians to enter the city.

Manuel Comnenus of Byzantium

An idealistic and chivalrous ruler, Manuel was also a statesman and ambitious soldier. He ruled the Byzantine empire for nearly 40 years (1143–1180) and made his capital the focus of culture and art in the Christian world. His ambition was to reunite the eastern and western empires of Rome by reconquering Italy and overthrowing the Holy Roman emperors. The result was constant conflict in the west, especially with the Normans. The price Comnenus paid was to weaken his empire in the east where there was a resurrection of Turkish Seljuk power. Nonetheless his reign was one of the last great periods in the long history of Byzantium.

China

Although often a period of political confusion the 12th century saw great advances for China in the arts and sciences. The end of the 11th century was the golden age of landscape painting among the northern Sung. Sung ceramics reached a degree of perfection that has perhaps never since been equalled. Explosives were first used in battle in 1161, a development whose effects when later used in Europe hastened the end of the feudal age. Philosophical debate was also explosive. Chu Hsi (1130–1200), whose teachings were scientific, was opposed by Lu Chiu-yuan who stressed the teachings of Mencius – that goodness comes from within. Finally, the delicate art of drinking tea spread through northern China.

The Mongols

Mongol camp in central Asia. Now, as in the 13th century, they lived in felt tents called *yurts*, moving from winter pasture to summer pasture with their flocks and herds. Mongol soldiers had three or four mounts and carried two or three bows, three quivers of arrows, an axe, rope and a sword.

The Mongol empire of Genghis Khan and Kublai Khan was one of the largest in world history. Yet at the beginning of the 13th century the Mongols were a group of nomadic tribes confined to the windy steppes north of China. Following the death of Kublai Khan in 1294 their empire was soon to break up. But in that 100 years, the Mongol empire had awesome power.

The empire was founded by Temujin (1155–1227) who was proclaimed Genghis Khan in 1206. He rapidly expanded the areas under Mongol control using a military machine that for its time was unmatched. The Mongols were very mobile – their horsemen charged silently into battle so that only the thunder of hooves was heard – a tactic that struck terror into their enemies. They also developed superior siege equipment.

The empire reached its greatest extent under Ogadai (1229–1241). At the time of Ogadai's death the Mongols had swept across Russia, the Middle East and into Austria.

Christian Europe was deeply divided at the time. In an age of uncertainty and superstition Batu Khan, the Mongol general who had led the invasion of Europe, was seen as 'the punishing Rod of God'. To the relief of Europe, on

EUROPE	MONGOLS	ELSEWHERE
1203 John, king of England (1199–1216), has his nephew Arthur murdered.	**1206** Temujin is proclaimed Genghis Khan – 'Emperor within the Seas'.	**1200** Mexico: Hunac Ceel revolts against the Maya of Chichen Itza – he establishes a new capital at Mayapan.
1207 Pope Innocent III (1198–1216) appoints Stephen Langton Archbishop of Canterbury. King John does not allow him to take office.	**1210** Mongols invade China.	Africa: Jews given special privileges in Morocco.
1208 Innocent lays England under Interdict.	**1218** Genghis Khan captures Persia.	**1202–1204** Fourth Crusade – crusaders unable to pay Venice for transport, capture Constantinople and sack it in order to pay Venetians – instal Latin (Roman) ruler.
1209 Innocent excommunicates King John.	**1219** Mongols conquer Bokhara.	
1210 Innocent excommunicates the emperor Otto IV, Holy Roman emperor (1198–1212).	**1223** Mongols invade Russia.	**1206–1290** India: Dynasty of 'Slave Kings'.
1212–1250 Frederick II, Holy Roman Emperor.	**1227** Death of Genghis Khan – empire divided among sons.	**1217–1222** Fifth Crusade fails to capture Egypt.
1213 Pope Innocent declares King John deposed – John makes peace.	**1229–1241** Ogadai is elected khan.	**1219–1333** Japan: Hojo Clan rules, after the end of Minamoto family.
1215 Magna Carta – barons force King John to agree a statement of their rights.	**1234** Mongols annex the Chin empire.	**1228–1229** Sixth Crusade – crusaders recapture Jerusalem under Emperor Frederick II.
1216–1272 Henry III, king of England at age nine.	**1240** Mongols capture Moscow, destroy Kiev.	
1223–1226 Louis VIII, king of France.	**1241** Mongols invade Hungary and cross Danube into Austria – they withdraw from Europe on the death of Ogadai.	**1240** Africa: Old Empire of Ghana is extinguished and incorporated in new kingdom of Mali.
1224–1227 War between England and France.		
1226–1270 Louis IX (St Louis), king of France.		
1227 Henry III begins personal rule without regents in England.	**1242** Batu sets up Mongol kingdom of the 'Golden Horde' on the lower Volga River.	**1243** Egyptians capture Jerusalem from the Christians.
1240 Battle of Neva – Alexander Nevski of Novgorod defeats the Swedes.	**1246–1251** Guyuk is khan.	
1245 Synod of Lyons called by Pope Innocent IV (1243–1254) declares Frederick II deposed.	**1251–1259** Mongka is khan – empire divided.	**1248–1270** Seventh Crusade by Louis IX of France.
1247–1250 War in Italy between Frederick and the papal allies.	**1258** Mongols pillage Hanoi.	
1250–1254 Conrad IV, Holy Roman emperor.	**1260** Kublai, Mongol leader, has himself elected khan by his army although he only took title of khan in 1271.	**1250** Saracens capture Louis IX in Egypt – he is ransomed.
1254–1273 The Great Interregnum – struggle for the crown of the Holy Roman emperor.		
1256 Pope Alexander IV founds the Augustinian Order from several groups of hermits.		
Llewellyn ap Griffith drives out the English – adopts new title 'Prince of Wales'.		
1263 Norway surrenders Hebrides to Scots.		
1264 Simon de Montfort and other English barons defeat Henry II at Lewes.		
1265 De Montfort parliament – burgesses summoned to parliament from major towns for first time.		
Battle of Evesham – de Montfort defeated and killed by Edward (son of Henry III).		

1200 AD

1260 AD

Ogadai's death, the Mongol generals were recalled to decide upon his successor.

Kublai Khan (1260–1294) was the greatest of the khans and we get our picture of his empire most vividly from the writings of Marco Polo, the Venetian explorer who travelled to the khan's court and then entered his service from 1275 to 1292. Marco Polo travelled widely in the khan's domains and later provided Europe with accurate knowledge of Asia.

Kublai Khan gave special attention to economic and social affairs. Canals were repaired. Imperial roads were improved making the postal service of 200,000 horses the swiftest known up to that date. Charitable relief was provided for orphans and the sick, for whom hospitals were also built. Inspectors examined the crops and bought surplus grain to store against famine. The use of paper currency was greatly improved and extended.

When Marco Polo was in China (and for many years afterwards) the deep sea port of Zayton (Ch'uan-chou) was the busiest in the world. The Mongols traded with Java, Malaya, Ceylon, India and Persia. Kublai Khan showed considerable tolerance in religious matters. He favoured Buddhism but allowed Muslim communities in his empire and gave full protection to Christians. In 1289, for example, he created a special bureau for Christianity under the care of the Franciscan friar John of Montecorvino, whom he made Archbishop of Peking.

China, conquered by the Mongols, was the centre of their empire, and Kublai Khan ruled it according to Chinese custom. Both literature and art were encouraged and in this period the novel and drama were introduced.

After Kublai's death his grandson Temur Oljaitu ruled China to 1307. But Temur was the last effective Yuan ruler and the Yuan dynasty of Kublai Khan petered out in 1368.

The seal of King John upon the Magna Carta. At Runnymede on the River Thames on June 15 1215, barons and church leaders assembled to force King John to sign the Magna Carta. It was a major step away from the absolute power of the crown. A power much abused, particularly by King John. The document guaranteed tax collection only by legal means, justice to all men and no imprisonment without trial.

EUROPE	MONGOLS	ELSEWHERE
1268–1271 Papacy vacant. **1270** Louis IX of France dies on Seventh Crusade. **1270–1285** Philip III, king of France. **1272–1307** Edward I, king of England. **1273–1291** Rudolf I, Holy Roman emperor. **1274** Synod of Lyons – Pope Gregory X (1271–1276) recommends conclaves (meetings) to be secret to avoid corruption. **1277** Llewellyn submits to Edward I. **1278** Rudolf I defeats and kills Ottokar of Bohemia at Marchfeld. **1279** Rudolf surrenders his claims to Sicily and the papal states. **1283** Edward I completes conquest of Wales. Llewellyn killed in skirmish and his brother David executed. **1285–1314** Philip IV, the Fair, king of France. **1286–1290** Margaret, the 'Maid of Norway' proclaimed queen of Scotland in absence. **1290** Death of Margaret on way to Scotland causes confusion – 13 claimants to Scottish throne. Edward I expels Jews from England. **1291** Scots accept Edward I as suzerain (nominal controller) – arbitrates in succession dispute. **1292** Edward nominates John Balliol as king of Scotland. **1292–1298** Adolf, Count of Nassau, Holy Roman emperor. **1295** Edward I holds Model Parliament and summons knights and burgesses from shires and towns – the first representative parliament. **1296** Edward I deposes John Balliol of Scotland – who rebelled against the English – interregnum to 1306. **1296–1303** Conflict between Philip of France and Pope Boniface (1294–1303) over papal powers in France. **1297** Battle of Cambuskenneth – William Wallace of Scotland defeats English army. **1298** Edward defeats Wallace at Falkirk and reconquers Scotland.	**1260–1368** Yuan (Mongol) dynasty in China. **1264** Kublai Khan captures his brother and then reunites the Mongol empire. Transfers capital to Yen-ching and builds Khanbalig (modern Peking). **1268–1279** Mongols obtain control of all China. **1271–1285** Marco Polo, the Venetian traveller (1254–1324), travels to court of Kublai Khan. **1274** Mongol invasion of Japan fails. **1275** Marco Polo enters service of Kublai Khan as a travelling envoy. **1281** Second Mongol invasion of Japan ends in disaster. **1287** Mongols pillage Pagan, capital of Burma. **1289** Friar John of Montecorvino becomes first Archbishop of Peking. **1292–1293** Mongol expedition to Java fails. **1294** Death of Kublai Khan. **1295–1307** Temur Oljaitu (Ch'eng Tsung) grandson of Kublai Khan is emperor of China – last effective ruler of Yuan dynasty.	 Gothic interior of Ste-Chapelle, Paris. Louis IX, its builder, was a wise king and a great soldier – he led the 7th crusade. He was also devoted to the church and was canonized in 1297. **1261–1282** Byzantium: Emperor Michael VIII, restores Byzantine authority. **1290–1320** India: Firuz, Turkish leader, founds the Khalji dynasty in Delhi. **1291** Saracens capture Acre, last Christian stronghold in the Holy Land – this ends period of Crusades. **1297** Louis IX canonized.

The Black Death

The Black Death was a fearful epidemic of bubonic plague which caused havoc throughout Europe. It originated in China and was carried along the trade routes to Europe by the fleas on rats. It reached Cyprus in 1347 and soon swept across all Europe, affecting Italy, France, Germany and England in 1348. In 1349 it was in Scotland, Poland and Scandinavia. Russia was ravaged in 1351. Half Europe's population, about 25,000,000 people, are estimated to have died. Many more died in Asia and China.

The old economic and social order in Europe was thrown into chaos. The immediate result was a desperate shortage of labour, for the lower classes were by far the worst affected by the plague, and as a result wages soared. In England, for example, wages rose 50 per cent for men and as much as 100 per cent for women. In 1351, because of the labour demands, the English parliament passed the Statute of Labourers which fixed both wages and prices – it was an attempt to compel able-bodied men to accept work when and where this was offered. But the Statute of Labourers strengthened the position of the humbler workers and hastened the end of the feudal system. There was now free land to be rented and more jobs. A growing sense of freedom emerged in the ranks of peasants and labourers.

In France a major manifestation of this new relationship between the upper and lower classes came with the Jacquerie rising of French peasants in 1358. They rebelled at the imposition of heavy war taxes to pay the ransoms of the nobility, captured by the English at Poitiers in 1356. The revolt was put down mercilessly by the nobility.

In England, much later, came the Peasants' Revolt of 1381. Although this could hardly be attributed directly to the Black Death, it was the result of the changes in attitude which followed it. Efforts by landlords to force the peasants back into a system of servile tenure sparked off the revolt which was led by Wat Tyler and John Ball. It was mainly centred upon the south east (Kent and Essex). The peasants burnt manor houses, destroyed records of tenure and wrecked game parks. A mob of 100,000 marched on London where they sacked and burnt John of Gaunt's home – the Savoy Palace. They dispersed when the young Richard II promised reforms. Violent retribution followed but attempts to restore the old system of villeinage failed. The Peasants' Revolt was a further sign of the changing times and another crippling blow to the old feudal order which by then was crumbling fast.

European Art

The movement away from feudalism was also evident in the arts. Before the 14th century artists had been simply employed craftsmen. By the end of the 15th century artists, sculptors and architects were known far and wide by name. Men like Leonardo da Vinci and Michelangelo were received as honoured guests by powerful men.

The city of Florence led Europe in the arts. There Dante, Petrarch, Boccaccio and Giotto (1266–1337) and others were representatives of this new adventurous spirit known as the Renaissance. Dante (1265–1321) established the Tuscan dialect (Florentine language) of Italy – his *Divine Comedy* was his greatest work. Petrarch (1304–1374) is one of the greatest Italian poets – a man of astonishing range. Boccaccio (1313–1374) is the father of Italian prose and did much to revive interest in the ancient Greek and Roman writers. His masterpiece is the *Decameron*.

In England Geoffrey Chaucer (1340–1400) greatly developed English poetry. He was a diplomat and worked in the circle of men who surrounded John of Gaunt, Edward III's son. He brought some of the sophistications of the continent to the less polished Anglo-Saxon language. His greatest work, *The Canterbury Tales*, marks the transition from Middle English to 'modern' English and from his time onwards writers worked in their own tongue rather than in French or Latin as they had done. In France, the best illuminated (painted) manuscripts and tapestries were being made and Jean Froissart wrote the *Historical Chronicles*.

Maesta by Duccio; (Siena 1260-1319). In 1250 Italy was split into many separate city states. Through trade those in the north became wealthy and powerful and could afford to have beautiful pictures painted to decorate their churches and buildings. The city states of Florence, Siena and Pisa were close together and all had their own schools of painting. Their reputation as centres of art and science drew scholars and painters from all over Europe. They brought with them the latest advances in learning. One result of this was that people, especially in northern Europe, began to question the traditional teachings of the church. This questioning gradually caused the church to split into Catholics and Protestants.

EUROPE

1301 Edward I invests his son, Edward, as Prince of Wales.
1302 Battle of Courtrai – Flemish burghers defeat French knights and prevent occupation by France.
1305 Execution of Scottish patriot, William Wallace, by English.
1305–1377 Papal See moved to Avignon.
1306 Philip IV expels Jews from France.
Robert Bruce leads Scottish rebellion against English – crowned at Scone.
1307–1327 Edward II, king of England.
1314 Battle of Bannockburn – Robert Bruce defeats the weak Edward II and makes Scotland independent.
1316–1334 John XXII Pope – the papacy sends eight Dominican friars to Ethiopia in search of Prester John – the Christian emperor.
1317 France adopts Salic law which excludes women from succession to the throne.
1326 Queen Isabella and Roger Mortimer sail from France with an army to rebel against Edward II of England.
1327 Parliament declares Edward II deposed – Edward III succeeds his father. Edward II is murdered.
Louis IV, Holy Roman emperor (1314–1347) invades Italy and declares Pope John XXII deposed.
1328–1350 Philip VI, king of France founds House of Valois.
1333 Edward III defeats Scots who had rebelled at Halidon Hill.
1337 Edward III, provoked by attacks on his French territories, declares himself king of France – the beginning of the '100 Years' War'.
1338 Declaration of Rense – electors of Holy Roman empire declare the empire to be independent of the papacy.
Treaty of Coblenz – alliance between England and empire.
1340 Battle of Sluys – English defeat French and gain control of the Channel.
English parliament passes statutes that taxation may only be imposed by parliament.
1346 Edward III invades France and defeats French at Crécy.
1347 English capture Calais.
1349 Persecution of Jews in Germany.
1353 Statute of Praemunire – English parliament forbids appeals to the pope.
1356 Battle of Poitiers – Edward the Black Prince, son of Edward III, defeats the French and captures King John II.
1358 Jacquerie revolt by French peasants is suppressed by the regent Charles, son of John II.
1360 Treaty of Brétigny ends the first stage of the '100 Years' War' – Edward III gives up his claim to the French throne.
1367 Confederation of Cologne – 77 Hanse towns prepare to fight Denmark.
1369 Renewed war between France and England.
1370 Peace of Stralsund establishes the power of the Hanse towns with the right to veto Danish kings.
Sack of Limoges by Black Prince.
1371 Robert II, king of Scotland – the first Stuart monarch.
1372 French recapture Poitou and Brittany from English.
1374 John of Gaunt, son of Edward III, rules England – the king is too old and the Black Prince is ill.
1376 Good Parliament of Edward, the Black Prince, introduces many reforms of government.
Death of Black Prince.
1377 Pope Gregory XI returns to Rome.
1377–1399 Richard II, king of England on death of Edward III.
1381 Peasants' Revolt in England.
1382 Scots with a French army attack England.
1389 Truce halts fighting between English, French and Scots until 1396.
1397 Union of Kalmar brings Norway, Denmark and Sweden under one King, Eric of Pomerania.
1399 Henry Bolingbroke, on death of John of Gaunt, his father, deposes Richard II to become Henry IV, king of England.

OTTOMAN TURKS

1290–1326 Osman I, founder of the Ottoman dynasty based on the Black Sea coast of Asia Minor.
1301 Osman defeats the Byzantines.
1326 Bursa becomes Ottoman capital.

Edward III's army of nearly 13,000 defeated Philip IV's army of 40,000 at the battle of Crecy in 1346. This was mainly because the English army had longbow archers capable of loosing 16 arrows a minute compared to 2 or 3 crossbow arrows a minute from the French. Following this and other victories, Edward secured a large part of France by treaty. However by 1453 only Calais was left.

1326–1359 Orkhan I – first clear ruler and organizer of Ottoman Turks.
1345 Ottomans first cross the Bosporus into Europe.
1354 Turkish settlements in Europe; they spread through Thrace (N. Greece).
1369–1372 Ottomans conquer Bulgaria.
1371 Ottomans defeat Serbs and conquer Macedonia.
1389 Battle of Kossovo – Ottomans defeat a coalition of Serbs, Bulgars, Bosnians, Wallachians and Albanians.
1390 Ottomans complete the conquest of Asia Minor.
1391–1398 First siege of Constantinople by Turks. Constantinople pays tribute.
1396 Abortive crusade by about 20,000 European knights against Turks – defeated at Nicopolis.
1397 Turks invade Greece.

ELSEWHERE

1300–1400 S. America: Period of expansion by Incas.
1320–1413 India: Tughluk dynasty founded by Ghidyas-ud-din Tughluk at Delhi – encourages agriculture, reforms taxes, creates postal system.
1324 Africa: Mansa Musa, king of Mali (1307–1332), travels to Mecca. His wealth and magnificence of his court astonish those who see him.
1325 Mexico: Foundation (traditional) of Tenochtitlan (now Mexico City) by the Aztecs.
1325–1351 India: Muhammad Tughluk – a military genius but his policies lead to constant revolts.
1333–1336 Japan: Emperor Daigo II overthrows the Hojo family of shoguns and starts personal rule.
1336 Japan: Revolution – Daigo II exiled. Ashikaga family rule as shoguns – to 1568 but a period of civil war to 1392.
1338 India: Muhammad Tughluk loses Bengal in north east.

1351 Firuz Tughluk – restores administration in Delhi kingdom.
1363 Tamerlane, descendant of Genghis Khan (Timur the Lame), begins conquest of Asia.
1368–1644 China: Ming dynasty founded by Yuanchang who drives Mongols from Peking.
1369 Korea submits to Ming dynasty.
Tamerlane becomes king of Samarkand.

1388 Mongols driven out of their capital, Karakorum, by Chinese.
1391 Tamerlane defeats Toqtamish, Mongol khan of the 'Golden Horde'.
1392–1910 Korea: I dynasty.
1393 Tamerlane takes Baghdad and reduces Mesopotamia.
1398–1399 Tamerlane invades the kingdom of Delhi which he desolates – 100,000 prisoners massacred, then Tamerlane leaves.

THE FEUDAL AGE AD 1400–AD 1453

1400 AD

1453 AD

ENGLAND & FRANCE

1400 Richard II murdered
Owen Glendower
leads rebellion of the Welsh.
1402 Henry IV invades
Wales.
1403 Henry IV defeats the
Percy family at Shrewsbury.
1405 French land in Wales
to support Glendower.
1406 Henry, Prince of
Wales, defeats Welsh.
1406–1437 James I, king of
Scotland, (captive in
England 1406–1423).

1415 Henry V revives
English claim to French
throne and invades France –
defeats French at Agincourt.
1416 Death of Owen
Glendower.
1419 Henry allies with
Philip II of Burgundy
(Burgundy is independent
from France).
1420 Treaty of Troyes –
Henry V acknowledged heir
to the French throne by the
insane French king, Charles
VI. Henry marries Catherine,
daughter of Charles VI.
1422 Death of Henry V and
Charles VI – War flares up
again.
1422–1461 Infant Henry VI,
king of England.
Charles VII, king of France
(Dauphin to 1429).
1424 Battle of Cravant –
Duke of Bedford (regent)
defeats the French.
Last of the great English
victories in '100 Years' War'.
1428 English besiege
Orléans.
1429 Joan of Arc, in
command of French forces,
raises the siege of Orléans.
1430 Burgundians capture
Joan of Arc and hand her
over to the English.
1431 Joan of Arc is burnt at
Rouen, Normandy, as a
witch.
Henry VI of England
crowned king of France in
Paris under treaty.
1436 English troops withdraw from Paris.
1449 Charles VII enters
Rouen.
1451–1453 England swept
from France. Only Calais is
retained by English.
End of '100 Years' War'
between France and
England.
1453 Henry VI becomes
insane (for two years).

REST OF EUROPE

1409 Gregory XII pope in
Rome (to 1415). Benedict
XIII – anti-pope based at
Avignon – recognized by
France, Scotland and parts
of Germany and Italy.
Council of Pisa called to
resolve the Great Schism.
Deposes the rival popes and
elects a third – Alexander V –
anti-pope at Pisa. All the
popes refuse to resign. The
schism is now a triple one.
1410–1415 John XXIII,
anti-pope at Pisa.
1414–1417 Council of Con-
stance, called by Pope John
XXIII, deposes John,
persuades Gregory to resign
and isolates Benedict XIII.
1417–1431 Pope Martin V –
end of Great Schism.

Joan of Arc, the young
peasant girl who put new
heart into France during the
'Hundred Years' War', at the
siege of Paris in 1430. Joan
believed she heard voices
guiding her to go to the
uncrowned king of France
and demand to lead his
soldiers. In 1430 she was
captured by the Burgundians
who handed her over to the
English. They burned her as
a witch.

1431–1447 Pope Eugene
IV.
1434 Cosimo Medici
becomes ruler of Florence.
1439 Council of Basle
deposes Pope Eugene IV –
Felix V anti-pope to 1449.
1447–1455 Pope Nicholas
V.
1451 Birth of Christopher
Columbus, dies 1506.

NEAR EAST

1401 Tamerlane takes
Damascus and Baghdad.
1402 Battle of Angora –
Bayazid, the Turkish sultan,
defeated and captured by
Tamerlane. He overruns
most of the Ottoman empire
which saves Byzantium.
1403 Tamerlane withdraws
from Anatolia.
1404–1447 Shah Rukh
(fourth son of Tamerlane)
rules Persia – reign of
splendour.
1405 Death of Tamerlane on
way to China to convert
them to Islam. Mongol
empire disintegrates.
1405–1413 Civil war in
Ottoman empire.
1411–1442 Ahmad Shah in
western India builds
Ahmadabad as his capital –
it becomes one of most
beautiful cities in world.
1413–1421 Muhammad I
consolidates Ottoman
power.
1421–1451 Sultan Murad II
– rivalry between Ottomans
and Venice.
1428 Byzantines conquer
Morea in Greece except for
the Venetian ports – this
becomes the most valuable
and extensive part of the
Byzantine empire for its final
period.

Ming dynasty jade belt
ornament. The Ming dynasty
was founded in 1368 by Chu
Yuan-chang, who overthrew
the Mongols, bringing order
to China.

1444 Second western
crusade against the Turks is
crushed at Varna.
1448–1453 Constantine XI
last Byzantine emperor.
1451–1481 Muhammad II,
sultan of Turkey.
1453 The fall of Constantinople to the Turks after a
siege of 54 days marks the
end of the Byzantine empire
and is usually regarded as
the end of the Middle Ages.

ELSEWHERE

1392–1494 Korea: Period of
great prosperity.
1403–1424 China: Reign of
Ch'eng Tsu.
1403–1433 China sends a
series of naval expeditions
through the south seas as far
as Sumatra, Ceylon,
Hormuz, Aden.

The siege of Constantinople
in 1453. Sultan Muhammad
II's Turkish forces battered
the walls with cannon fire for
six weeks before attacking it
on three sides. Its capture
marked the end of the
Byzantine empire. Under
Turkish rule its lands became
the most backward in
Europe.

1418–1419 Portuguese
exploration of the Madeira
Islands.
1421 Chinese transfer
capital to Peking.
1431 S. E. Asia: Khmer city
of Angkor is abandoned.
1433 Africa: Tuaregs from
Sahara sack Timbuktu.
1438 S. America: Inca
empire at its height in Peru.
1442 S. America:
Portuguese find gold at Rio
de Oro.
1444 W. Africa: Huno
Tristan reaches the Senegal
River – the first green coastline (not desert).

Ottoman Turks

The Ottoman Turks established their power in Asia Minor during the 14th century. The Ottoman dynasty was founded by Osman I (1290–1326). In the middle of the century they first crossed into Europe and in 1389 defeated a coalition of Balkan peoples who tried to stop their advance. By 1391 the Turks had completed their conquest of Asia Minor and established a major bridgehead in the Balkans. Then they besieged Constantinople for the first time (1391–1398), but failed to capture it.

The astonishing rise of the Mongol military genius, Tamerlane, who defeated the Turks at the battle of Angora (Ankara) in 1402 very nearly destroyed Ottoman power completely. But the next year Tamerlane withdrew from Anatolia and two years later died. There followed a period of civil war but by 1451 the Ottomans had reunited their empire, consolidated their power and expanded further into the Balkans. Then Muhammad II became sultan. He was a ruthless, brilliant soldier but also a cultivated man, patron of arts and subsequently a great ruler. At the beginning of his reign he was determined to take Constantinople, then still regarded as the greatest city of the Christian world. The siege in 1453 is one of the epics of history and though Byzantium had become weak and disorganized, its last emperor Constantine XI showed great gallantry in his defence of the city. He died in the fighting after the walls had been breached. Muhammad renamed the city Istanbul and made it his capital.

The Incas

The Inca empire, centred upon Peru in South America, had flourished for centuries before the Spanish conquests at the beginning of the 1500s. It had a population of between 6 and 8 million. It was an absolute despotism – all power resided in the hands of the Inca who was both ruler, and representative of the Sun Deity, the God of the Incas. There was a well-advanced system of provincial and local administration and everyone had his place fixed in Inca society. A large army and a highly-developed system of communications ensured central control.

The Incas were the most politically-advanced people of the New World. Navigation and trade along the coasts of Peru and Chile were well-developed, and there was a great tradition of oral poetry and music. But most of all the Incas were great builders. Huge sections of vast buildings still stand where more modern ones have been destroyed by the frequent earthquakes that plague Peru.

On his death, Huayna Capac divided the Inca empire between his son Huascar and his illegitimate son Atahualpa with the result that a civil war followed. Atahualpa had just gained control of the whole empire when the Spanish Conquistadores arrived led by Francisco Pizarro in 1533.

The fall of Constantinople ended an era and had momentous consequences for Europe which regarded the event as a major cataclysm. It meant the end of the Byzantine empire, the inheritor of the traditions of Rome, which had lasted for 1000 years. Many scholars from Constantinople fled to Europe where their teaching and fresh ideas were to play an important part in the Renaissance. It cut the overland trade routes to the east which forced Europeans to look west to America and to search for new routes by sea to the east.

Even though the Ottomans were more tolerant towards Christians than European Christians had ever been towards Muslims, they remained a constant threat to Europe until the Peace of Karlowitz in 1699, when the Ottoman empire went into decline.

Prince Henry the Navigator of Portugal (1394-1460) organizing an expedition to sail down the west coast of Africa. Before Henry, people believed that the sea boiled near the equator and that ships fell off the edge of the world. By the time he died ships had reached as far south as the coast of Sierra Leone, and he had founded a school of navigation in Portugal.

The Incas were experts at building fortresses made of huge blocks of stone. They were built near all cities, as safe places in times of trouble. This is the greatest Inca fortress at Sacsahuaman overlooking Cuzco. The architects of the time had no paper on which to draw plans. Instead they made models of clay or stone for the workmen to follow. For the building they used huge blocks of stone, some weighed more than 100 tonnes. No mortar was used to bind the blocks together so the stones were cut until they fitted the spaces so exactly that even a thin knife blade could not be forced between them.

New Horizons AD 1453–AD 1650

EUROPE AND AMERICA

1453 AD

An early microscope (c. 1650) a tool which led to a new understanding of the nature of diseases.

1455–1485 Wars of the Roses in England.
1467 Charles the Bold, duke of Burgundy.
1469 Unification of Spain follows the marriage of Ferdinand of Aragon and Isabella of Castile.
1485 Battle of Bosworth – Henry VII founds Tudor dynasty in England.
1492 Spain conquers Granada and ends Muslim influence in the Iberian peninsula.
Christopher Columbus crosses Atlantic and discovers the West Indies.
1493 Pope divides New World between Spain and Portugal.
1497 John Cabot discovers Newfoundland.
1500 Pedro Cabral claims Brazil for Portugal.
1501 Negro slaves introduced to the Spanish Indies.
France and Spain occupy Naples.
1511–1515 Spanish conquer Cuba.
1518 Cortes begins conquest of Mexico (Aztecs).
1519–1556 Charles V, Holy Roman emperor.
1529 Peace of Cambrai between France and Spain – France renounces her claims to Italy.
1533 Pizarro captures Cuzco – collapse of Inca empire.
1547 Ivan IV (The Terrible) is crowned tsar of Russia.
1548 Charles V annexes the Netherlands.
1555 Peace of Augsburg allows Protestant princes freedom of worship in Holy Roman empire.
1562 John Hawkins starts English slave trade from west Africa to the Indies.
1568 Netherlands revolt against Spain.
1571 Battle of Lepanto – Papal-Venetian fleet defeats Turks.
1580 Spain conquers Portugal.
1581 Union of Utrecht.
1584 Raleigh founds a colony in Virginia.
1588 Spanish Armada against England is defeated.
1598 Edict of Nantes ends religious wars in France.
1607 John Smith founds English colony at Jamestown, Virginia.
1615 French missionary work begins in Quebec.
1618 Defenestration of Prague leads to the Thirty Years' War.
1620 *Mayflower* reaches Cape Cod – New Plymouth (later Boston) is founded.
1624–1642 Richelieu first minister of France.
1626 Dutch found New Amsterdam (later New York).
1628 Petition of Right – Charles I accepts statement of civil rights in return for funds.
1632 Battle of Lützen – death of Gustavus Adolphus of Sweden.
1640 Portuguese revolt against Spain.
1642 French found Montreal.
1642–1646 Civil war in England.
1648 Treaty of Westphalia ends the Thirty Years' War – Holland and Switzerland to be independent.
1649 Execution of Charles I.
Commonwealth in England.

1650 AD

ELSEWHERE

1456 Ottomans: Turks capture Athens.
1467 Japan: Start of civil wars.
1468 Africa: Sunni Ali takes Timbuktu from Tuaregs – rise of Songhay empire.
1472 Ottomans: Turks defeat Persians at battle of Otlukbeli.
1475 Ottomans: Turks conquer Crimea.
1514 Ottomans: War between Turkey and Persia – the beginning of a long duel.
1517 Ottomans: Turks capture Cairo – end of Mameluke empire.
1526 Mongols: Battle of Panipat – Babar the Mongol defeats sultan of Delhi and founds Mughal empire in north India.
1534 Ottomans: Turks capture Tunis, Baghdad and Mesopotamia from Persia.
1541 Ottomans: Turks conquer Hungary.
1557 Portuguese establish a settlement at Macao in China.
1570 Japan: Nagasaki opened to foreign trade.
1573 Venice abandons Cyprus.
1577 India: Akbar the Great, Mughal emperor, unifies north India.
1590 Hideyoshi unifies Japan.
1591 Africa: Moroccans defeat army of Songhay empire which then disintegrates.
1593 Japanese withdraw from Korea after invading it in 1592.
1595 Japan: Dutch settle on Guinea coast.
1600 Japan: Tokugawa period.
India: English East India Company founded.
1603 Japan: Shogun Ieyasu.
1604 India: French East India Company founded.
Russians settle Siberia.
1638 Japan: Slaughter of Japanese Christians.
1644 China: Manchu dynasty founded.
1645 Ottomans: Turks and Venice at war over Crete.

Johannes Gutenberg, inventor of printing from movable metal type, checking a printed sheet. This relief shows a printing shop with ink daubers, and sheets hanging up to dry and a press of the kind Gutenberg designed in 1454 (which stayed virtually unchanged until the 1800s). His invention consisted of a type-mould for casting the individual letters, a press adapted from the wine-press of the day, and a suitably sticky ink. The press could print about 300 sheets a day. Printing enabled books to be produced more quickly, cheaply, and accurately than by hand-copying, so boosting the spread of knowledge.

CULTURE & RELIGION

1453 Turks convert basilica of St Sophia, Constantinople into a mosque.
1454 Gutenberg prints his first bible.
1465 First printed music.
1466–1536 Erasmus of Rotterdam, Dutch scholar regarded as leader of learning in Renaissance in northern Europe.
1475–1564 Michelangelo Buonarotti, Italian artist.
1477 William Caxton prints Chaucer's *Canterbury Tales.*
1477–1576 Titian, Italian painter.
1478–1535 Thomas More, English Catholic humanist.
1483–1520 Raphael, Italian painter.
1484 Botticelli (1444–1510) paints his *Birth of Venus.*
1490 First beginnings of ballet at Italian courts.
1492 By order of the Spanish inquisitor, Torquemada, Jews are given three months to accept Christianity or leave the country.
1492–1556 Pietro Aretino, Italian author and satirist.
1494 Italian preacher, Girolamo Savonarola holds power in Florence until 1497 when burned at the stake.
1494–1553 François Rabelais, French writer and humanist.
1497 Famine in Florence.
1500 Beginning of High Renaissance.
1503 Leonardo's *Mona Lisa.*
1508–1512 Michelangelo paints Sistine Chapel ceiling.
1517 Luther at Wittenberg sets off the Reformation.
1521 Diet of Worms – Martin Luther (1483–1546) is condemned as a heretic by Rome and excommunicated.
1532 John Calvin starts Protestant movement in France.
Religious Peace of Nuremberg – Protestants allowed to practise their religion freely.
1534 Act of Supremacy in England makes Henry VIII supreme head of the English Church.
Ignatius Loyola founds Jesuits.
1541 Knox brings the Reformation to Scotland.
1545 Council of Trent opened by Pope Paul III to reform Catholic Church under Jesuit guidance.
St Francis Xavier introduces Christianity to Japan.
1547–1616 Miguel de Cervantes, Spanish writer.
1549 Book of Common Prayer in England.
1550 Beginning of early Baroque period.
1555 England returns to Catholicism under Mary.
1561–1626 Francis Bacon, English philosopher and statesman.
1563 39 Articles set out agreed beliefs of Church of England.
1564–1616 William Shakespeare.
1566 *Notizie Scritte*, one of first newspapers, in Venice.
1572 Mass murder of Protestants (Huguenots) in France on St Bartholomew's Day.
1573–1652 Inigo Jones, English architect.
1577–1640 Peter Paul Rubens, Flemish painter.
1586 Beginning of Japanese Kabuki theatre.
1592 Pompeii ruins discovered.
1593–1665 Nicholas Poussin, French painter.
1596–1650 René Descartes, French philosopher.
1598 Edict of Nantes allows Huguenots equal rights with Catholics in France.
1606–1669 Rembrandt van Rijn, Dutch painter.
1611 King James' Authorized Version of the Bible.
1618–1648 Thirty Years' War devastates central Europe.
1621–1695 Jean de la Fontaine, French poet.
1622–1673 Jean-Baptiste Molière, French dramatist.
1628–1650 Taj Mahal built in Agra, India.
1629 Shah Jahan, the Great Moghul, orders the making of the Peacock Throne.
1632–1723 Christopher Wren, English architect.
1639–1699 Racine, French dramatist.
1642 Abel Tasman, Dutch mariner, discovers Van Diemen's Land (now Tasmania).

DEVELOPMENTS

1464 Louis XI establishes imperial mail service.
1473–1543 Nicolaus Copernicus, European astronomer, who first stated that the earth and other planets turn around the sun.
1488 Bartholomew Diaz rounds Cape of Good Hope.
1489 Symbols + (plus) and − (minus) come into use.
1492 First globe constructed by Nuremberg geographer, Martin Beheim (1459–1507).
1498 Modern toothbrush first described in Chinese encyclopedia.
Vasco da Gama reaches India.
1500 First Caesarean operation performed by a Swiss sow-gelder, Jacob Nufer, using his sow-gelding instruments.
1501 Amerigo Vespucci explores coast of Brazil.
1502 Peter Henlein of Nuremberg constructs the first watch.
1503 Pocket handkerchief comes into use.
1503–1566 Nostradamus, French astrologer.
1507 Waldseemuller's map shows South America separate from Asia, proposes the New World be called America after Amerigo Vespucci.
1510–1590 Ambroise Paré, French surgeon – one of the greatest of all time.
1513 Vasco Nuñez de Balboa discovers Pacific Ocean.
1517 Coffee in Europe for the first time.
1520 Chocolate brought from Mexico to Spain.
1521 Manufacture of silk introduced to France.
1522 First circumnavigation of the world by Magellan's expedition.
1533 First lunatic asylums.
1535 First diving bells.
1553 Tobacco brought from America to Spain.
1554–1618 Sir Walter Raleigh, English explorer, author and courtier.
1561 Forerunners of hand grenades made for the first time.
1562 Milled coins introduced in England to counteract clipping.
1564–1642 Galileo Galilei, great Italian scientist.
1565 First graphite pencil described by Swiss, Konrad Gaesner.
1577 Francis Drake sails round the world.
1582 Gregorian calendar introduced in Catholic countries.
1585 Antwerp loses its importance as international port to Rotterdam and Amsterdam.
1589 Knitting machine invented by Englishman, William Lee.
Water closet installed by Sir John Harington at his home.
1595 Heels first appear on shoes.
1596 Galileo invents thermometer.
1598 Korean admiral Vesunsin invents iron-clad warship.
1600 Dutch opticians invent the telescope.
1606 Willem Jansz sights Australia.
Galileo invents proportional compass.
1609 Keppler's laws of planetary motion.
1610 Thomas Harriett discovers sunspots.
1619 William Harvey announces his discovery of the circulation of the blood.
1624 Submarine consisting of skin of greased leather over a wooden frame, made by Dutchman, Cornelius Drebbel.
1630 Beginning of public advertising in Paris.
1635 Sale of tobacco in France restricted to apothecaries – only on doctor's prescription.
1637 First umbrella known, in France.
1638 Torture abolished in England.
1639 First printing press in N. America at Cambridge, Mass.
1642 Income and property tax introduced in England.
1643 Italian physicist Torricelli invents the barometer.
1650 World population estimated at 500 million.

1453
AD

1650
AD

The Renaissance

During the Middle Ages, the Christian Church was the main source of scholarship and the main sponsor of the arts. For this reason, all learning had a strong religious bias. But in the 1200s the foundation of the universities of Bologna, Paris, and Oxford brought study to a much wider group of people. The breadth of their knowledge was increased by a revival of interest in the writings of ancient Greece and Rome, a revival which led historians of the 1800s to describe the movement as the *Renaissance*, the rebirth of learning.

A key date in the Renaissance was 1397, when Manuel Chrysoloras of Constantinople became the first professor of Greek at Florence University. Italian scholars quickly seized on the works of the ancient philosophers, which dealt with questions not answered by the Christian Church. From this came *humanism*, the belief that man, and not God, controlled his own fate.

The example of Greek and Roman sculptors, with their realistic portrayal of the human form, led to major changes in art. The Florentine painter Giotto (1266–1337) pioneered the change from a stiff, formal style of medieval art to showing men and women on canvas as they really are. In the *quattrocento* – the 1400s – Italian art produced great masters like the painter Massacio, the sculptor Donatello – who made the first bronze statue since Roman times – and the architect Brunelleschi.

The period of the 1500s is known as the High Renaissance, during which Italian artists produced their finest work. The period is dominated by three men: Michelangelo, Leonardo da Vinci, and Raphael. All three were skilled in many arts, the Renaissance ideal being a 'universal man', but the greatest all-rounder was Leonardo, who was a superb painter, sculptor, architect, engineer, musician, and inventor.

The Songhay Empire

For centuries great empires in west Africa flourished almost unknown outside the continent because of their isolation behind the barrier of the Sahara desert. In the 15th century a new empire arose. Sunni Ali, a great warrior king, was to transform his small trading kingdom of Songhay based on Gao into a great empire. He did so largely at the expense of the declining empire of Mali. Gao was at the southern end of an ancient caravan route across the Sahara but Sunni Ali developed new trade with the forest peoples to the south. Then he organized the empire into provinces each with its own governor and civil service. He ruled from 1464 to 1492 and by his death the empire included cities such as Timbuktu and Jenne.

On his death, Askia Muhammad, seized power and ruled until 1528. He built on the base that Sunni Ali had established and extended Songhay power still further. Under his rule trade flourished. But the empire faced a growing problem (one still found in Africa today) – the conflict between the interests of the towns and the countryside. The traders of the towns were wealthy and mainly Muslims. The farmers of the countryside kept their older traditional beliefs and resented the power and influence of the towns on their lives. So all Songhay rulers had to spend much of their time trying to balance the interests of these two groups. They did this by making country men into ministers.

Because Timbuktu was a great centre of learning at this time, its scholars spent time writing histories of the Songhay empire. So we know that at the end of the 16th century in 1591 the Songhay army was defeated in battle by the Moroccans. The empire had already passed its zenith and it rapidly broke up.

Discovering America

From the time of Prince Henry the Navigator, Portuguese seamen were exploring the west coast of Africa, seeking a sea route to India. Believing in theory that the earth was round, a Genovese navigator, Christopher Columbus (1451–1506) conceived the idea of reaching the Indies by sailing due west. He persuaded Queen Isabella of Spain to finance the expedition. Columbus was using ancient, inaccurate maps and thought the world much smaller than it is. In 1492 he sailed across the Atlantic Ocean and discovered a group of islands which he called the Indies (now the West Indies), believing them to be his goal.

Columbus never did realise he had found a whole new continent, even though a later explorer, Amerigo Vespucci reported that this must be so in 1502, four years before Columbus died.

The American continent was to dominate European imperial rivalries for the next three centuries.

Vasco da Gama left Lisbon on July 8th, 1497 to sail to the east. An Arab pilot took him to Calicut on the west coast of India. He took presents for the Hindu ruler but he demanded gold. The journey back took nearly 3 months and 30 of his crew died of scurvy.

EUROPE

1454 Richard, duke of York is regent in England while Henry is insane.
1455 Henry VI recovers. Richard of York is replaced.
1455–1485 Wars of the Roses in England between the royal houses of York (Richard) and Lancaster (Henry VI).
1460 Battle of Westfield – Richard of York is killed.
Earl of Warwick captures London for the Yorkists.
Battle of Northampton – Henry VI is captured by Yorkists.
Battle of Roxburgh – James II of Scotland killed, James III reigns to 1488.
1461 Edward of York defeats the Lancastrians to become Edward IV – to 1483.
1462 Castile captures Gibraltar from Arabs.
1462–1505 Ivan III (the Great), Duke of Moscow, laid the foundations of the Russian empire.
1465 League of the Public Weal – French dukes conspire against King Louis XI (1461–1483).
1466 Peace of Thorn – Poland gains large area of Prussia from the Teutonic Knights.
Warwick quarrels with Edward IV and allies with Louis XI.
1467 Charles the Bold becomes duke of Burgundy – main rival to Louis XI of France.
1468 Charles the Bold marries Margaret of York.
1469 Marriage of Ferdinand of Aragon and Isabella of Castile ensures future unification of Spain.
1470 Warwick turns Lancastrian, defeats Edward IV and restores Henry VI.
1471 Battle of Barnet – Edward IV defeats and kills Warwick; Henry VI dies in the Tower (probably murdered).
Vladislav of Poland elected king of Bohemia on death of Podiebrad.
1474 War between Louis XI and Charles the Bold (now allied to Edward IV).
Isabella succeeds to the throne of Castile.
1474–1477 Charles the Bold of Burgundy at war with the Swiss Federation, who object to Charles attempting to extend his lands.
1475 Edward IV invades France – Peace of Piéquigny follows.
1476 William Caxton sets up his printing press at Westminster.
1477 Battle of Nancy – Charles the Bold is defeated and killed by the Swiss.
1478 Ferdinand and Isabella establish the Spanish Inquisition with consent of Pope Sixtus IV (1471–1484). Its main aim is to punish so-called converted Jews who still practise their old faith in secret.
Ivan III incorporates Novgorod into duchy of Moscow.
Hungary gains Moravia and Silesia.
1478–1492 Lorenzo de Medici rules Florence.
1479 Spain formally united by union of Aragon and Castile – Ferdinand V of Castile, king of Aragon to 1516.
1483 Death of Edward IV – Richard of Gloucester deposes Edward V to become Richard III. Edward V and his brother are murdered in the Tower, but when and by whom is uncertain.
1485 Battle of Bosworth – Henry Tudor, Earl of Richmond defeats and kills Richard III. He becomes Henry VII, king of England and first of the Tudor monarchs.
Hungary takes Vienna and lower Austria to become most powerful state in central Europe.
1488–1513 James IV, king of Scotland.
1494 Charles VIII of France (1483–1498) invades Italy.
1495 Charles VIII enters Naples, he is forced to withdraw by the Holy League – Milan, Venice, Emperor Maximilian, Pope Alexander VI and Ferdinand V of Castile.
1498 Florentine preacher and brief ruler, Savonarola burned at stake.
1499 Louis XII of France (1498–1515) invades Italy.
1500 Louis XII conquers Milan. Treaty of Granada – Louis and Ferdinand V agree to divide Naples.

ELSEWHERE

1449–1490 Japan: Rule of Shogun Yoshimasa – period of creative art.
1453–1478 Persia: Uzun Hasan – period of expansion; ally of Venice.
1456 Ottoman Turks capture Athens.
1459 Turks conquer Serbia.
1460 Turks conquer Morea.
1461 Turks conquer Trebizond – the last ancient Greek state.
1463–1479 War between Turkey and Venice.
1464–1492 Africa: Sunni Ali rules Songhay empire in west Africa.
1467 Japan: Beginning of 100 years of civil wars.
Africa: Sunni Ali of Songhay recaptures Timbuktu from Tuaregs.
1470 Turks take Negroponte from the Venetians.
1471 Africa: Portuguese seize Tangier from Muslims.
1472 Venetians destroy Ottoman town of Smyrna. Battle of Otlukbeli – Turks defeat Persians, the chief allies of the Venetians.
1473 Persia: Uzun Hasan of Persia defeated by Turks at Ersindjam.
1475 Turks conquer Crimea.

1478 Turks conquer Albania.
1478–1490 Persia: Jaqub rules – a period of enlightened rule.
1479 Treaty of Constantinople ends war between Turkey and Venice. Venice agrees to pay tribute to Turks for trading rights in Black Sea.
1480 Turks occupy Otranto in southern Italy.

1492 Africa: Death of Sunni Ali – conflict until Muhammad Turay seizes power, rules to 1528.
1493 Africa: Songhay empire reaches its height, absorbs much of Mandingo empire.

EXPLORATION

1450s Great impetus to exploration was trade. Overland trade too expensive, so alternative routes sought.
1455–1456 Cadamosto, Venetian sailor explores the Senegal and Gambia rivers and discovers Cape Verde Islands.

Ivan III (1462-1505), known as 'the Great', laid the foundations of the Russian empire.

1472 Portuguese discover Fernando Po, an island off present day Cameroun in Africa.

1482–1484 Portuguese navigator, Diego Cao explores the Congo River. Portuguese settlement on Gold Coast (Ghana).
1487 Portuguese reach Timbuktu overland from coast.
1488 Diaz rounds Cape of Good Hope.
1490 Portuguese ascend River Congo, about 200 miles, 'convert' king of Congo to Christianity.
1492 Genoan-born Christopher Columbus makes first landfall in West Indies – Cuba – on behalf of Spain.
1493 Pope Alexander VI divides New World between Spain and Portugal.
1497 Italian explorer John Cabot discovers Newfoundland.
1498 Vasco da Gama of Portugal reaches India. Columbus discovers Trinidad and South America.
1500 Pedro Cabral claims Brazil for Portugal.

1453
AD

1500
AD

EUROPE	REFORMATION	EXPLORATION AND IMPERIALISM
1501 France and Spain occupy Naples. **1501–1503** Russia and Poland at War – Russia gains Lithuania and other border territories. **1503** Spain defeats France at the battles of Cerignola and Garigliano. **1505** Treaty of Blois – France keeps Milan but cedes Naples to Spain which now controls all southern Italy. **1508** League of Cambrai – Louis XII, Ferdinand V and Emperor Maximilian – against Venice. **1509** Earthquake destroys Constantinople. **1509–1547** Henry VIII, king of England. **1510** Pope Julius II and Venice form Holy League to drive Louis XII out of Italy. **1511** Henry VIII and Ferdinand V of Spain join Holy League. **1512** Swiss join League – drive French from Milan. **1512–1520** Selim I, sultan of Turkey. **1512–1522** Russia and Poland at War. **1513** Battle of Novara – French driven from Italy. Battle of Flodden Field – James IV of Scotland killed by English; James V king to 1542. **1515** Thomas Wolsey, Archbishop of York is made Lord Chancellor of England and a cardinal. **1515–1547** François I, king of France. Battle of Marignano – French defeat Swiss and regain Milan. **1516** Treaty of Noyon between France and Spain – France relinquishes claim to Naples. **1516–1556** Charles I, king of Spain. **1519** Charles I becomes Charles V, Holy Roman emperor. **1520** Field of Cloth of Gold at Calais – meeting of Henry VIII and François I fails to gain Henry's support against Charles V. Henry VIII makes secret treaty with Charles V. **1520–1566** Suleiman I, sultan of Turkey – empire at its height in his reign. **1521** Ottoman Turks capture Belgrade. **1521–1529** France and Spain at war again over Italy. **1522** Battle of Biocca – Charles V drives French from Milan. Turks capture Rhodes.	**1517** Martin Luther, Augustinian monk, nails his 95 Theses (reasons) challenging the sale of indulgences (pardons for sins), to the door of the church in Wittenberg. **1521** Diet of Worms – Luther is condemned as a heretic and excommunicated by the pope. Henry VIII is named 'Defender of the Faith' by Pope Leo X for his opposition to Luther. **1529** Henry VIII dismisses Cardinal Wolsey (Lord Chancellor) for his failure to obtain the pope's consent to his divorce from Catherine of Aragon. Sir Thomas More appointed Lord Chancellor. Henry summons 'Reformation Parliament' and begins cutting ties with Rome. **1530** Death of Wolsey. Civil war in Switzerland between Roman Catholic and Protestant cantons – Protestants defeated. **1532** Sir Thomas More resigns over Henry's divorce. Religious Peace of Nuremberg – Protestants	**1501–1502** Amerigo Vespucci explores the coast of Brasil. **1502** Columbus discovers Nicaragua. **1502–1524** Shah Ismail founds the Safavid dynasty in Persia. **1505** Francisco de Almeida sent out as first Portuguese governor of India. **1506** Africa: Portuguese settlements in Mozambique – take Sofala and Kilwa from Arabs. **1509** Almeida destroys a Muslim fleet at the battle of Diu and gains control of Indian seas. **1513** Portuguese reach Canton, China. Vasco Nuñez de Balboa crosses Panama isthmus to sight Pacific. Africa: Portuguese ascend the Zambezi River and establish posts at Sena and Tete. **1518** Hernan Cortes begins conquest of Mexico. **1519** Ferdinand Magellan begins circumnavigation of the globe – dies en route, 1521.

1500 AD

1521 AD

The Reformation

The revival of learning known as the Renaissance played a large part in the religious movement which we know as the Reformation. Already many people questioned the teachings of the Catholic Church as well as criticizing its leadership and the way it was run. There had been previous attempts to reform the Church such as that by John Wyclif of England during the 14th century but the Church remained too powerful. But by the early 1500s the Roman Catholic Church had come into disrepute – following the 'Babylonian Captivity' and the Great Schism with its rival popes. Rising nationalism in countries like England led to resentment at the political rôle now played by the pope and the Church.

It was Martin Luther's famous protest in 1517 when he nailed a protest against the sale of indulgences (pardons for sins) to the door of the church in Wittenberg that finally started the Reformation. Although Pope Leo X and Charles V tried to suppress the new movement, Luther quickly found support. Other men – Calvin in France and Knox in Scotland – began similar movements of *protest*: those who opposed the old Catholic Church became known as Protestants. These new 'heretical' sects had as their hallmark simple services and greater reliance on the teachings and texts of the Bible. As a result, the services were translated into English and German from Latin which the common people could not understand.

In England, the break with Rome came when Pope Clement VII refused to allow Henry VIII to divorce his wife Catherine of Aragon. Henry VIII never adopted the new religion himself. But he was determined to divorce his wife because she had not provided him with a male heir. By the Act of Supremacy of 1534 Henry became the head of the English Church. Henry dissolved (closed down) the monasteries and confiscated their wealth, thus depriving the Catholic Church in England of its power.

The Counter-Reformation

The Reformation led to a Counter-Reformation by the Catholic Church. The most powerful Catholic figure in Europe was Charles V, the Holy Roman emperor, but for much of this time he was engaged in wars with Francis I of France. However, a Spanish soldier, Ignatius Loyola (1491–1556), founded the Society of Jesus (the Jesuits) in 1534 and this became the principal arm of the Catholic Church in its fight against the rise of Protestantism.

The Reformation had a profound effect upon all Europe dividing it into two religious camps. In the main the north became Protestant while the Latin countries remained Catholic.

Right: Beautiful ornaments that lured the Spanish to South America in search of gold.

EUROPE

1524 France invades Italy – retakes Milan.
1525 Battle of Pavia – François I is captured.
1526 Treaty of Madrid – François I gives up claim to Milan, Genoa, Naples; subsequently does not keep treaty.
Battle of Mohacs – Turks defeat and kill Louis II of Bohemia and Hungary.
League of Cognac formed against Charles V by François I, Pope Clement VII, Milan, Florence and Venice.
1527 Spanish and German mercenary troops sack Rome – Pope Clement VII is captured.
1529 Peace of Cambrai between France and Spain – France renounces claims to Italy.
Unsuccessful siege of Vienna by Turks.
1532 Turks invade Hungary but are defeated.
1533 Peace between Turkey and Austria.
1536 Anne Boleyn executed – Henry VIII marries Jane Seymour. She dies after the birth of a son in 1537.
France invades Savoy and Piedmont in Italy. France forms alliance with Turkey.
1540 Henry VIII marries Anne of Cleves (arranged by Thomas Cromwell), divorces her and marries Catherine Howard. Cromwell executed for treason.
1542 Catherine Howard is executed.
Battle of Solway Moss – James V of Scotland killed by English, Mary Stuart, queen of Scotland to 1567.
1543 Alliance of Henry VIII and Charles V against France and Scotland.
Henry marries Catherine Parr.
1547 Death of Henry VIII – Edward VI, king of England to 1553 with Duke of Somerset as protector.
Battle of Muhlberg – Charles V defeats Schmalkaldic League (group of Protestant German rulers).
Ivan IV (the Terrible) is crowned tsar (emperor) of Russia.
1547–1559 Henri II, king of France.
1548 Charles V annexes the Netherlands.
1548–1572 Sigismund II, king of Poland. Polish possessions stretch from Baltic to Black Sea.

REFORMATION

allowed to practise their own religion.
John Calvin starts Protestant movement in France.
1533 Henry VIII marries Anne Boleyn and is excommunicated by the pope. Thomas Cranmer is made Archbishop of Canterbury.
1534 Act of Supremacy – Henry VIII declared supreme head of Church of England. Ignatius Loyola founds the Society of Jesus (Jesuits).
1535 Sir Thomas More executed for failing to take Oath of Supremacy.
1536 Calvin leads Protestants in Geneva. Thomas Cromwell supvervises the suppression of the monasteries in England – to 1539.
Catholic uprising in the north of England – The Pilgrimage of Grace – suppressed.
1541 John Knox brings the Reformation to Scotland.
1545 Council of Trent opened, which, under Jesuit guidance, is to reform the Catholic Church.
1549 Book of Common Prayer in England brings uniform Protestant services.

EXPLORATION AND IMPERIALISM

1521 Cortes captures Aztec capital, Tenochtitlan and soon ends Aztec power. Mexico City erected on site of Tenochtitlan to become seat of Spanish government.
1521–1549 Spanish colonize Venezuela.
1522 One of Magellan's ships completes the first circumnavigation of the world.
1522–1533 Spanish exploration of Pacific coast of South America under Francisco Pizarro.
1533 Pizarro captures the Inca capital, Cuzco and conquers Peru.
1535–1536 Jacques Cartier navigates the St Lawrence River in Canada.
1541 Hernando de Soto discovers the Mississippi River.
1546–1550 Emperor Charles V, fearful of a separatist movement among the Spanish colonies of South America, appoints Pedro de la Gasca as governor who unites them.

1521 AD

1550 AD

Left: Inca gold ceremonial knife, intricately worked and decorated with turquoise.
Right: Inca gold puma.

The Spanish in America

At the beginning of the 16th century, the two ancient empires of the Aztecs and Incas existed in South America unknown to Europe or the rest of the world. Both were to collapse in the space of a few years before the ruthless energy of a handful of Spanish explorer-adventurers we have come to call the *Conquistadores*. Columbus discovered the West Indies only in 1492 yet by 1550 all South and Central America had been colonized by Spain except for Brazil which had been taken by Portugal.

Because the Spaniards had the advantage of horses and firearms, both new and strange to the Indians of these two empires, Cortes needed only 500 men to overcome the Aztec empire of King Montezuma. While Pizarro had less than 200 men to conquer the empire of the Incas, centred on Peru. The *Conquistadores* also benefited from deep divisions and civil wars in the Aztec and Inca empires. Nonetheless the achievement was astonishing. In half a century Spain had created one of the greatest of the European overseas empires which was to last for three hundred years.

1550 AD

1600 AD

EUROPE AND AMERICA

1551 Archbishop Cranmer in England publishes the 42 Articles of Religion.
1552–1556 War between Henri II of France and Charles V.
1553 Death of Edward VI – Duke of Northumberland, the Lord Protector, proclaims Lady Jane Grey queen for 9 days.
Mary I is queen until 1558 – restores Catholic bishops.
1554 Execution of Lady Jane Grey.
Mary marries Philip, heir to the throne of Spain.
1555 England returns to Catholicism – about 300 Protestants, including Cranmer, burnt at stake.
Peace of Augsburg – Protestant princes in Holy Roman empire allowed freedom of worship and right to introduce Reformation in their territories.
1556 Abdication of Charles V.
Philip II, king of Spain, its colonies, the Netherlands and Italian possessions.
Ferdinand (brother to Charles) becomes emperor and ruler of Habsburg lands.
1557 Battle of St Quentin – France defeated by Spain and England.
1557–1582 Livonian war – Russia, Poland, Denmark, Sweden dispute succession to Balkan territories.
1558 England loses Calais – its last possession in France.
1558–1603 Elizabeth I, queen of England repeals Catholic legislation.
1560 Treaty of Edinburgh between England, Scotland and France.
Charles IX, king of France to 1574.
1562–1568 John Hawkins takes cargoes of slaves from west Africa to Hispaniola.
1563 39 Articles complete establishment of Church of England.
1564–1576 Maximilian II, Habsburg Holy Roman emperor.
1565 Portuguese attack French settlement in South America and then found Rio de Janeiro (1567).
1567 Murder of Lord Darnley (husband of Mary, Queen of Scots) probably by Earl of Bothwell whom the queen at once marries. She is imprisoned and forced to abdicate.
1567–1625 James VI, king of Scotland.
1568 Mary Queen of Scots flees to England and is imprisoned by Queen Elizabeth.
1572 Massacre of 20,000 Huguenots in France on St Bartholomew's day.
1575 Population figures: Paris 300,000, London 180,000, Cologne 35,000.
1576 Pacification of Ghent – the Netherland provinces unite to drive out the Spanish.
Protestantism forbidden in France.
1578 Duke of Parma of Spain subdues southern provinces of Netherlands.
1579 Union of Utrecht formed by northern provinces of Netherlands.
1580 Spain conquers Portugal.
1581 Union of Utrecht declares itself the Dutch Republic – elects William (the Silent) of Orange as ruler.
1584 Murder of William of Orange – England aids Netherlands.
1585–1589 War of three Henrys in France: Henry III (Catholic), Henri of Guise (Holy Catholic League) and Henri of Navarre (Protestant).
1587 Execution of Mary Queen of Scots. England at war with Spain – Drake destroys Spanish fleet at Cadiz.
1588 Spanish Armada against England.
Henri of Guise is murdered.
1589 Murder of Henri III – Henri of Navarre becomes king of France as Henry IV – to 1610.
1590 Henri IV defeats French Catholics at battle of Ivry.
1597–1601 Irish rebellion under Hugh O'Neill, Earl of Tyrone.
1598 Edict of Nantes ends civil war in France – gives Huguenots equal rights with Catholics.
Treaty of Vervins between France and Spain – all conquests restored to France.
1599 Defeat of Earl of Essex by Irish rebels in Ireland.

ASIA

1551–1562 War between Turkey and Hungary.
1552 Russians annex khanate of Kazan and begin expansion into Asia – Astrakhan 1556, Siberia 1581 onwards.
1554–1556 Turks conquer north African coast.
1556 Battle of Panipat – Akbar the Great defeats the Hindus.
1556–1606 Akbar consolidates the Mughal empire in north India.

1562 Truce between Turkey and the Holy Roman empire.
1565 Turks besiege Malta – but without success.
1566 Death of Suleiman – the Turkish empire now at its greatest extent.
1566–1574 Selim II, sultan of Turkey.
1570 Turks attack Cyprus.
1571 Battle of Lepanto – Turkish fleet under Ali Pasha destroyed by Don John of Austria and Papal-Venetian fleet.
1572 Turks rebuild fleet.
1573 Venice abandons Cyprus and makes peace with Turkey.
Don John recaptures Tunis from Turks.
1574 Turkey regains Tunis from Spain and ravages coasts of western Mediterranean despite the defeat of Lepanto.
1577 Akbar completes the unification and annexation of northern India.
1581 Peace between Turkey and Spain – confirmed in 1585.
1585 Start of decline of Turkish empire, rise of the Janissaries (Turkish soldiers).
1587–1629 Shah Abbas I, the Great, of Persia – period of Persian greatness after decline.
1590 Abbas of Persia makes peace with Turkey – Turkish frontiers now on the Caucasus and Caspian.
1592 Akbar conquers Sind.
1593–1606 Turkey at war with Austria.
1596 Battle of Keresztes – Turks defeat Hungarians.

ELSEWHERE

1557 China: Portuguese establish a settlement at Macao.

1568–1600 Japan: Period of national unification – revival after civil wars.
1570 Japan: Nagasaki opened to foreign trade – Japan's greatest port.
1571–1603 Africa: Bornu empire (Sudan) reaches greatest extent under Idris.
1574 Africa: Portuguese begin to settle the coast of Angola.
1577 So-nam gya-tso reforms Tibetan Buddhism – becomes Dalai Lama.
1578 Africa: Battle of Al Kasr Al-kabil – the Portuguese are defeated by Muslims in Morocco. Ahmed al Mansur establishes the Sharifian dynasty in Morocco.
1581 Moroccans begin penetration of Sahara.

Medal to commemorate the defeat of the Spanish Armada in 1588.

1583 Sir Humphrey Gilbert takes possession of Newfoundland for England.
1591 Moroccans aided by Portuguese and Spanish mercenaries defeat forces of the Songhay empire which then disintegrates.
1592 Japan under Hideyoshi invades Korea – plans attack on China.
1595 Africa: Dutch settle on the Guinea coast.
1598 Dutch take Mauritius off south-east coast of Africa.
1600 Battle of Sekigahara – Tokugawa Ieyasu defeats rivals and becomes ruler of Japan. He establishes his headquarters at Edo (Tokyo).

The Habsburgs

Charles V (1500–1558) was the most powerful member of the German Habsburg family, which controlled the Holy Roman empire for more than 300 years. From his father, Philip of Burgundy, Charles inherited Burgundy and most of present-day Belgium and the Netherlands. In 1516 he inherited the thrones of Aragon and Castile through his mother, Juana of Castile, and ruled Spain as Charles I.

In 1519 Charles's paternal grandfather, the Emperor Maximilian I, died. Charles inherited the vast Austrian lands, and in 1520 was crowned Holy Roman emperor. By 1550, with the new Spanish empire in America, Charles V ruled a greater empire than anyone since Charlemagne 700 years before. The empire was increased when Charles's brother, Ferdinand, inherited Bohemia and Hungary.

In 1556 Charles abdicated, leaving Spain and the Netherlands to his son, Philip II, and the empire to his brother, Ferdinand I. Italy was soon added to the Habsburg empire when in 1559 Spain defeated the French (who held Italy) after 65 years of fighting.

By 1520, the Ottoman Turks, the other Mediterranean power and Spain's great enemy, had defeated their Muslim enemies and could now attack Christian Europe again. In 1522, their sultan, Suleiman the Magnificent led an expedition across the River Danube into Hungary, where he won a great victory at Mohacs in 1526. In 1529 Suleiman advanced towards the imperial capital of Vienna and besieged it. If Vienna had fallen, all Central Europe might have passed under Ottoman control. As it was, the Turks were driven back.

The Ottomans then concentrated on north Africa and by 1550 ruled the whole of the north African coastal plain. The next step was to dominate the Mediterranean by sea, so in 1570 they invaded the island of Cyprus, owned by Venice. So Pope Pius V assembled a fleet of 208 galleys and six galleasses (huge oar-driven ships with 44 guns), from the navies of Venice, Spain, and the papal states, under the command of Charles V's son, Don John of Austria. This fleet met 230 Turkish galleys off Lepanto, Greece, on October 7, 1571. The fight lasted three hours. All but 40 of the Turkish galleys were destroyed or captured; the Christians lost only 12 ships. Lepanto was the end of the Turkish threat to Europe from the sea.

Meanwhile in the north of the Habsburg empire, the Dutch had become Protestant. Philip II, a devout Catholic, was determined to stamp it out. In 1567 he made the cruel Duke of Alva governor hoping to crush the opposition by terror. The resulting revolt was brutally put down. Across the Channel, the execution of the Catholic Mary Queen of Scots in 1587 led Philip II of Spain, long an enemy of Protestant England, to plan an invasion of the island to restore the English to the faith of Rome. He assembled a huge fleet, which the proud Spaniards called the *Invincible Armada*.

Sir Francis Drake destroyed part of this Armada in Cadiz Harbour, but Philip rebuilt his fleet and despatched it in July 1588. The Spanish commanded by the inexperienced Duke of Medina Sidonia, sailed first to pick up an army from the Spanish territory of the Netherlands.

A scratch English fleet under Lord Howard of Effingham, including Drake, was waiting for the Armada and harried it up the English Channel. After a hard-fought battle off the French port of Gravelines, the English drove the Armada into the North Sea. Sidonia sailed round Britain back to Spain; more than half his ships were lost, many wrecked by storms.

In 1543 Nicolaus Copernicus, a Polish astronomer, established that the Earth revolved around the sun and how long it took. This preoccupation with the universe and measurement of time was important to 16th century scientists. Up to that time the calendar in use, introduced by Julius Caesar in 46 BC, had provided for a year that was 11 minutes and 14 seconds longer than the actual year, the time the earth takes to orbit the sun. After more than 1600 years, the calendar was 10 days ahead of the seasons. So on Pope Gregory XIII's orders, October 5th, 1582 was made October 15th, 1582 which corrected the error. To prevent it recurring, he decreed that century years which could not be divided by 400 would not be leap years (i.e. not have an extra day as expected).

Akbar the Great

The Mughal empire in northern India was established by Babar in the 1520s. He was a descendant of the Mongol conqueror Tamerlane. The greatest of Babar's successors was Akbar who ruled from 1556 to 1605. He extended and consolidated his empire to cover an area corresponding to most of modern India, Pakistan and Bangladesh. Akbar was an enlightened ruler. In 1562, for example, he abolished the tax on non-Muslims in his Muslim empire and by marrying a Hindu Rajput princess he showed his wish to be impartial to all his subjects. He was tolerant of other religions too and introduced a new *Divine Faith* but this did not last after his death.

Akbar was responsible for some of the most beautiful and perfect examples of Muslim architecture including the lovely city of Fatepur Sikri. The Mughal Empire achieved its greatest extent and influence during his reign and was to last another century before disintegrating in the early 1700s.

European Expansion

The 17th century was a period of expansion for Europe. The foundations of the big overseas empires of Holland, England and France were laid. Already Latin America had been colonized by Spain and Portugal. Now explorers revealed more and more secrets of the world's geography. In Canada the Frenchman, Champlain, went up the St Lawrence River while the Englishman, Hudson, discovered the bay which bears his name. On the other side of the world the Dutchman, Willem Jansz, first sighted Australia while Russian explorers reached the Pacific across the vastness of Siberia.

It was also a period of rivalry between the European powers as the profitable nature of colonies became more obvious. Thus in the Moluccas which they regarded as their own, the Dutch massacred an English settlement at Amboyna in 1623. The Dutch went on to establish control over most of these East Indian islands (modern Indonesia).

These splendid opportunities for profit were left to private enterprise rather than to government and so chartered companies were formed. The three most important of these were the English East India Company which was granted its charter by Elizabeth I in 1600, the Dutch East India Company (1602) and the French East India Company (1604). The Dutch company was largely responsible for colonizing the Dutch East Indies. The English and French companies became intense rivals in India. The two powers fought for more than a hundred years before Britain became supreme on the sub-continent.

In 1620 the little ship *Mayflower* sailed from Plymouth in England with 102 passengers – men, women and children bound for the New World and religious freedom. Most of them were Puritans who had fallen foul of the religious laws of England; some had been in exile in the Netherlands. The expedition reached Cape Cod Bay in Massachusetts after 65 days, and landed on part of the rocky shore which had been given the name Plymouth a few years earlier. By the time the party reached its proposed settlement, numbers were reduced to 99 – five people had died and two babies had been born. These early settlers, forerunners of the colonists who were to form the independent United States 150 years later, are generally known as the Pilgrim Fathers.

European contact often had devastating effects upon the people of the countries colonized. Already in Central and South America the arrival of the Spanish had destroyed the Aztec and Inca civilizations. The North American Indians were to fare little better as they faced the advancing Europeans. While the slave trade from west Africa, which supplied labour for the new American and West Indian colonies, had an immense influence upon the way Africa developed over the next two hundred years. This period saw the beginning of a world dominated by Europe.

Above: Gustavus Adolphus, the 'Lion of the North', king of Sweden from 1611 to 1632. In 1630, acknowledged as one of the great warriors of the age, he intervened in the Thirty Years' War on the Protestants' side. He overwhelmed one of the most successful Catholic generals, the Count of Tilly. Gustavus won by splitting up his army into small, mobile units supported by light and equally-mobile artillery.

The Arts and Sciences

The greatest scientific figure of the time was the Italian Galileo Galilei (1564–1642) who was to assert the truth of Copernicus' theory that the Earth revolved round the Sun. It was still an age of religious intolerance, however, and the Inquisition forced Galileo to withdraw such an 'heretical' (unorthodox) view. The Frenchman, René Descartes, (1596–1650) laid the foundations of much modern thought with his insistence upon reason as the basis for philosophy rather than Church teachings.

Many scientific advances were made. Sir William Harvey (1578–1657) demonstrated the circulation of the blood; John Napier (1550–1617) developed logarithms; Torricelli (1608–1647) invented the barometer.

The Baroque period in art was dominated by three great painters – Sir Anthony Van Dyck (1599–1641), Sir Peter Paul Rubens (1577–1640) and Diego Velazquez (1599–1660). The first operas were produced during this period and the oratorio form was also developed. The Venetian, Claudio Monteverdi (1567–1643) was the leading composer of the time.

Left: This canopy or *baldacchino* by Bernini (1598-1680) built in 1624-1633 towers over the high altar in St Peter's in Rome. Other great architects of the period were Frances Borromini (1599-1667); and Inigo Jones (1573-1652), who went against the prevailing trend by producing simple but elegantly-proportioned buildings.

EUROPE

1603–1625 James VI of Scotland becomes James I of England. He believes in the 'Divine Right of Kings'. This upsets parliament who start to rebel against monarchy.
1604 England and Spain at peace after fighting since 1587. James I bans Jesuits.
1605 Failure of 'Gunpowder Plot' to blow up House of Lords during James I's state opening of parliament.
1607 Union of England and Scotland rejected by parliament.
1608 Formation of Protestant Union in Germany – led by Frederick IV.
1609 Twelve Years' truce between Spain and United Provinces means virtual independence for Netherlands.
Formation of Catholic League – led by Maximilian of Bavaria.
1610 Assassination of Henry IV, king of France.
James I to receive annual income of £200,000.
1614 Estates-General summoned in France by Maria, queen regent of France, to curb power of nobility.
1617 Treaty of Stolbovo between Russia and Sweden.
1618 'Defenestration of Prague' (incident when Bohemians claiming independence throw two Catholic governors from a window) starts Thirty Years' War of religion – general conflict in Europe until 1648.
1622 Spain and France at war, until 1630.
1624 Richelieu becomes First Minister of France – 1642.
1625 Denmark enters Thirty Years' War on Protestant side.
1625–1649 Charles I, king of England. Parliamentary opposition continues on number of counts: (i) Charles stating himself to be above the law; (ii) favouring bishops while others want a more Puritan worship; (iii) in desperate need of money for armies, he imposes taxes.
1626 Battle of Dessau – Catholic forces defeat Protestants.
1627–1628 Siege of La Rochelle (Huguenots) by Richelieu – Charles I provides loan to Huguenots.
1628 Petition of Right – Charles I accepts parliament's statement of civil rights in return for finances.
La Rochelle surrenders – end of political power for Huguenots.
1629 Charles I dissolves parliament – personal rule until 1640.
Treaty of Lübeck between Ferdinand II, Holy Roman emperor, and Christian IV of Denmark.
1630 King Gustavus Adolphus II of Sweden enters war against Ferdinand II.
1631 Catholics under Tilly sack Magdeburg.
Battle of Leipzig – Swedes and Saxons defeat Tilly.
1632 Battle of Lützen – Swedish victory over Catholic forces but Gustavus Adolphus killed.
1634 Battle of Nordlingen – imperial forces defeat Swedes.
1635 Treaty of Prague: Ferdinand II makes peace with Saxony – accepted by most Protestant princes.
1640 Charles I summons Short Parliament – which he dissolves when it fails to grant him money.
1640–1653 Long Parliament in England.
1641 Revolt of Irish Catholics – 30,000 Protestants massacred.
Charles I marches to Westminster to arrest 5 members of the Commons. Attempt fails, he flees to Hampton Court.
1642 Outbreaks of Civil War in England between Royalists (Cavaliers) and Parliamentarians (Roundheads).
Battle of Edgehill indecisive.
1643–1645 Denmark fights Sweden for Baltic supremacy.
1644 Battle of Marston Moor – Prince Rupert defeated.
1645 Cromwell forms Model Army: Battle of Naseby – Parliamentarians defeat Charles I.
1646 Charles I surrenders to the Scots.
1647 Charles handed over to Parliamentarians. Escapes and makes secret treaty with the Scots.
1648 Scots invade England – defeated at Preston by Cromwell.
Treaty of Westphalia: end Thirty Years' War – Dutch and Swiss Republics recognized as independent.
1648–1649 *Fronde* (Parliamentary) rebellion in Paris against Louis XIV.
1649 Execution of Charles I – the Commonwealth (Republic) to 1660.

EXPANSION

1603–1608 John Mildenhall of British East India Company at Agra trying to obtain concessions.
1604 Foundation of French East India Company.
1607 Henry Hudson voyages to Greenland and up Hudson River.
1610 Hudson discovers Hudson Bay.
1615 Four Recollet friars begin French missionary work in Quebec.
1616 Willem Schouten, Dutch navigator, rounds Cape Horn.
British East India Company trades with Persia from Surat (seat of British in India).
1619 Representative assembly at Jamestown, Virginia – first in American colonies.
First Negro slaves arrive in Virginia.
1620 Puritan Pilgrim Fathers from England reach Cape Cod in *Mayflower* and found New Plymouth (later Boston).
1621 Dutch take Goree (W. Africa) from Portuguese.
1622 English (with Persians) capture Hormuz (S. Iranian port) from Portuguese – obtain special privileges.
1623 Dutch massacre English at Amboyna in Spice Islands (Moluccas, Indonesia).
1624 Virginia becomes a crown colony.
1625–1664 French settlements in West Indies.
1626 Dutch found New Amsterdam (later New York).
French establish St Louis on mouth of Senegal River (W. Africa).
First French settlements in Madagascar.
1627 Company of the Hundred Associates organized by Richelieu to colonize New France in Africa.
1630–1644 16,000 English colonists settle in Massachusetts, America.
1637 Dutch take Elmina (W. Africa) from Portuguese and build fort on Gold Coast.
1642 French found Montreal.
1645 Capuchin Monks ascend Congo River.

ELSEWHERE

1600 Japan: Power struggle ends at battle of Sekigahara which Tokugawa wins.
1602–1618 War between Persia and Turkey.
1603 Tokugawa appointed shogun in Japan.
1605–1627 India: Jahangir, Mughal emperor.
1606 Treaty of Zsitva-Torok: Austria abandons Transylvania and ceases to pay tribute to Turkey.
1615 China: Tribes in north form military organization – later called *Manchus*.
1621 China: Nurhachi expels the Ming and sets up Manchu capital at Loyang.
1622–1624 Japan: Execution of Christian missionaries.
1623–1640 Ottoman Turk revival under Murad IV.
1627 China: Manchus overrun Korea.
1628–1658 India: Shah Jehan – poor ruler but responsible for Taj Mahal (1632–1653) as tomb for his wife.
1629–1642 Persia: Shah Safi – a period of decline.
1630 Ottoman Turks under Murad IV take Hamadan (Persia).
1638 Turks conquer Baghdad.
Shimbara uprising and slaughter of Japanese Christians virtually exterminates Christianity in Japan.
1641 Japan: Only Dutch retain a trading post on an island in Nagasaki Harbour. Japan is virtually cut off from world until 1854.
1644 Last Ming emperor hangs himself when Peking is seized by a bandit, Li Tzu-ch'eng.
1644–1912 Manchu (Tu Ch'ing) dynasty in China.
1645–1664 War between Turkey and Venice, principally for Crete.
1650 Ali Bey makes himself hereditary bey (governor) of Tunis.

1600 AD

1650 AD

Balance of Power AD 1650–AD 1840

EUROPE

1650 AD

1652–1654 Anglo-Dutch War.
1660 Restoration of Charles II (Catholic) to throne of England.
1661 Louis XIV absolute monarch in France.
1665 Great Plague of London.
1665–1667 Second Anglo-Dutch War.
1666 Great Fire of London.
1672 William III (of Orange), ruler of the Netherlands.
1685 Louis XIV of France revokes the Edict of Nantes. All religions except Catholicism banned.
1686 League of Augsburg – coalition of European princes against Louis XIV, who was claiming one of the German states.
1688 The 'Glorious Revolution' in England.
William III of the Netherlands invited to save England from Catholicism. James II flees to France. William III and his wife Mary II become joint rulers of England and Scotland.
1689–1725 Peter I, tsar of Russia.
1690 William III defeats exiled James II at the Battle of the Boyne in Ireland.
1697 Treaty of Ryswick ends war against France by League of Augsburg.
1700–1721 Great Northern War for supremacy in the Baltic.
1701 Act of Settlement establishes Protestant Hanoverian succession in Britain.
1701–1713 War of Spanish Succession.
1707 Act of Union between England and Scotland – now named Great Britain.
1713 Treaty of Utrecht ends war of Spanish Succession.
1715 First Jacobite uprising in Scotland.

1740–1748 War of Austrian Succession.
1745 Jacobite rebellion (in Scotland).
1756–1763 Seven Years' War between Britain and France.
1762–1796 Catherine the Great, tsarina of Russia.
1772 First partition of Poland.
1773 Peasant uprising in Russia.
1783 Treaty of Paris recognises American independence.
1787 Assembly of Notables in France dismissed after refusing to introduce financial reforms.
1789 French Revolution begins.
1791 New constitution in France.
1792 France declared a republic.
1793–1794 Reign of Terror in France under Robespierre.
1795 Directory rules France.
Coalition of Britain, Austria, Russia, Portugal, Naples and Ottoman empire against France.
1799 Bonaparte sets up Consulate in France to replace Directory.
1801 Act of Union between Great Britain and Ireland to form United Kingdom.
1802 Bonaparte created First Consul.
1804 Bonaparte crowns himself Napoleon, emperor of the French.
1805 Battle of Trafalgar.
1806 Napoleon dissolves Holy Roman empire.
1807 Britain abolishes slave trade.
Treaty of Tilsit between Napoleon and Tsar Alexander. Napoleon at the height of his power in Europe.
1808–1814 Peninsular War – French occupy Spain.
1809 Battle of Corunna.
1812 Napoleon's Russian campaign.
1814 Napoleon abdicates and is exiled to Elba.
1815 Napoleon returns. Final defeat of Napoleon at Waterloo.
1830 July Revolution in Paris overthrows Charles X.
1832 Reform Act passed in Britain – extends vote to the middle classes.

1840 AD

ELSEWHERE

1652 Africa: Capetown founded by the Dutch.
1661 India: English acquire Bombay.
1664 America: English seize New Amsterdam from Dutch and rename it New York – leads to war.
1669 India: Aurungzeb prohibits Hindu religion.
Venice surrenders Crete to Turkey.
1670 America: English Hudson Bay Company founded.
1682 America: La Salle takes Mississippi Valley for France.
1689 Treaty of Nerchinsk between Russia and China.
1692 Salem witchcraft trials in New England.
1699 America: French establish colony of Louisiana.
1707 India: Death of Aurungzeb leads to disintegration of Mughal empire.
1739 Britain captures Porto Bello in West Indies from Spain.
1744–1748 America: War between Britain and France – King George's War.
1745 Canada: Britain captures Louisburg.
1751 India: Clive takes Arcot – beginning of British ascendancy.
1759 Canada: British capture Quebec from French.
1763 Peace of Paris ends Seven Years' War – Britain gains Canada and most land west of the Mississippi.
America: Chief Pontiac leads Indian uprising.
1767 America: Townshend Acts impose tax on imports.
Mason-Dixon line divides free states from slave states.
1768 James Cook discovers Australia.
1770 America: Boston massacre – British troops fire on mob.
1773 America: Boston Tea Party.
1774 India: Warren Hastings appointed first Governor-General.
1775–1783 American War of Independence.
1776 American Declaration of Independence.
1777 Christianity introduced in Korea.
1783 America: Britain recognizes independence of the Thirteen Colonies.
India Act gives Britain control of political affairs of India.
1787 Britain establishes colony of Sierra Leone in Africa.
1788 First British convicts transported to Australia.
1789 George Washington, first president of United States (USA)
1791 Canada Act – divides Canada into English and French-speaking territories.
1794 Persia: Aga Muhammad founds Qaja dynasty.
America: Jay's Treaty – commercial treaty with Britain.
1795 Africa: British take Cape of Good Hope from the Dutch.
1803 America: Louisiana Purchase – France sells Louisiana to USA.
1804 Haiti becomes independent of France.
1810 Argentina independent.
1811 Paraguay and Venezuela independent.
1814 Japan: Kurozumi sect founded in Japan (first modern Shinto sect).
1815 France prohibits slave trade.
1818 Chaka the Great founds Zulu empire in southern Africa.
1819 Bolivar secures the independence of Great Colombia.
Spain cedes Florida to USA.
1820–1822 Egyptians conquer Sudan and found Khartoum.
1821 Peru and Mexico independent.
1822 Brazil independent of Portugal.
1823 Proclamation of the Monroe Doctrine by the president of USA warning Europe not to interfere in American politics.
1825 Bolivia independent.
1826 Russia and Persia at war.
1830 French invade Algeria.
1833 Abolition of slavery in British empire.
1835–1837 Great Trek by Boers from Cape to found Transvaal.
1836 Texas independent of Mexico after battle of Alamo.
1839–1842 First Opium War between Britain and China.
1839 British occupy Aden.

56

TECHNOLOGY

1661 Robert Boyle defines chemical elements.
1665 Isaac Newton experiments with gravitation; invents differential calculus.
1666 First Cheddar cheese.
1667 French army uses hand grenades.
1668 Reflecting telescope invented by Newton.
1680 Dodo, flightless bird, extinct.
1701–1744 Anders Celsius, Swiss astronomer who invents centigrade thermometer (1742).
1705 Edmund Halley correctly predicts the return in 1758 of the comet seen in 1682.
1714 D. G. Fahrenheit constructs mercury thermometer with temperature scale.
1718 Machine gun patented by James Puckle of London.
1733 John Kay patents his flying shuttle loom.
1735 Linnaeus writes his classification of nature.
1752 Benjamin Franklin invents lightning conductor.
1760 Botanical Gardens opened at Kew, London.
1766 Henry Cavendish, English scientist, discovers hydrogen less dense than air.
1767 First successful spinning machine invented by James Hargreaves.
1769 Arkwright's water powered spinning machine.
1774 Joseph Priestley discovers oxygen.
Austrian physician, F. A. Mesmer (1733–1815) uses hypnosis for health purposes.
1775 James Watt, Scottish scientist, perfects his invention of the steam engine.
1780 Scheller constructs first fountain pen.
1783 Montgolfier brothers ascend in hot air balloon at Annonay, France.
1784 George Atwood, English mathematician, accurately determines acceleration of a free-falling body.
Andrew Meikle, Scottish millwright, invents threshing machine.
1785 Salsano invents seismograph.
Power loom invented by Cartwright.
1790 Lavoisier produces his table of 31 chemical elements.
1793 Eli Whitney invents the cotton gin in USA.
1794 First telegraph – Paris-Lille.
First technical college – École Polytechnique – opens in Paris.
1795 Francois Appert designs preserving jar for foods.
1796 Edward Jenner, English physician, introduces vaccination against smallpox.
1800 Alessandro Volta produces the first electric battery.
1802 John Dalton, English physicist, introduces atomic theory into chemistry.
1803 Robert Fulton propels a boat by steam power (also inventor of torpedo).
Henry Shrapnel invents shells.
1808 J. L. Gay-Lussac's *The Combination of Gases.*
1815 Humphrey Davy, English chemist, invents miner's lamp.
1818 Jeremiah Chubb invents detector lock.
1819 Steamship *Savannah* crosses the Atlantic.
Stethoscope invented by René Laennec.
1822 Shell gun invented by Henri J. Paihans of France.
1825 Opening of Stockton-Darlington railroad – first line to carry passengers.
1829 George Stephenson's engine: 'The Rocket'.
1830–1833 *Principles of Geology* by Sir Charles Lyell.
First railroads in France and U.S.A.
1831 Dynamo and transformer invented by Michael Faraday.
1835 Photography – negative/positive process developed by William Fox Talbot.
1836 Invention of revolver by Samuel Colt.
1840 Introduction of the Penny Post in Britain.

CULTURE

1660 Famous 'Café Procope' opens in Paris.
1662 Louis XIV begins to build Palace of Versailles.
1664 French furniture prevails in European houses.
1666 Antonio Stradivari labels his first violin.
1608–1674 John Milton, English poet writes 'Paradise Lost' (1667–1674).
1667–1745 Jonathan Swift, Irish author of *Gulliver's Travels* (1726).
1675 Paris becomes centre of European culture (with approximately ½ million inhabitants).
1675–1741 Antonio Vivaldi, Italian composer of *The Four Seasons.*
1677 Ice cream becomes popular in Paris.
1680 Comédie Française formed.
1684–1721 Jean Antoine Watteau, French painter.
1685–1750 J. S. Bach, German composer.
1685–1759 George Frederick Handel, German composer.
1694–1778 Voltaire, French writer and philosopher.
1698 Tax on beards in Russia.
1700 Unmarried women taxed in Berlin.
1700–1715 Approximate start of late Baroque period.
1707–1793 Carlo Goldoni, Venetian dramatist.
1709 Invention of the pianoforte by Bartolomeo Cristofori.
1718 Porcelain manufactured for first time in Vienna.
1724–1804 Immanuel Kant, German philosopher.
1730 Rococo art movement in its fullest form.
1731 10 Downing Street, London residence of British Prime Ministers built.
1732 Covent Garden opera house opens.
1732–1799 Beaumarchais, French dramatist.
1732–1806 Jean Honoré Fragonard, French painter.
1746–1828 Francisco de Goya, Spanish painter.
1748–1825 Jacques Louis David, French Classical painter.
1749–1832 Johann Goethe, German Romantic writer.
1750 Neoclassicism spreads as a reaction against Baroque and Rococo.
1755 Samuel Johnson (1709–1784) writes *Dictionary of the English Language.*
1756–1791 Wolfgang Mozart, Austrian composer.
1762 Jean Jacques Rousseau (1712–1778): *Social Contract.*
1770–1827 Ludwig van Beethoven, German composer.
1770–1850 William Wordsworth, English poet.
1775 Jane Austen, English writer.
1775–1851 J. M. W. Turner, English painter.
1776 *An Inquiry into the Nature and Causes of the Wealth of Nations* by Adam Smith.
1785 *The Times* newspaper begun by John Walter.
1788–1824 Lord Byron, English poet.
1790–1824 Théodore Géricault, French painter.
1793 The Louvre, Paris, becomes national art gallery.
1795–1821 John Keats, English poet.
1798 Essay on population by Thomas Robert Malthus.
1799 Rosetta stone found near Rosetta, Egypt, makes the deciphering of hieroglyphics possible.
1799–1850 Honoré de Balzac, French writer.
1799–1863 Delacroix, French painter.
1802 Period of the Empire style in France.
1802–1885 Victor Hugo, French writer.
1803–1882 Robert Waldo Emerson, U.S. philosopher.
1804–1849 Johann Strauss, Austrian composer.
1812 Elgin Marbles brought to England.
1813–1883 Richard Wagner, German composer.
1819–1877 Gustave Courbet, French painter.
1821–1880 Gustave Flaubert, French writer.
1828–1910 Leo Tolstoy, Russian writer.
1833–1891 Pedro Antonio de Alarcon, Spanish writer.

Salon de la Guerre, Palace of Versailles, 1680s. Versailles was designed to provide a suitable setting for the Sun King, Louis XIV. Louis made Versailles the centre of European culture – theatre, opera and the ceremony of court. It also displayed the power and glory of the French crown. But there was little comfort in the palace. The private chambers were dark and airless, the plumbing was poor and baths unheard of. Instead men and women splashed themselves with perfume.

France under Louis XIV

Cardinal Richelieu (1585–1642), the great chief minister of Louis XIII, laid the foundations of French power for the second half of the 17th century. At home he broke the domination of the old nobility and concentrated all decision-making in the hands of the king. Abroad, by diplomacy and money as well as war, he restored France's influence in Italy, the Netherlands, Germany and Sweden.

Louis XIV came to the throne as a child of five in 1643 and the following years were troubled ones for France. Cardinal Mazarin had replaced Richelieu as chief minister, but he did not command either the power or respect of his great predecessor. There were rebellions against the crown (known as the *fronde*) and these made a deep impression upon Louis as a boy. When Mazarin died in 1661, Louis assumed full control of the state which he ruled without restraints imposed by the constitution. He once summed up his position in the words, 'L'état, c'est moi' – I am the state.

Wars dominated much of Louis' reign. Under a series of great generals such as Turenne, Condé and Vauban, France was repeatedly successful in battle. But France's success worked against her because the rest of Europe, fearing French domination, banded together to defeat Louis' plans for expanding his empire. They formed the League of Augsburg. The chief members were the Holy Roman Emperor Leopold I, the kings of Sweden and Spain and the electors of Saxony, Bavaria and the Palatinate in Germany. Eventually the pope, Netherlands

The Rest of Europe

In England the monarchy was restored under Charles II. But fears that his brother James II intended to restore Catholicism led parliament to invite the Protestant William III of Orange to take the throne which he did in 1689.

At the other end of Europe, Tsar Peter the Great (1672–1725) expanded Russian territory to the north and south. But Peter's greatest achievement was the modernization of Russia. He reorganized the army, founded a navy, developed trade, industry and built canals and roads until Russia had been transformed into a great power in western Europe.

To the east of Europe, Turkey achieved her greatest influence and power. Most of this period she was at war – with the Venetians, the Holy Roman empire, the Austrians and Poland. But finally in 1699 the Turks were subdued and though the Ottoman empire remained formidable for another two centuries it never again threatened Europe.

In many respects it was a destructive age – Europe was almost always at war. Yet it was also a time of intellectual advance and the foundations were laid for the following century which came to be called the 'Age of Reason'.

and England joined. The war lasted from 1689 to 1697. Finally the Treaty of Ryswick restored the conquered territories – only Alsace and Strasbourg remained French.

But Louis XIV is best remembered for the splendour of his reign. The great palace at Versailles was the wonder of the age. Louis' court set the example for all Europe and the king himself become known as *Le Grand Monarque*. In this grandeur, and Louis' concept of absolute power, lay the seeds of the Revolution that swept France in 1789.

Unfortunately, the cost of maintaining his army and his court was so great that by the time Louis died in 1715, France was a troubled and impoverished country.

Bacons Castle, Virginia, the headquarters of the Virginia Company, was built in 1655. The Virginia Company was given a charter by James I in 1607. Soon the colonists were growing and exporting tobacco and in 1624 Virginia was made a royal colony.

EUROPE

1650 Second *fronde* rebellion in France – suppressed.
Charles II lands in Scotland and is proclaimed king.
1651 Battle of Worcester – Charles II defeated by Cromwell and flees abroad again.
1652–1654 First Anglo-Dutch War.
1653 Cromwell becomes Lord Protector of England.
1658 Death of Cromwell – succeeded by son Richard.
1659 Richard Cromwell forced to resign by army – parliament restored.
Treaty of Pyrenees between France and Spain – confirms borders and supremacy of France over Spain.
1660 Charles II restored to throne by parliament in England – reigns to 1685.
1661 Clarendon Code in England – Charles II's parliament passes laws against Non-conformists.
Death of Cardinal Mazarin – Louis XIV becomes absolute monarch.
1665 Great Plague in London.
1665–1667 Second Anglo-Dutch War.
1666 Great Fire of London.
1667 Dutch fleet defeats English in river Medway.
Treaty of Breda between England, Holland, France, Denmark.
1668 Triple Alliance of England, Holland and Sweden against France.
Treaty of Lisbon – Spain recognizes independence of Portugal.
Treaty of Aix-la-Chapelle ends war between France and Spain.
1670 Secret Treaty of Dover between Charles II and Louis XIV to restore Catholicism in England.
1672 William III (Orange) becomes hereditary *Stadholder* (ruler) of Netherlands – to 1702.
1672 Third Anglo-Dutch War.
1672–1678 France at war with Netherlands.
1677 William III of Netherlands marries Mary, daughter of James, Duke of York, Catholic heir to the English throne.
1678 Popish plot in England – Titus Oates falsely accuses Catholics of plan to murder Charles II.
1679 Act of Habeas Corpus passed in England, forbidding imprisonment without trial.
Parliament's Bill of Exclusion against the Duke of York blocked by Charles II – Parliament dismissed. Charles II rejects petitions calling for a new parliament. Petitioners become known as *Whigs*, their opponents (royalists) known as *Tories*.
1680 Louis XIV establishes Chambers of Reunion – France occupies Strasbourg, Luxembourg, Lorraine.
1685 Louis XIV revokes the Edict of Nantes – all religions banned in France.
1685–1688 James II, king of England.
Charles II's illegitimate son, Duke of Monmouth, rebels against James – put down.
1686 League of Augsburg is formed against France.
1687 James II issues Declaration of Liberty of Conscience – toleration for all religions.
1688 The 'Glorious Revolution' in England – William III of Holland is invited to save the country from Catholicism. James flees to France.
1689 Bill of Rights in England – establishes principle of constitutional monarchy and bars Catholics from the throne. William III and Mary II joint rule to 1694.
England and Netherlands join League of Augsburg against France in Grand Alliance.
1689–1725 Peter I (the Great), tsar of Russia.
1690 Defeat of exiled James II by William III at battle of the Boyne in Ireland.
1692 Battle of La Hogue – Anglo-Dutch fleet defeats French.
1694 Death of Mary II – William III sole ruler of England to 1702.
1695 First penal laws against Catholics in Ireland.
1697 Treaty of Ryswick ends war of League of Augsburg against France.
1700 Charles II of Spain names Philip of Anjou, grandson of Louis XIV as his heir – Philip becomes the V of Spain to 1746.
Battle of Narva – Charles XII of Sweden defeats Russians.

TURKEY & EUROPE

1656 Venetians rout the Turks off the Dardanelles.
1661–1664 Turkey at war with the Holy Roman empire.
1664 Battle of St Gotthard – Austrians defeat Turks. Treaty of Vasvar ends war between Turkey and Holy Roman empire.
1669 Venice surrenders Crete to Turkey.

Sir Isaac Newton (1642-1727) in a burst of inspiration in 1665-1667, before he was 26, made three momentous discoveries: the theory of gravitation, white light is made up of rays of coloured light and a new branch of mathematics – calculus.

1672–1676 Turkey at war with Poland for control of Ukraine.
1676 Treaty of Zuravno – Turkey gains Polish Ukraine.
1677–1681 Turkey at war with Russia.
1681 Treaty of Radzin – Russia gains most of Turkish Ukraine.
1682–1699 Turkey at war with Austria.
1683 Turks besiege Vienna – city relieved by German and Polish troops.
1684 Pope Innocent XI forms the Holy League of Venice, Austria and Poland against Turkey.
1686 Venice takes Peloponnese from Turks.
1687 Battle of Mohacs – Turks are defeated and the Habsburg succession to the Hungarian throne is confirmed.
1688 Austrians capture Belgrade.
1690 Turks retake Belgrade from Austrians.
1697 Battle of Zenta – Eugène of Savoy defeats Turks.
1699 Treaty of Karlowitz – Austria receives Hungary from Turkey; Venice gains Peloponnese and parts of Yugoslavia; Poland takes Turkish Ukraine.

ELSEWHERE

1657 Japan: Great fire destroys Edo.
1658–1707 India: Aurungzeb, Mughal emperor – clever but ruthless leader and a bigoted Muslim. Imprisons his father and kills his brothers to gain throne.
1660 Africa: Rise of Bambara kingdom on upper Niger River.
1661 India: English acquire Bombay.
Chinese under Koxinga take Formosa (Taiwan).
1662 N. Africa: Portugal cedes Tangier to England.
1666–1688 India: Aurungzeb at war with Muhammadans in central India and with peoples of north-east India.
1669 India: Aurungzeb prohibits the Hindu religion and persecutes Hindus.
1676–1678 India: Sikh uprisings against Aurungzeb.
1680–1709 Tsunayohi, shogun of Japan.

1681 India: Prince Akbar in unsuccessful revolt against the misrule of his father, Aurungzeb.
1683 China: Koxinga's grandson surrenders Formosa to the Manchus.
1684 N. Africa: English abandon Tangier to sultan of Morocco.
French expeditions against Algerian pirates.
1685 India: Aurungzeb seizes Surat – expels English.
1686 Africa: Louis XIV proclaims French annexation of Madagascar.
America: Dominion of New England formed.
1688–1704 Japan: Rise of merchant class.
1690 India: English allowed to return to Bengal at Calcutta by Aurungzeb.
1691 China: Emperor reorganizes Mongolia.
1697 Africa: French complete their conquest of the Dutch in Senegal.
1699 USA: French establish colony of Louisiana.

1650 AD

1700 AD

EUROPE

1700 AD

1701 Act of Settlement establishes Protestant Hanoverian succession in England.
James II dies in exile.
1701–1713 War of Spanish Succession following failure of Charles II of Spain to produce an heir.
Grand Alliance of England, Netherlands, Holy Roman empire and German states against France.
Charles XII of Sweden invades Poland.
1703–1711 Hungarian revolt against Austria.
1704 British fleet captures Gibraltar from Spain.
Battle of Blenheim – John Churchill, duke of Marlborough and Prince Eugène of Savoy (commanding Austrian army) defeat French to save Vienna.
1706 Battle of Ramillies – Marlborough defeats French.
Battle of Turin – Eugène defeats French.
Treaty of Altranstadt between Augustus II of Poland and Charles XII of Sweden.
1707 Act of Union unites England and Scotland.
Battle of Almaza – Spain defeats the Alliance.
1708 Battle of Oudenarde – Marlborough and Eugène defeat French.
Charles XII invades Russia.
1709 Battle of Malplaquet – Alliance defeats French but at heavy cost of 20,000 men.
Battle of Poltava – Peter the Great of Russia defeats Charles XII of Sweden. Begins building new capital – St Petersburg.
1711 Duke of Marlborough is dismissed as Allied commander.
1713 Treaty of Utrecht ends War of Spanish Succession – France cedes Newfoundland, Nova Scotia and Hudson Bay to Britain and recognizes the Protestant Succession.
Britain gains Gibraltar and Minorca from Spain.
1714–1727 George I, first Hanoverian king of Great Britain.
1715 Jacobite rising in Scotland for James Edward, the Old Pretender, son of James II.
1720 Collapse of John Law's Mississippi Company in France.
South Sea Bubble in England – financial panic.
1721–1742 Sir Robert Walpole, the first British prime minister.
Treaty of Nystadt between Russia and Sweden.

1720 AD

MIDDLE ASIA

King Charles XII (1682-1718) of Sweden, the 'Swedish Meteor'. In 1700 Sweden had control of the Baltic. Denmark, Poland and Russia launched an attack to break its control. Within months Charles had crushingly defeated them.

1707 Death of Aurungzeb is followed by disintegration of Mughal empire.
1709–1711 Afghans rise against Persians – establish Afghan state.
1710–1711 Turkey and Russia at war – Peter the Great buys peace.
1715 English East India Company gains tax and other exemptions in India.
1718 Treaty of Passarowitz ends war between Turkey and Austria.

ELSEWHERE

1705 Africa: Hussein Ibn Ali founds the Husseinite dynasty in Tunis and throws off Turkish control.
1709–1745 Japan: Period of reform.
1712 China: Period of prosperity in China.
1713 S. America: Britain gains the *asiento* (contract) to supply slaves to Spanish America from west Africa – the most active period of British slave trade.
1714 Africa: Ahmed Bey makes himself bey (governor) of Tripoli – founds Karamanli dynasty.
1720 China: Imperial garrisons established in Tibet.
Japan: Ban removed on the study of Europe and European books but not religion.
1721 China: Revolt in Formosa.
Edo (Tokyo) has population of 800,000, largest city in the world.
1723 Africa: Bartholomew Stibbs takes possession of Gambia region for the British Africa Company.
1723–1735 China: Peace at home but war against the Mongols.

The Slave Trade

Portuguese explorers first brought African slaves to Europe in the 15th century but only in small numbers. It was the development of sugar plantations in the West Indies, and cotton plantations in what later became the southern American states which made this imported labour so valuable. Countries like Britain earned enormous wealth by supplying slaves from west Africa to the Americas. Africans enslaved each other in their wars and the victors sold their captives to the European traders. These were then transported on the dreaded 'middle passage' to the Indies or America. Nine to ten million slaves were transported across the Atlantic in the 18th century.

The effects of the slave trade can still be seen today in the racial attitudes of whites towards blacks in the USA and the United Kingdom. It has shaped social attitudes in the West Indies. The effects of depopulation upon parts of Africa retarded development until the era of independence. The slave trade was one of the most destructive of all developments which arose out of European contact with Africa.

The Agrarian Revolution

In England, until the 18th century the purpose of agriculture had been to provide enough food to maintain the population at a level of comfortable survival. The old strip system of open fields was used. Yeoman farmers and cottars who owned their own land – even if only a few acres each – worked together as a community.

But by 1700 there was a need for more food to maintain a growing population. Soon the thought of farming for profit took root. The idea of enclosing land to improve crop yield was introduced. In the 17th century this was often achieved by agreement between landlords and tenants but by the 18th century the favoured device was the private act of parliament. Since parliament in the 18th century was dominated by the landlord class the small farmers had little chance of preventing the enclosures. They had their land taken from them. Some of them could work for the big landlords but the rest often suffered appalling hardships. They migrated to the new towns of the industrial revolution, providing cheap labour in the factories.

Once the land had been enclosed under single ownership, it was possible for the big farmer to introduce reforms. One of the most famous of the big landowning

EUROPE

1725 Treaty of Vienna between Austria (Savoy) and Spain. Catherine, widow of Peter I, becomes Catherine I of Russia.
1727–1729 Spain at war with Britain and France.
1733 Family pact between Bourbons of France and Spain.
1733–1735 War of Polish Succession after death of Augustus II – elector of Saxony and king of Poland. Sweden and France, supported by Spain and Sardinia, favour Stanislaus Leszczynski for king, but Russia and Austria force Poles to accept Augustus's son, Augustus III.

1738 Treaty of Vienna settles War of Polish Succession.
1739–1741 War of Jenkin's Ear between Britain and Spain.
1740–1786 Frederick II (the Great), king of Prussia – briefly seizes Silesia (1740), the richest Austrian province sparking off War of Austrian Succession.
1740–1748 War of Austrian Succession caused by death of last male descendant of Habsburg family, Charles VI and failure by rivals, Bavaria, Spain and Saxony (supported by Poland and France) to recognize Maria-Theresa as empress, (supported by Hungary, Britain and Netherlands).
1742–1745 Charles VII of Bavaria, Holy Roman emperor.
1743 Battle of Dettingen – French defeated by Hanoverians and Britain.
1744 Frederick the Great (Prussia) invades Bohemia but is defeated by Austrian and Saxon forces.
1745 'Forty Five' rebellion by Charles Edward Stuart, the Young Pretender, in Scotland.
Alliance by Austria, Britain, Netherlands and Saxony against Prussia.
Bavaria is defeated and withdraws claim to Austrian throne.
Battle of Fontenoy – French defeat British in War of Austrian Succession.
Francis I, husband of Maria Theresa, is elected Holy Roman emperor (to 1765) securing Maria Theresa's postion in Europe.
1746 Battle of Culloden – Jacobites are defeated in Britain.
1748 Treaty of Aix-la-Chapelle ends the War of Austrian Succession – Prussia keeps Silesia.

MIDDLE ASIA

1724 Russo-Turkish agreement to dismember Persia.
Hyderabad (central India) achieves independence from the Mughal empire.
1726 Persia defeats Turks.
1730–1735 Maratha government gains ascendancy in India.
1735 Russians give up their Persian conquests and unite with Persians against Turkey.
1736–1739 Turkey at war with Russia and Austria.
1738 Nadir Shah, ruler of Persia (1736–1747), invades northern India – captures Kandahar.
1739 Nadir Shah sacks Delhi to reach height of his power – a great soldier but not a statesman.
Treaty of Belgrade ends war between Turkey, Austria and Russia – Austria gives up Serbia and Belgrade to Turkey.
1746 French capture Madras from English.
1747 Nadir Shah is assassinated and a period of anarchy follows in Persia to 1750.
1748 English regain Madras – the beginning of Anglo-French rivalry in India.

ELSEWHERE

1727 China: Kiakhta Treaty fixes borders between China and Russia.
1732–1733 Japan: Great famine in western Japan.
1733 USA: Foundation of Georgia, the last of the Thirteen Colonies in North America.
1736–1795 China: Imperial control is extended throughout central Asia – a period of wealth.
1742 Japan: Codification of criminal law.
1744–1748 USA: War between Britain and France – King George's War.
1745 Canada: British capture Louisburg, French fortress.

Austrian commander, Prince Eugène of Savoy.

---

farmers was Lord Townshend. He already rotated his crops – planting crops that took different food (nutrients) from the soil in rotation so that the soil was never exhausted of one particular nutrient. He had the idea of planting a field of turnips to make possible the winter feeding of cattle. He also improved his land by manuring and better drainage. Other farmers experimented with different grasses and the storage of water. The new English methods were copied by farmers all over Europe. All of this changed the landscape of England. The countryside was broken up into hundreds of fields surrounded by hedges.

By 1750, the agrarian revolution and the industrial revolution were fuelling each other. Landlords who made fortunes from the new agriculture invested in the new industries; and industrialists put some of their profits back into the land. It turned Britain into the most urban-based (town-based) society in the world. England became the 'workshop of the world' and the most powerful nation in the 19th century.

Portuguese arriving in Japan. The first Portuguese ship reached Japan in 1542. Merchants were followed by missionaries who made many converts to Christianity – 150,000 by 1580. But the shogun regarded this as a dangerous threat to Japanese beliefs, so there was a brief, violent and successful persecution. By 1650 Christianity was almost completely wiped out. The Japanese were forbidden to build ocean-going ships and so remained cut off from the rest of the world until 1854.

BALANCE OF POWER AD 1750–AD 1800

EUROPE	ASIA	ELSEWHERE

1750 AD

1800 AD

EUROPE

1756 Treaty of Westminster – alliance of Britain and Prussia.
Treaty of Versailles – alliance of France and Austria.
Beginning of the Seven Years' War – result of Anglo-French rivalry in the colonies and Austro-Prussian antagonism in Europe.
1757 Russia joins the French alliance.
Battles of Rossbach and Leuthen – Prussians defeat French and Austrians.
1758 Battle of Zorndorf – Prussians defeat Russians.
1759 Battle of Quiberon Bay – British fleet defeats the French.
Battle of Kunersdorf – Austrian victory.
1762 Britain declares war on Spain.
Treaty of St Petersburg between Russia and Prussia.
1763 Peace of Paris between Britain, France and Spain ends Seven Years' War.
Peace of Hubertsburg between Prussia, Saxony and Austria.
1771 Russia conquers Crimea.
1772 First partition of Poland among Austria, Prussia and Russia.
1773–1775 Cossack Pugachev leads peasant uprising in Russia – suppressed.
1775 Beginning of American War of Independence.
1778 France joins American War against Britain.
1779 Spain joins American War against Britain.
1779–1783 France and Spain besiege Gibraltar but fail to capture.
1780 Armed Neutrality of the North: Russia, Denmark, Sweden, Netherlands join to protect neutral shipping from British interference.
1781 Joseph II introduces religious toleration in Austria and abolishes serfdom.
1783 Treaty of Paris ends American War of Independence.
Russia annexes Crimea.
1787 Assembly of Notables dismissed in France after refusing to introduce financial reforms.
1789 Estates-General called in France.
Storming of the Bastille – beginning of French Revolution.
Third Estate forms a National Assembly which governs France as a Constituent Assembly until 1791.
1792 France at war against Austria and Prussia – Prussians defeated at battle of Valmy.
1792–1795 National Convention governs France which declares itself a republic on September 21, 1792.
1793 Louis XVI then his wife, Marie Antoinette, executed.
Revolutionary France declares war on Britain, the Netherlands and Spain.
Second partition of Poland between Prussia and Russia.
1793–1794 Reign of Terror in France – Robespierre and Committee of Public Safety rule the country.
Conscription is introduced for the French revolutionary army.
1794 French invade Dutch Republic; occupy Netherlands.
Execution of Danton and Robespierre – ends Reign of Terror.
1795 Treaty of Basle between France and Prussia; Spain makes peace with France; the 5-man Directory rules France.
Third partition of the remainder of Poland between Austria, Prussia and Russia.
1796–1797 The Corsican, Napoleon Bonaparte, leads French army to conquer most of Italy.
1797 British naval mutinies at Spithead and Nore.
Battle of Cape St Vincent – British defeat Franco-Spanish fleet.
1798 Rebellion in Ireland (Battle of Vinegar Hill) wanting separation from Britain.
French occupy Rome and establish Roman republic.
French invade Switzerland and set up Helvetic republic.
1799 Coalition of powers (Britain, Austria, Russia, Portugal, Naples and Turkey) against France; battles of Zürich, Trebbia and Novi – French driven from Italy.
Bonaparte returns to France, overthrows Directory and sets up Consulate which he heads to 1804.
1800 French defeat Austrians at the battles of Marengo and Hohenlinden.

ASIA

1751 India: Robert Clive takes Arcot – ends French plans for supremacy in south.
1756 India: Black Hole of Calcutta – Suruj-ud-Daulah, nawab of Bengal, imprisons 146 British in small room, most die.
1757 India: Clive captures Calcutta.
Battle of Plassey – Clive defeats the nawab of Bengal.
Start of British ascendancy.
1757–1843 China restricts foreign trade to Canton.
1761 India: Battle of Panipat – Afghans defeat Marathas.
1774 Turkey: Treaty of Kuchuk Kainarji – Russia gains Black Sea ports and the right to represent Greek Orthodox Church in Turkey.
India: Regulating Act – British India to be ruled by a Governor-General and Council. Warren Hastings appointed first Governor-General.
1775–1782 India: British at war with Marathas.
1782 India: Treaty of Salbai ends British-Maratha war.
1784 India Act: British government in Westminster to control political affairs.
1786–1787 Indonesia: Chinese suppress a revolt in Formosa.
1787 Japan: Rice riots at Edo, following great famine.

1793 India: Lord Cornwallis, Governor-General, stabilizes the revenue and reorganizes law courts on British lines.
1794–1925 Persia: Aga Muhammad founds the Qaja dynasty.
1796 British take Ceylon from Dutch.
1799 India: Tippoo Sahib, ruler of Mysore killed in battle fighting British – British control is established over southern India.

ELSEWHERE

1759 British capture Quebec.
1767 USA: Mason-Dixon line separates the free and slave states.
1770 USA: Boston Massacre – British troops fire on Boston mob and kill five citizens.
Repeal of the Townshend Tax Acts but a tax is retained by Britain on imported tea.
1773 Boston Tea Party – citizens, disguised as Indians, dump tea in Boston harbour.
1774 USA: 'Intolerable Acts' by British parliament.
First Continental Congress meets at Philadelphia to protest.
1775 American War of Independence to 1783.
Battles of Lexington and Concord – Americans led by George Washington.
British victory at Bunker Hill after retreat.
1776 USA: British troops evacuate Boston.
American Declaration of Independence.
1777 USA: Battle of Saratoga – the British surrender.
1778 USA: France joins the war on the side of the colonists against Britain.
1780–1783 S. America: Peruvian Indians under Inca, Tupac Amara, revolt against Spain.
1780 USA: British capture Charleston.
1781 USA: Surrender of British troops at Yorktown.
1783 USA: Treaty of Paris – end of American War of Independence. Britain recognizes independence of the 13 colonies.
1787 USA: New constitution is drawn up.
1789–1797 George Washington, first American president.
1791 Canada Act – divides Canada into English and French-speaking territories.
USA: Bill of Rights – the first 10 Amendments to US Constitution.
1798–1799 Africa: Bonaparte's expedition to Egypt – battle of the Pyramids; Cairo taken by the French.
Battle of the Nile – Nelson defeats the French fleet.
1799 Napoleon invades Syria.

The French Revolution

By the time Louis XVI came to the throne in 1774, France was deeply in debt, and badly governed by an elite of the nobility. While they escaped taxes and lived in luxury, poor people in their thousands lived in miserable poverty.

The system of monarchy which still prevailed in France was beginning to be questioned. The successful revolt of North American colonists against royalist England in the American War of Independence had a great impact upon thinking in France, especially as Frenchmen like the Marquis de Lafayette had taken part in the war.

Faced with national bankruptcy, the king decided to summon the Estates-General, a national parliament which had not met since 1614. It consisted of three 'Estates': 300 noblemen, 300 clergy, and 600 commoners. Each Estate had one vote, which meant that the nobility and the clergy could outvote the commoners. So the commoners formed a national Constituent Assembly, pledged to make a new constitution for France.

Louis planned to dismiss the Assembly. This aroused

George Washington, first president of the United States (1789-1799). The American War of Independence lasted from 1775 to 1783. At the end of it 13 ex-British colonies formed the United States of America. The war started after the British had tried to impose taxes to maintain a standing army in America which the colonists objected to. British troops were sent from Britain to destroy an arms cache held by the colonists at nearby Concord. Just after dawn on April 19, 1775, at Lexington on the road to Concord, the troops were confronted by armed colonists. The opening 'shot heard round the world' was fired and war began. The end came when the British, under Cornwallis, surrendered to the American commander-in-chief, George Washington, at Yorktown, Virginia, on October 19, 1781.

the fury of the Paris mob, which stormed the fortress-prison of the Bastille on July 14, 1789. Louis had to give way, and the people's Assembly made many reforms.

In June 1791, Louis tried to flee the country. He was captured and taken back to Paris. In August the Paris mob attacked the king in the Palace of the Tuileries, butchering his guards and imprisoning him. A new assembly, the National Convention, declared the monarchy abolished and set up a republic on September 21.

Power in the Convention passed to a political group called the Girondins, who had Louis tried for treason and executed. But during 1793 a more extremist group, the Jacobins, gained power. The Girondins were executed, and a Committee of Public Safety ruled the country, headed by Maximilien Robespierre. Under his influence anyone suspected of opposing the new regime was executed in a bloodbath known as the 'Reign of Terror'. In July 1794 Robespierre himself was accused and guillotined, and the Terror gradually died away. In 1795 a new two-chamber assembly was elected, and order returned gradually to France.

The impact of the Revolution was enormous. In 1792 France offered aid to the people of any country who wished to overthrow their governments. As a result France was soon at war with most of Europe. Carnot, described as the 'organiser of victory', was responsible for the French revolutionary armies and in 1793 there was a levy of the entire male population capable of bearing arms, revolutionizing warfare. These new armies proved successful against the standing armies of the monarchical states.

The three catchwords of the Revolution – Liberty, Equality and Fraternity – enshrined ideas which influenced the major political movements of the following century and later.

Age of Enlightenment

The *Social Contract* by Jean-Jacques Rousseau and the writings of Voltaire were part of the 'Enlightenment', the new relationship in which the poor were not always ruled by the rich. The Englishman Thomas Paine gave great support to the revolutions of America and France. In *The Rights of Man* and *The Age of Reason* he supported ideas of colonial freedom and republicanism. The widely travelled Adam Smith wrote *Wealth of Nations* (published in 1776), the basis of modern economics. Arguably one of the most important theses ever published was the essay which appeared in 1798 by the English clergyman, Thomas Robert Malthus – *Essay on Population*. It argued that the world's resources were limited and that the rise in population must ultimately lead to disaster.

But in the emotional upheaval of the social revolution, the Age of Enlightenment gave way to a Romantic movement in the arts which favoured emotions before reason, and free individual expression. Romanticism was embodied by French painters of the following century such as Théodore Géricault (1791–1824) and Eugène Delacroix (1798–1863).

Simon Bolivar, liberator of six South American republics and first president of Colombia and Peru. In 1812 inspired by the revolutions in North America and Europe, the young Creole aristocrat set out from Venezuela with a small untrained army to cut the bonds with Spain. Because of the superior numbers of the Spanish army, Bolivar relied on guerrilla tactics. In 1813, with only 600 men and 5 cannon, he invaded Venezuela and defeated 5 Spanish units and captured 50 cannon.

The Napoleonic Wars

Following the wars against France during and immediately after the French Revolution, there was another attempt to curb the overweening ambition of Napoleon Bonaparte, who in May 1804 was voted the title of emperor. Britain was joined by Austria, Naples, Russia and Sweden.

Napoleon massed an invasion fleet to attack England. But in October 1805 a British fleet led by Horatio Nelson destroyed a combined French and Spanish fleet at Trafalgar, ending the invasion threat.

Napoleon switched his armies to attack Austria, which he crushed at the battle of Austerlitz in December 1805. He went on to invade Prussia and defeat Russia.

In 1808 Napoleon attacked Spain and Portugal, and made his brother Joseph king of Spain. The Spanish people appealed to Britain for aid. British troops landed in Portugal and advanced into Spain. Napoleon forced them to retreat to Corunna, in northern Spain. Arthur Wellesley, later duke of Wellington, then took command of the British forces in the Peninsular War. In a series of battles Wellesley wore down the French, and forced Napoleon to keep a large army in Spain. Finally in 1814 the British crossed the French frontier and won a resounding victory at Toulouse on April 10.

Napoleon was determined to crush Russia, and invaded it with 600,000 men in June 1812. He captured Moscow, which the Russians had set on fire, but found himself short of supplies and in the grip of a Russian winter. He had to retreat, losing almost all his men. In October 1813 a combined Russian, Prussian and Austrian force heavily defeated Napoleon at Leipzig. In April 1814 he abdicated and was exiled to Elba.

In March 1815 Napoleon escaped from Elba and returned to France. The French king, Louis XVIII, fled, and Napoleon was soon in power again. An allied army was hastily gathered, and under the command of Wellington and the Prussian Marshal Gebhard von Blucher it defeated Napoleon finally at Waterloo in Belgium in June.

Industrial Revolution

The term 'Industrial Revolution' was coined in the 1830s by French historians to describe the change from a world in which farming was the most important occupation, to one dominated by factories.

The Industrial Revolution, which began in the 1700s, developed in Britain first. During this period Britain enjoyed certain commercial advantages, as well as having some very skilled inventors, which gave Britain a lead over her main competitors.

The invention which started the revolution was the flying shuttle, made by John Kay in 1733. Now weavers produced cloth quickly and in greater widths.

The new machines were too big to drive by hand, so factories were built beside rivers where water-wheels could provide power. By the early 1800s, nearly all spinning and weaving was being done in factories.

The first steam engines built in the late 1600s to pump water were very inefficient. James Watt, a Scottish engineer, devised the first satisfactory steam-engine in 1769, and in 1775 with Matthew Boulton he formed a company to make them. This new source of power speeded up production.

The Industrial Revolution changed the face of the countryside. The new machines were housed in large factories, and towns sprang up around these to provide homes for the workers. Before the revolution, most workers could grow their own food. In the new towns, they lived in cramped conditions with no gardens, depending on their wages for everything.

Battle of Navarino, October 1827, was a key point in the war for Greek Independence from Turkey. An allied fleet of British, Russian and French ships defeated a Turkish-Egyptian fleet in Navarino Bay, south west Greece, destroying 60 vessels and killing 8000 men. The allies lost no ships and about 176 men.

ELSEWHERE

1804 Bonaparte crowns himself Napoleon I, emperor of France.
Third Coalition formed against France by Britain, Russia, Austria and Sweden.
1804–1813 Serbs revolt against Turks.
1805 Battle of Trafalgar – British fleet under Nelson defeats Franco-Spanish fleet.
Battle of Austerlitz – French defeat Austro-Russian forces.
1806 Napoleon dissolves the Holy Roman empire and replaces it with the Confederation of the Rhine.
Berlin Decree by Napoleon attempts an economic blockade of Britain.
1807 Battle of Friedland – French defeat Russians; Treaty of Tilsit between Tsar Alexander and Napoleon.
1808 French occupy Spain.
Peninsular War in Spain to 1814 – British troops with Spanish and Portuguese guerrillas oppose the French.
1809 Battle of Corunna – French defeat British.
1811 Luddite riots in England against mechanization of textile industry, followed by passing of harsh laws in 1812.
George III declared insane, Prince of Wales becomes Regent.
1812 Battle of Salamanca – British victory in Spain.
Napoleon invades Russia with the Grand Army – the battle of Borodino – French occupy Moscow, but then have to retreat and only 100,000 of 600,000 of the army survive.
1813 Battle of Vittoria – French driven from Spain by Wellington.
Allied forces invade France and enter Paris in March 1814.
1814 Napoleon abdicates and is exiled to Elba.
Treaty of Paris ends Napoleonic wars.
1814–1815 Congress of Vienna – heads of state discuss settlement of post-war Europe.
1815 The Hundred Days – Napoleon escapes from Elba and marches on Paris.
Battle of Waterloo – Napoleon defeated by British under Wellington and exiled to St Helena. He dies in 1821.
Congress of Vienna reconvened.
Second Treaty of Paris restores France's boundaries to those of 1790.
Quadruple Alliance of Britain, Austria, Prussia and Russia to maintain the Congress system.
English Corn Laws restrict imports.
1818 Congress of Aix-la-Chapelle allows France to join the great powers, to form the Quintuple Alliance.
1819 Peterloo Massacre in England – cavalry charge political meeting in England, several killed.
1820 Cato Street conspiracy, in London, to assassinate cabinet ministers fails.
Liberal revolutions occur in Spain, Portugal and Italy.
1821–1829 Greek War of Independence from Turkey – succeeds.
1823 Spanish revolution is crushed.
1824 Repeal of Combination Acts in Britain allows the growth of trade unions.
Decembrist uprising against the Tsar Nicholas (1825).
1829 Catholic Emancipation Act in Britain – Catholics allowed to hold public office.
1830 July Revolution overthrows Charles X of France.
Revolution against Dutch rule in Belgium.
Revolution in Poland – crushed by Russia.
1832 Reform Act in Britain extends vote to middle classes.
1833 Factory Act in Britain – children under nine may not be employed.
Slavery abolished throughout British empire.
1834 Tolpuddle Martyrs – 6 Dorset labourers transported for trying to form a trade union.
1834–1839 Carlist Wars in Spain – the Pretender, Don Carlos, attempts to gain Spanish throne.
1836 Beginning of Chartist Movement in Britain which demands votes for all adult males.
1839 'Newport Rising' of armed Chartists suppressed.

EUROPE

1800 Ottoman empire: In decline along with Persia. Russia fought wars against both and detached territory from northern border of Persia.
Africa: North Africa remains under Ottoman rule.
European trading stations along west Africa flourish through the slave trade.
1803 Australia: Flinders circumnavigates.
USA: Louisiana Purchase – France sells Louisiana Territory for $15m.
1804–1805 American explorers Meriwether Lewis and William Clark explore north-west USA and reach the Pacific.
1805 Egypt: Selim III, sultan of Turkey, appoints Muhammad Ali as pasha of Egypt.
China: Christian literature is banned.

1811 Egypt: Ruling Mamelukes are massacred in Cairo by Muhammad Ali.

The Penny Black of 1840. Before 1840 it was expensive to send a letter. The simple solution of a prepaid adhesive stamp meant that poor people could communicate with friends or relatives in other parts of the country or abroad. The British example was soon imitated by most other countries.

1818 Africa: Chaka the Great founds Zulu empire in south.
USA: 49th parallel is fixed as the boundary between USA and Canada.
1819 India: Sikh leader, Ranjit Singh, conquers Kashmir.
Far East: Sir Stamford Raffles founds the British colony of Singapore.
1820 Africa: 4000 British settlers at Albany (Durban) on east coast of South Africa.
USA: Missouri Compromise – admission of several states to the Union including Missouri as a slave state (1821).
1822 Africa: Liberia in west is founded as a colony for freed US slaves.
1823 US President James Monroe issued Monroe Doctrine warning European powers not to intervene in the Americas.
1824–1826 Burma: First Anglo-Burmese war – Britain begins annexation.
1824–1827 Africa: First Ashanti War between Britain and the Ashanti of the Gold Coast (Ghana).
1825 Africa: Alexander Laing, the Scot, crosses Sahara from Tripoli to Timbuktu.
1829 S. America: Greater Colombia is divided into Colombia, Venezuela, Ecuador, New Granada.
1830 Africa: French invade Algeria and depose the ruler *(dey)* – ten years of warfare follow; beginning of French colonization of Algeria.
1833–1835 Voyage of Captain Fitzroy and Charles Darwin in the Beagle to Tahiti and New Zealand (scientific).
1835 Africa: Turkish forces land in Tripoli and bring its independence to an end.
1835–1837 Africa: Great Trek of Boers in South Africa inland from the Cape – the foundation of Transvaal.
1838 Battle of Blood River – Boers in Natal defeat the Zulus.
1839 British occupy Aden.
1839–1842 First Opium War between Britain and China after Chinese commissioner Lin destroyed opium shipments. War put pressure on weak Manchus to open its doors to European trade.
1840 Treaty of Waitangi – New Zealand becomes a British Crown Colony.

The Modern World AD 1840–AD 1983

1840 AD

1983 AD

EUROPE & AFRICA

1846 Zulu reserves set up in Natal, South Africa.
1848 Year of revolutions in Europe.
1853–1856 David Livingstone crosses Africa.
1866 Austro-Prussian War over Schleswig – Holstein. Austria defeated.
1869 Suez Canal opened.
1870–1871 Franco-Prussian War because of French resentment at growing power of Prussia – defeat of France and emergence of united Germany.
1871 Unification of Italy.
1877 Russia at war with Turkey over the Balkans. Transvaal (South Africa) annexed by Britain.
1879 Britain and France assume control of Egyptian affairs. Zulu War.
1881 Boers defeat British at Majuba Hill and make Transvaal independent.
1882 Britain occupies Egypt.
1882–1914 Triple Alliance of Germany, Italy and Austria-Hungary.
1884 Berlin Conference signals the 'Scramble for Africa'.
1885 German East Africa established.
1893 Ivory Coast becomes a French protectorate.
1895 Rhodesia founded by Cecil Rhodes.
1896 Ethiopians defeat the Italians at Adowa.
1897 Greece and Turkey at war over Crete.
1898 Battle of Omdurman. British defeat Sudan nationalists.
1899–1902 Anglo-Boer War.
1900 Britain conquers Nigeria.
1904 *Entente cordiale* between Britain and France.
1909 Act of Union of South Africa.
1911 Italy invades Libya.
1914–1918 First World War.
1916 Easter Rising in Ireland.
1917 October revolution in Russia.

1919 League of Nations formed.
1922 Egypt independent of Britain and France.
Mussolini becomes prime minister of Italy, which becomes a Fascist state (1923).
1926 General strike in Britain.
1933 Hitler becomes chancellor of Germany.
1935 Italians invade Ethiopia.
1936–1939 Spanish Civil War brings Franco to power.
1939–1945 Second World War.
1945 Formation of United Nations.
1949 South African government adopts policy of *apartheid*.
Formation of NATO.
1952 Mau Mau rebellion in Kenya.
1955 Formation of Warsaw Pact in opposition to NATO.
1956 Dispute over Suez Canal.
1957 Treaty of Rome starts European Common Market.
1960 17 African colonies become independent.
1961 Berlin Wall built.
1965 Rhodesian government declares independence.
1967 Six Day War between Arabs and Israel.
1967–1970 Nigerian civil war.
1968 Soviet troops invade Czechoslovakia.
1975 October War between Arabs and Israel.
Independence for Portuguese colonies follows the 1974 coup in Portugal.
1979 Downfall of Amin in Uganda.
1980 Rhodesia becomes independent as Zimbabwe.
1981 President Sadat of Egypt assassinated.
Martial Law declared in Poland.
1982 Falklands War – Britain reoccupies islands after Argentine invasion.

ELSEWHERE

1848 Treaty of Guadeloupe Hidalgo gives California and New Mexico to the USA.
1854 Commodore Perry forces Japan to conclude commercial treaty with the USA.
1856–1860 Anglo-Chinese War.
1857 Indian Mutiny.
1858 India Bill transfers government of India to British Crown.
1860 Anglo-French forces occupy Peking.
1861–1865 American Civil War.
1865 President Lincoln assassinated.
1867 USA buys Alaska from Russia.
1876 Battle of Little Big Horn.
1895 Treaty of Shimonoseki between China and Japan – Japan gains Formosa, Korea independent of China.
1898 American-Spanish War – Cuba becomes independent.
1900 Boxer (Nationalist) rebellion in China.
1904–1905 War between Japan and Russia.
1911 Revolution in Mexico.
1917 USA enters World War I.
1920 Jewish state of Palestine established.
Prohibition of alcohol in USA.
1924 Sun Yat-sen establishes Chinese Republican government.
1927 Civil war in China.
Charles Lindbergh makes first solo flight across Atlantic.
1929 Collapse of American stock market triggers off world-wide depression.
1931 Japanese occupy Manchuria.
1932 Ottawa Conference – Britain gives trading preferences to Commonwealth.
1934 Mao Tse-tung leads Communists on Long March.
1937 Japanese invade China.
1940 Japan joins Axis powers.
1941 Japan attacks American fleet at Pearl Harbor, Hawaii. USA declares war on Axis powers.
1945 First atomic bombs are dropped on Japan.
1946 Civil war in Indo-China between nationalists and French.
1947 Marshall Plan for economic recovery in Europe.
India becomes independent – splits into India and Pakistan.
Indonesia becomes independent.
1948 State of Israel is formed.
1949 Communists control all China.
1950 American Senator McCarthy begins inquiry into 'un-American activities' (communism, homosexuality, etc).
1950–1953 Korean War.
1954 French defeated at Dien Bien Phu – Vietnam.
1957 Race riots in southern USA.
1959 Castro comes to power in Cuba.
1960 J. F. Kennedy becomes US President. Assassinated 1963.
1962 Cuban missile crisis.
1964 Civil Rights Bill in USA.
1965 USA sends troops to Vietnam.
India and Pakistan at war.
1966 'Cultural Revolution' in China.
1968 Martin Luther King and Robert Kennedy assassinated.
1969 American astronauts land on moon.
1971 East Pakistan becomes independent as Bangladesh.
1973 Military overthrow communist Allende in Chile.
USA withdraws from Vietnam.
World-wide oil crisis follows October War (Arab-Israeli).
1974 Watergate scandal forces President Nixon to resign.
1976 Death of Mao Tse-tung.
1979 Collapse of Shah's regime in Iran – Ayatollah Khomeini sets up an Islamic state.
1980 War between Iran and Iraq.
1982 Israel invades Lebanon.

TECHNOLOGY

1844 Anaesthetic used by US dentist Horace Wells.
Morse transmits the first telegraph message.
1853 Hypodermic syringe invented by C. G. Pravaz (France).
1856 Method of mass-producing steel announced by H. Bessemer (GB).
1858 Domestic sewing machine designed by Isaac Singer (US).
1860 Invention of Winchester repeating rifle (US).
1862 Machine gun used in American Civil War, invented by R. J. Gatling.
1864 Electromagnetic theory of light – J. C. Maxwell (GB).
1866 Dynamite invented by Alfred Nobel (Swed) – he founded the Nobel prizes from the fortune he made from his invention.
1867 Typewriter invented by Christopher Sholes (US).
1874 Riveted Jeans made in San Francisco by J. Davis and Levi Strauss for miners and cowboys.
1876 Telephone invented by Alexander Graham Bell (Scot).
1877 Record player invented by Thomas Edison (US).
Fingerprinting used by W. Hirschel of the Indian civil service to stop army pensioners drawing their pensions twice.
1897 Thomas Edison burned the first successful incandescent filament light bulb for 13½ hours.
1881 Louis Pasteur (Fr) applies immunization to rabies.
1885 First successful petrol-driven car test driven by its inventor Karl Benz (Germany) – on sale in 1888.
First successful submarines are built.
1886 Coca Cola invented by Dr J. Pemberton (US). Launched as 'Esteemed Brain Tonic and Intellectual Beverage'!
1887 Contact lenses invented by Dr Frick (Swiss).
1892 Zip fastener invented by W. L. Judson (US).
1893 First modern breakfast cereal – shredded wheat – invented by H. D. Perky (US).
1895 Sigmund Freud (Aust) publishes first work on psycho-analysis.
Wireless invented by G. Marconi (It.).
Motion pictures presented publicly on screen for the first time by A. L. Lumière in Paris.
William Roetgen (Ger) discovers X-rays.
1901 Safety razor-blades by King Camp Gillette (US).
1903 First aeroplane flight by Wilbur and Orville Wright (US).
1911 Ernest Rutherford (GB) discovers the proton.
1914 Tank invented by Ernest Swinton (GB).
1915 Einstein (Swiss) offers his Theory of Relativity.
1920 Tea bags produced by J. Krieger of San Francisco.
1925 Television invented by John Logie Baird (Scot).
Frozen food process developed by C. Birdseye (US).
1928 Alexander Fleming (GB) discovers penicillin.
First robot built by Captain Richards and A. H. Refell (GB).
1930 Jet engine invented by Frank Whittle (GB).
Planet Pluto is located.
1936 Helicopter designed by Professor Focke (Ger).
1939 First jet aircraft – Heinkel 178 – designed by Dr Okain.
First jet fighter – Messerschmitt Me262 – flew in July 1942.
1943 Ball-point pen patented by Hungarian journalist L. Biro.
1944 Automatic digital computer designed by H. Aiken (US)
1948 Transistors devised by Drs Bardeen, Brattain and Shockley (US).
1953 Watson, Crick and Wilkins (GB) discover DNA.
1954 First nuclear submarine USS *Nautilus* launched.
1955 Hovercraft principal patented by C. Cockerell (GB).
Oral contraceptive developed by Dr G. Pincus (US).
1961 Yuri Gagarin (USSR) – first man in space.
Silicon chip integrated circuit patented by Texas Instruments.
1967 Dr Christiaan Barnard (SA) performs heart transplant.
1978 First test-tube baby born following fertilization in a laboratory conducted by Dr Steptoe and Dr Edwards (GB).
1981 First re-usable space shuttle *Columbia* flies.

CULTURE

1848 Holman Hunt, Millais and D. G. Rossetti found the Pre-Raphaelite Brotherhood in England.
1869 Paul Verlaine (1844–1896; Fr) writes *Fêtes Galantes*.
1872 C. Monet (1840–1926; Fr) paints *Impression: Sunrise*.
1874 First Impressionist exhibition in Paris.
1880 *The Thinker* by August Rodin (1840–1914; Fr).
1881 Henry James (1843–1916; USA) writes *Portrait of a Lady*.
1883 R. L. Stevenson (1850–1894; GB) Writes *Treasure Island*.
1886 Vincent Van Gogh (1853–1890; Dutch) moves to Paris and meets the French Impressionist painters.
1889 Émile Zola (1840–1902; Fr) writes *Germinal*.
1891 Thomas Hardy (1840–1928; GB) writes *Tess of the d'Urbervilles*.
1893 Anton Dvòrak (1841–1904; Czech) composes *The New World Symphony*.
1895 *Swan Lake* ballet by Tchaikovsky (1840–1893; Russ).
1899 Edward Elgar (1857–1934; GB) composes *Enigma Variations*.
1900 Giacomo Puccini (1858–1924; It) composes *Tosca*.
1901 W. B. Yeats (1865–1939; Irish) assumes leadership of Irish literary revival.
1902 Rudyard Kipling (1865–1936; GB) writes *Just So Stories*.
1904 Anton Chekhov (1860–1904; Russ) writes *The Cherry Orchard*.
1907 First Cubist exhibition in Paris.
1909 Sergei Diaghilev (1872–1929; Russ) forms the *Ballet Russe* in which Nijinsky appears.
1911 Richard Strauss (1864–1949; Austr) composes the opera, *Der Rosenkavalier*.
1912 George Bernard Shaw (1856–1950; GB) writes *Pygmalion*.
1913 Marcel Proust (1871–1922; Fr) starts writing *Remembrance of Things Past*.
Igor Stravinsky (1882–1971; Russ) composes *The Rite of Spring*.
1922 *Ulysses* by James Joyce (1882–1941; Irish).
First commercial talking film *Der Brandstift* made in Berlin.
The Waste Land by T. S. Eliot (1885–1965; GB).
1923 George Gershwin (1898–1937; USA), the jazz composer, writes *Rhapsody in Blue*.
Franz Kafka (1883–1924; Ger) writes *The Trial*.
Virginia Woolf (1882–1941; GB) writes *To The Lighthouse*.
1929 Salvador Dali (1904–; Sp) joins Surrealist group of painters.
Ernest Hemingway (1899–1961; USA) writes *A Farewell to Arms*.
1936 Aldous Huxley (1894–1963; GB) writes *Eyeless in Gaza*.
1937 Pablo Picasso (1881–1974; Sp) exhibits his mural *Guernica* which conveys horrors of Spanish Civil War.
1939 Clark Gable and Vivian Leigh star in *Gone with the Wind*.
1941 Henry Moore (1898–; GB) produces a series of drawings of refugees in a London air raid shelter.
1942 Albert Camus (1913–1960; Fr) writes *The Stranger*.
1943 Jean-Paul Sartre (1905–1981; Fr) writes existential treatise *Being and Nothingness*.
1945 Benjamin Britten (1913–1976; GB) writes *Peter Grimes*.
1948 Bertold Brecht (1898–1956; Ger) writes *The Caucasian Chalk Circle*.
1949 George Orwell (1903–1950; GB) writes *1984*.
1952 Samuel Beckett (1906–; Irish) writes *Waiting for Godot*.
1959 Gunter Grass (1927–; Ger) writes *The Tin Drum*.
1963 Andy Warhol (1930–; USA) and others feature in a show of Pop Art in New York.
1982 Steven Spielberg's film *E.T.* is most financially successful film in the history of the cinema.
Gabriel Garcia Marquez, author of *One Hundred Years of Solitude*, wins Nobel prize.

1840 AD

1983 AD

The Year of Revolutions – 1848

By 1848 Europe was ready to explode. Food shortages, trade recessions and nationalist feelings were the main causes of discontent. In France, in February an uprising of citizens drove out Louis Philippe and set up the Second Republic.

In March, there followed an uprising in Vienna against the Austrian chancellor, Prince Metternich, who had dominated the empire's affairs for thirty years. He was a reactionary who had firmly repressed popular movements. He had to be smuggled out of Vienna in a laundry basket. Emperor Ferdinand abdicated in favour of his more liberal-minded nephew, Franz Joseph.

Hungary, an uneasy part of the Austrian empire, proclaimed itself a republic under the popular leader Kossuth. The revolt was put down within the year, but not before Austria called in the Russian army to assist her.

Revolutions in parts of Italy, then still under Austrian rule, were suppressed. These were the rumblings of a movement that led to the unification of Italy twelve years later.

The revolution in Paris acted as a catalyst for half Europe. There was widespread discontent in Germany, then still divided into a number of small states. The revolts were nationalist and liberal, with demands for constitutional changes and other reforms. In Austria the revolutionary aim was to destroy the power of the Habsburg monarchy. In Germany the aim was to unify the various German states into a kingdom. At first the German rulers gave way to the demands made upon them and debates about unification were held. But at the end of 1850 the Conference of German States at Dresden re-established the old Germanic Confederation and German unity had to await the leadership of Prussia's Bismarck in 1871.

Britain was partially isolated from developments on the continent but the Chartist movement had its last revival in 1848. The Chartists were working men's associations demanding the vote – at that time such demands appeared revolutionary. Their leader, Feargus O'Connor, wanted to present a monster petition of 5 million signatures to Parliament. The government was so worried that the old Duke of Wellington was called upon to defend the capital against a possible insurrection. In the event, the petition was a farce and Britain's rulers were able to relax again. It was 1867 before Britain extended the franchise (right to vote) with the Second Reform Act.

Perhaps the most significant event of 1848 was the publication of *The Communist Manifesto* by Marx and Engels. This was to become the 'Bible' of the Communist movement which was to split the world into two rival camps in the 20th century.

A British party lavishly entertained by an Indian prince. But many Indians were embittered by British invasion of state after state and alarmed at the threats to the Hindu caste system. Discipline and administration of the Indian army was slack. Mutiny in 1857 was finally sparked off by the introduction to the Bengal army of cartridges greased with pig and cow fat, offensive to both Muslims and Hindus.

American Civil War

The Civil War (1861–1865) between the north and south of the United States has sometimes been called the first modern war. Casualties were enormous – 618,000 died. In the end the north won because of its greater numbers and because it possessed the manufacturing industries essential to support a modern war machine.

It has been a myth of history that the Civil War was fought in order to end slavery – it was not. The north (Union) fought to prevent the southern (Confederate) states from breaking away from the union and thereby weakening the USA as a whole.

The turning point of the war was the Union victory at the battle of Gettysburg in 1863. Two years later the south surrendered. Once the war was over the USA rapidly developed so that by the end of the century she had become the greatest industrial power in the world.

Starving Irish peasants at the gates of a workhouse in 1846. The British Corn Laws, of 1815 banned the import of wheat to protect farmers from competition, but this made the price of bread too high for poor people. In Ireland, the poor lived on potatoes. But in 1845 and 1846 a disastrous blight ruined the potato crop. An estimated million Irish died. About two million left Ireland for America bearing a great deal of ill-will towards England. The effects of the famine led to the repeal of the Corn Laws in 1846.

EUROPE

1846 Potato famine in Ireland.
Repeal of Corn Laws in Britain.
1848 Year of Revolutions in Europe:
Revolution in Paris – Louis Philippe abdicates and the Second Republic is set up with Louis Napoleon as president.
Revolutions in Milan, Naples, Venice and Rome which are mainly suppressed within the year.
Revolutions in Berlin, Vienna, Prague, Budapest have initial success.
Prince Metternich resigns in Austria and Emperor Ferdinand abdicates.
Frankfurt National Assembly discusses German unification.
Russia suppresses uprising in Wallachia (Romania).
Insurrection in Tipperary (Ireland) is put down.
1849 Revolutions in Italy and Hungary crushed.
1850 Don Pacifico incident – British foreign secretary, Lord Palmerston, defends rights of British citizens abroad.
1852 Louis Napoleon establishes the Second Empire in France as Napoleon III, emperor of France.
1854–1856 Crimean War – Britain, France and Turkey against Russia as a result of Russian invasion of Turkish territory demanding passage for its warships through the Dardanelles.
1854 Russians defeated at battles of Balaclava and Inkerman.
Russian navy immobilized at Sevastopol.
Liberal revolution in Spain overthrows government.
1855 Florence Nightingale reforms British army nursing.
1858 Secret alliance between Napoleon III and Count Cavour, prime minister of Piedmont in Italy, determined to liberate Italy from Austrian control.
Irish emigrants in the USA found the Fenian Society.
1859 France and Piedmont at war against Austria: battles of Magenta and Solferino – Austria defeated.
Treaty of Zurich between France and Austria – Piedmont gains Lombardy.
1860 Parma, Modena, Tuscany and Romagna unite with Piedmont.
Italian patriot, Giuseppe Garibaldi and the 1000 Redshirts conquer Sicily and Naples, allying all southern Italy with Piedmont.
1861 Italy, except for Venice and Rome, is united to become a kingdom under Victor Emmanuel, king of Piedmont.
Serfs freed in Russia.
Death of Prince Albert, husband to Queen Victoria.
1863–1864 Polish insurrection fails.
1864 Austria and Prussia take Schleswig-Holstein from Denmark.
1866 Prussia forms alliance with Italy.
Austro-Prussian war over Schleswig-Holstein.
Battle of Sadowa – Prussian victory.
Battles of Custozza and Lissa – Italy defeated by Austrians, but gains Venice.
Treaty of Prague ends Austro-Prussian war after 7 weeks – Austria have to withdraw from German affairs.
1867 Second Reform act in Britain widens the franchise (right to vote).
North German confederation is formed under Prussian leadership.
Formation of Austro-Hungarian monarchy – Franz Joseph of Austria is also created monarch of Hungary.
1869 Disestablishment Act passed in Britain – Irish Church ceases to exist in 1871.
1870 Irish Land Acts – compensation for eviction but this fails to ease the Irish problem.
Kingdom of Italy annexes papal states and Rome becomes the capital of Italy.
1870–1871 Franco-Prussian War when Prussia appears to support the claim of a German prince to the throne of Spain. Bismarck, the prime minister of Prussia, insults the French in a telegram, inciting war which Bismarck hopes will unite Germany behind Prussia. It works.
Battle of Sedan – French defeated, Napoleon III captured, Prussians besiege Paris, end of Second French Empire.

AFRICA & AMERICA

1842 Webster-Ashburton Treaty – settles boundary between the USA and Canada.
1843 Natal becomes a British colony.
1845 Texas joins the USA.
1846 Zulu reserves set up in Natal.
1846–1847 Bantu-British war in South Africa – defeat of Bantus.
1846–1848 War between the USA and Mexico.
1848 California gold rush.
First convention of Women's Rights in New York.
1852 Sand River Convention – Britain recognizes an independent Transvaal.
1853 Livingstone begins crossing Africa – comes across Victoria Falls.
1854 Convention of Bloemfontein – the British withdraw south of the Orange River and Boers establish the Orange Free State.
1860 South Carolina withdraws from the Union (USA).
1861 Abraham Lincoln, president of the USA.
Confederate states of America formed by South Carolina and ten other southern states.
1861–1865 Civil War in USA between Confederates and the Union (north).
1861 Confederates win the battle of Bull Run.
1863 Lincoln proclaims abolition of slavery in USA.
Battle of Gettysburg – Confederate defeat.
French occupy Mexico City.
1864 Union army wins control of Georgia.
1865 Confederate General Lee surrenders to Union General Grant – end of American Civil War.
President Lincoln assassinated.
1867 Dominion of Canada is established.
France forced to withdraw from Mexico.
1868 British expedition to Magdala (Ethiopia) forces release of diplomats.
1868–1878 Ten Years' War – Cuba attempts to win independence from Spain but fails.
1869 Opening of Suez Canal.

ELSEWHERE

1842 Afghanistan: British withdraw from Kabul.
China: Treaty of Nanking between Britain and China – China cedes Hong Kong to Britain.
1845–1848 India: Anglo-Sikh wars – British annexation of the Punjab in north west.
1850 Australian Colonies Act – can set up their own legislatures.
1850–1864 China: T'ai Ping rebellion – revolt against the Manchu dynasty.
1852–1853 Second Anglo-Burmese War – British victory, take Pegu.
1854 Japan: Commodore Perry of the US Navy forces Japan to make first commercial treaty with the USA – the Treaty of Kahagawa.
1856 Afghanistan: Persia captures Herat – leads to war with Britain.
Anglo-Chinese War.
1857 Persia: Treaty of Paris ends Anglo-Persian war.
Indian Mutiny – Sepoys (native soldiers) rebel in Bengal army. They take Cawnpore and besiege Lucknow.
1858 India: Relief of Lucknow – end of Indian Mutiny.
India Bill – government of India passes from East India Company to the Crown.
Russia: Treaty of Aigun – gains the Amur region from China.
China: Treaties of Tientsin open 11 Chinese ports to western trade.
1860 China: Anglo-French force occupies Peking and burns the summer palace – end of Third Anglo-Chinese war.
1862 China: French establish protectorate over Cochin-China – obtain western provinces in 1867.
1863 French establish a protectorate over Cambodia.
1864 Expedition of British, Dutch, French and Americans bombard Shimonoseki, Japan.
1864–1880 Russia conquers Turkestan.
1868–1912 Meiji period in Japan – ends the anti-foreign policy.

1870 AD

ELSEWHERE

1876 Korea opened to Japanese trade.
1877 Queen Victoria proclaimed 'Empress of India'.
Satsuma rebellion in Japan is crushed.
1878–1880 Second Afghan war to prevent Russia gaining control. Britain gains control of Afghan affairs.

1885 New Guinea is divided between Britain and Germany.
France establishes protectorates over Annam and Tonkin (Indochina).
1885–1886 Third Burmese war – Britain annexes upper Burma.
1889 New constitution in Japan leads to first general elections in 1890, though only a tiny minority has the vote.
1893–1906 Richard Seddon as Prime Minister of New Zealand introduces social reforms considered the most advanced in the world.
1893 Women's suffrage in New Zealand.
1894 China and Japan fight over Korea.
Sun Yat-sen founds first of several revolutionary societies in China.
1895 Treaty of Shimonoseki – Japan gains Formosa, China recognizes Korea's independence.
1896 Anglo-French agreement settles boundaries in Siam (Thailand).
1897 Germans occupy Kiaochow, China.
1898 China cedes Port Arthur to Russia.
USA annexes Hawaii.
Scramble for trading concessions by the European powers precipitates Boxer rebellion in China.
1900 Boxers, fanatical nationalists, attack Europeans and foreign legations. Rebellion is suppressed by an international force of soldiers from Europe, Japan and USA. China forced to pay huge compensation.

AFRICA & AMERICA

1876 Battle of Little Big Horn – Sioux Indians beat General Custer and his men.
1879 British-Zulu war in South Africa – Zulus are defeated at the battle of Ulundi.
1881 American President James Garfield is assassinated.
Battle of Majuba Hill – Boers defeat British.
Treaty of Pretoria makes Transvaal independent of Britain.
1882 British fleet bombards Alexandria and British occupy Cairo to suppress nationalists.
French withdraw from Egypt.
Anti-Egyptian revolt in Sudan is led by Muslim leader, Mahdi Muhammad Ahmed.
1884 British General Gordon sent to rescue Egyptian garrisons in Sudan – besieged in Khartoum by Mahdi.
1885 Fall of Khartoum and death of Gordon.
1886 Gold is discovered in South Africa.
1889 Brazil becomes a republic.
Cecil Rhodes founds British South Africa Company.
Panama scandal – collapse of Panama Canal Company causes financial scandal in France.
Durand Agreement settles north-west frontier of India with Afghanistan.
1895–1896 War between Italy and Ethiopia.
1895–1896 Jameson Raid.
1895–1898 Cuban revolt against Spanish rule.
1896 Treaty of Addis Ababa – Italy recognises the independence of Ethiopia.
1898 Battle of Omdurman – British General Kitchener defeats the Sudanese and establishes joint rule over Sudan.
Fashoda incident – confrontation between British and French in Sudan, French withdraw.
USA and Spain at war over Cuba.
Treaty of Paris – Cuba gains independence; Spain cedes Puerto Rico, Guam and the Philippines to the USA.
1899–1902 Boer War in South Africa.

EUROPE

Alexander Graham Bell, Scottish-American teacher of the deaf and inventor of the telephone, inaugurating the New York-Chicago line in 1892. In 1876 at the Centennial Exposition at Philadelphia, Bell gave the first demonstration by setting the transmitter and receiver 150m apart and declaring into the handset: "To be or not to be that is the question."

1871 Britain legalizes trade unions.
Franco-Prussian War: Paris surrenders following 132-day siege. Commune set up in opposition to the national government and the peace terms. Government troops crush the Commune.
Treaty of Frankfurt officially ends the Franco-Prussian war – Alsace-Lorraine is ceded to Germany.
France has to pay an indemnity of 5000 million francs.
New German *Reich* (empire) is created with William of Prussia as its *Kaiser* (emperor) and Bismarck as chancellor.
1873–1874 First republic in Spain.
1874 Spanish monarchy restored.
1875 Disraeli, Britain's Prime Minister, purchases 42 per cent of the Suez Canal shares from Egypt.
Insurrection against Turkey by Herzegovina and Bosnia (now Yugoslavia) – annexed by Austria in 1908.
1876 Bulgarian 'atrocities' – thousands massacred by Turks following insurrection.
Serbia and Montenegro (now Yugoslavia) declare war on Turkey but are defeated.
1877 Russia and Turkey at war in the Balkans.
1878 Treaty of San Stefano ends Russo-Turkish war – Turkey loses Montenegro, Serbia, Bulgaria and Romania who become independent.
1879 Irish Land League is formed by Stewart Parnell MP.
1882 Phoenix Park murders – Lord Frederick Cavendish, Chief Secretary for Ireland and the Under-Secretary, Thomas Burke murdered in Dublin.
1882–1914 Triple Alliance of Germany, Austria and Italy.
1883 Sickness insurance introduced in Germany.
1884 Third Reform Act passed in Britain.
Berlin Conference signals the partitioning of Africa.
1886 Prime minister Gladstone introduces the first Irish Home Rule bill – defeated.
1889 Georges Boulanger (former French war minister) plots against the Third Republic in France – flees.
1890 William II German emperor, dismisses his Chancellor, Otto von Bismarck.
1893 Gladstone reintroduces Home Rule for Ireland – defeated in House of Lords.
Independent Labour Party founded in Britain by Keir Hardie.
1894 Dreyfus affair in France – Alfred Dreyfus, a Jewish officer in the French army, convicted of treason (military secrets to Germany) and deported. Many people convinced of his innocence, campaign for a new trial. One of Dreyfus' accusers admitted forging documents. A new trial found Dreyfus guilty but reduced sentence. In 1906 an appeal court cleared him.
1894–1917 Nicholas II, last tsar of Russia.
1895 Massacre of Armenians, by Turks, in Constantinople.
1897 Greece and Turkey at war over Crete.
1899 First Hague peace conference aims to settle international disputes peacefully.
1900 German Navy Law calling for a massive increase in German sea power starts arms race with Britain.

1900 AD

Colonial Power

Following her victories at the end of the Napoleonic wars Britain became a deciding influence in Europe for much of the 19th century. By 1897 when Queen Victoria celebrated her Diamond Jubilee, Britain controlled about one quarter of the world's land surface and peoples. From 1870 to 1900 Britain annexed thirty-nine separate territories.

Victorian Britain was a vigorous, inventive and thrusting society. British engineers had built half the world's railways, British money had financed the development of the new dominions like Canada, as well as much of the growth in the USA. British wealth and power seemed, to her opponents, impregnable. Under Lord Salisbury, who was Prime Minister from 1886 to 1892 and again from 1895 to 1902, the country for a time was to pursue a policy known as 'splendid isolation'. Britain spurned alliances of the kind formed in continental Europe. She did so in part because of the security she enjoyed as an island protected by her huge navy. Under Salisbury it was laid down that the Royal Navy must equal the navies of any two other powers.

Yet during this same period first the USA and then Germany were to pass Britain in industrial output. The defeat of France by Prussia in 1870 led to the emergence of a united Germany under King William I and his remarkable Chancellor Bismarck. Germany was at once formidable. At the same time Italy was finally united. Europe had changed significantly and each power sought its 'place in the sun'. The 'Scramble for Africa', as it became known, had started.

Africa was the last great area of the world weak enough to be brought under imperial control. In 1884 Germany's Chancellor Bismarck, called a conference of the powers in Berlin – 15 nations attended. No representative was invited from Africa. At Berlin the Europeans laid down the rules for the coming partition of the continent. It was agreed that the power which controlled a strip of coastline was entitled to take over the land behind it – the hinterland. 'Spheres of influence' were also agreed and the policy of 'effective occupation' was established.

What then happened was one of the most remarkable power 'grabs' in history. Between 1884 and 1900 almost the entire African continent was partitioned between the main imperial powers – Britain, France, Germany and Portugal – and to a lesser extent Belgium, Spain and Italy. The only serious defeat suffered by the Europeans was at Adowa in 1896 when the Italian army was beaten by the Ethiopians and their Emperor Menelik was able to keep his country independent.

Detail of *Impression: Sunrise* (1872) by Claude Monet (1840-1926). Impressionism was a movement in painting in France in the 1870s and 1880s. Its followers included, Monet, Paul Cézanne, Edgar Degas and Pierre Renoir. They aimed to produce a natural effect by the precise analysis of colour and light. The group held their first exhibition in 1874. A derisive journalist coined the name 'Impressionism' for them from the title of this picture.

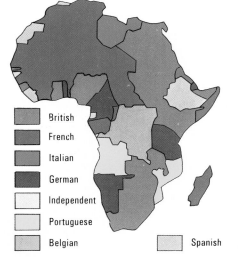

British
French
Italian
German
Independent
Portuguese
Belgian
Spanish

Following the Berlin Conference in 1884-1885, Germany occupied Togoland, Cameroons, S.W. Africa and German E. Africa. Belgium occupied Congo. France added Ivory Coast and Madagascar to her empire in west Africa; and Britain added Nigeria, Bechuanaland, Rhodesia, Zanzibar, Uganda and British East Africa to her empire in east and south Africa.

The South African Wars

In 1877 Britain annexed the Transvaal, with Boer agreement. But on December 30, 1880, Paulus Kruger and other Boer leaders proclaimed independence again. Boer forces defeated the British at the battles of Laing's Nek and Majuba Hill. On April 5, 1881, Britain signed the Treaty of Pretoria, restoring Transvaal's independence.

Gold was discovered in the Transvaal in 1886, and thousands of Uitlanders (foreigners) went there to dig for it. Denied civil rights by the Boers, the Uitlanders planned a revolt. Cecil Rhodes, prime minister of the neighbouring British Cape Colony, promised them a small force, led by Dr Leander Starr Jameson.

At the last moment the Uitlanders decided not to revolt, but Jameson, disobeying orders, went ahead with his raid. He had to surrender on January 2, 1896 after only four days. He was jailed; Rhodes resigned.

Further British efforts to persuade the Boers to give rights to Uitlanders led the Boers to declare war in October, 1899. Invading Cape Colony and Natal, they besieged the towns of Mafeking, Ladysmith, and Kimberley, and won several battles. In 1900 Britain sent in many more troops; the Boers reverted to guerrilla warfare prolonging the war until May 1902.

Britain had annexed the two Boer republics – Transvaal and Orange Free State – but eight years later amalgamated them with Cape Colony and Natal to form the independent dominion of South Africa.

1900 AD

1920 AD

THE GREAT WAR

1914 Jun 28: Assassination of the Archduke Ferdinand of Austria by a Bosnian student.
1914–1918 World War I: major Allied powers Britain, France, Russia, Italy, the USA – Central powers Germany, Austria-Hungary, Turkey.
1914 Jul 28: Austria invades Serbia.
Aug 4: Germans attack Belgium.
Aug 26: Battle of Tannenburg – Germans defeat the Russians.
Sept 5–9: Battle of Marne – Allies halt German advance on Paris.
Sept 6–15: Battle of Masurian Lakes – Russians retreat from East Prussia.
Oct 30–Nov 24: Battle of Ypres – the German push to the Channel ports is halted.
Trench warfare on the western and eastern fronts lasts to 1918.
Irish Home Rule Act – passed, separate Parliament in Ireland, some MPs at Westminster; position of Ulster (N. Ireland) to be decided after the war.
1915 Jan 5: Britain announces naval blockade of Germany.
Gallipoli campaign – Allies land on Gallipoli peninsula, Turkey, but fail to win Dardanelles Straits from Turks (to 1916).
Feb 18: German submarine blockade of Britain.
Apr 22–May 25: Second battle of Ypres – Germans use poison gas for first time.
May 7: Sinking of British liner, *Lusitania,* by German U-boat – many civilians including Americans drowned.
Sept: Offensive by Britain and France – battles of Artois, Champagne, Loos – fails.
Oct 15: Bulgaria joins Central powers.
1916 Feb 21: Battle of Verdun begins German offensive on western front – continues to July, terrible losses and the stalemate continues.
Apr 24: Easter Rising in Ireland suppressed after a week.
May 31: Battle of Jutland – the only major naval battle of the war between Britain and Germany – indecisive.
Jul 1: Battle of the Somme to Nov 18 – British offensive, over one million killed. Britain uses tanks for first time.
Dec 7: British prime minister, Lloyd George forms War Cabinet.
1917 February Revolution in Russia – Tsar Nicholas II abdicates; a provisional government set up.
Apr 6: USA declares war on Germany.
Jul 31: Third battle of Ypres (Passchendaele) – a major Allied offensive, German counter-attack, few gains.
Conquest of German colonies of Togoland and Cameroons by British and French forces.
British capture Baghdad from the Turks.
T. E. Lawrence takes over command of Arab revolt against Turks.
Oct 24: Battle of Caporetto – Italians defeated.
Nov 6–Nov 7: October Revolution – Bolsheviks led by Lenin seize power in Russia.
Nov 8: Balfour Declaration – Britain announces support for a Jewish state in Palestine.
Dec 9: British forces capture Jerusalem.
1918 Mar 3: Treaty of Brest-Litovsk between Russia and Germany – Russia withdraws from war.
Women over 30 get the vote in Britain.
Jul 15–Aug 2: Second battle of the Marne – the last major German offensive – fails.
Jul: Tsar Nicholas and family are murdered.
Aug 8: Allied offensive on western front breaks through the Hindenburg line of defences – Germans retreat.
Oct 24: Battle of Vittorio Veneto – Italian victory – Austria-Hungary surrenders.
German navy mutinies, Kaiser William II abdicates – a republic declared.
Nov 11: Armistice and World War I ends.

EUROPE

1903 Women's Social and political Union formed in Britain by the Suffragette, Mrs. Emmeline Pankhurst.
1904 *Entente cordiale* between Britain and France.
1905 End of union between Sweden and Norway.
'Bloody Sunday' in St Petersburg – Russian troops fire on workers, 500 killed.
1906 First Labour MPs returned to Parliament in Britain.
1912 *Titanic* liner sinks – 1513 die.
First Balkan War – Bulgaria, Greece, Serbia and Montenegro unite against Turkey, Balkans victorious.
1913 Third Irish Home Rule Bill passes the British House of Commons but is rejected by the Lords.
Second Balkan War – Serbia, Greece, Romania and Turkey unite against Bulgaria.
Macedonia is divided up between Greece and Serbia.

1919 Jan: Peace conference begins in Paris. Founding of the League of Nations.
June: Treaty of Versailles is signed by Germany – she loses Alsace-Lorraine and colonies and has to pay allies reparation.
Sept: Treaty of Saint-Germain is signed by Austria – end of Habsburg monarchy.
Austria recognizes independence of Czechoslovakia, Poland, Yugoslavia and Hungary.
Rebellion in Ireland led by nationalist Sinn Fein party.
1920 Civil War in Ireland – made worse by the British auxiliaries, the Black and Tans. Ireland partitioned into north and south. North staying in UK.
Poles repel Russian invasion.
Nov: Final collapse of counter-revolution in Russia.
Soviet government accepts existence of the newly-made border countries and makes treaties with them.
Treaty of Sèvres between Allies and Turkey – it is opposed by Turkish nationalists led by Mustafa Kemal (Atatürk).

ELSEWHERE

1902 S. America: British and German fleets seize the Venezuelan navy to force payment of debts.
Anglo-Japanese Alliance.
1904 Tibet: Sir Francis Younghusband leads an expedition from India – treaty opens Tibet to western (British) trade.
1904–1905 Russo-Japanese War over rival ambitions in Korea and Manchuria.
1905 Russo-Japanese War – Port Arthur, China, falls to Japan.
Battle of Mukden – Russians defeated by Japanese.
Battle of Tsushima – Russian fleet destroyed by Japanese.
Treaty of Portsmouth ends war.
India: Partition of Bengal favours Muslims and raises strong nationalist feelings.
1906 Morocco: Algeciras Conference – Germany recognizes France's rights.
USA: Severe earthquake in San Francisco.
1908 Africa: Belgian government takes over the Congo Free State from the king because of inadequacy of his rule – it becomes Belgian Congo.
1909 American explorer Robert Peary reaches North Pole.
US manufacturer Henry Ford begins assembly line production of cheap motor cars.
1911 China: Sun Yat-sen leads revolution and overthrows weak Manchu dynasty to form a republic (1912).
Norwegian explorer Roald Amundsen reaches South Pole.
1912 Africa: France establishes a protectorate in Morocco – the Spanish zone is defined.
Africa: Treaty of Ouchy ends the Italian-Turkish war – Turkey cedes Tripoli to Italy.
1919 India: Mohandas (Mahatma) Gandhi begins campaign of passive resistance against British.
Amritsar massacre – British troops fire on nationalist rioters.
1920 Palestine established as Jewish state under British administration.
USA: Prohibition to 1933.

The Great War

This terrible war – later called the First World War – cost 40 million lives. It marks a dividing line between the more leisurely pace of the 19th century and the frantic tempo of the 20th century.

One of the chief causes of the war was rivalry between groups of European powers over trade, colonies, and naval and military power. Countries formed defensive alliances, which meant an attack on one country automatically involved its allies. The two main alliances were the *Triple Entente* (Allied powers) – Britain, France, Russia; and the *Triple Alliance* (Central Powers) – Germany, Austria-Hungary, and Italy.

Germany was concerned about the weakness of its ally, Austria-Hungary. Austria knew that the many Serbs in the south of its empire wanted to join Serbia and felt threatened when Serbia greatly increased its territory in the Balkan Wars of 1912–1913. Austria wanted to fight and defeat Serbia and found an excuse when the Archduke Franz Ferdinand of Austria was assassinated at Sarajevo in Bosnia by a Serb nationalist.

Germany encouraged Austria to attack Serbia. Russia rallied to Serbia's support. France was allied to Russia, and Britain entered the war when Germany invaded Belgium on its way to France. The First World War had begun.

At first the Central powers were successful and Germany's initial advance brought her armies within 60 km of Paris. But the French and British halted the German advance at the battle of the Marne, and both sides dug in. Trench warfare had started. The fronts consisted of elaborate systems of trenches. Battles like the Somme in 1916 could cost a million lives and result in gains of only a few miles. There were three fronts in Europe – the western front stretched from Belgium to Switzerland, the eastern front from the Baltic to the Black Sea, and the southern front between Italy and Austria-Hungary.

In the Middle East in 1915 the Allies tried to capture the Dardanelles Straits from the Turks at Gallipoli. But the operation was bungled. The Allies fought the Turks in Mesopotamia and Palestine until the end of the war.

Following the October Revolution in 1917, Russia, after heavy losses and war weariness, made peace with Germany. Meanwhile German submarine attacks on merchant ships brought the USA into the war on the side of the Allies. Her massive supplies of armaments as well as fresh men tipped the balance in the Allies' favour.

Relatively new inventions such as the radio, aeroplane and car had rapidly developed. The war also saw the introduction of new weapons. The most important of these were poison gas, the tank, and the aeroplane which in the beginning was used for reconnaissance in support of ground attacks, but later was employed for bombing.

The outcome of the war changed the political face of Europe and the Middle East. Germany was reduced in size while its overseas colonies were taken over by the victorious powers. Finland, Estonia, Latvia, Lithuania, Czechoslovakia, Hungary and Yugoslavia emerged as new countries. Allied pressures upon defeated Germany, however, helped to bring about the situation of instability that allowed Hitler to achieve power in the 1930s.

Sackville Street, Dublin after the Irish Easter Week Rising of 1916. The people of Ireland protested at being ruled from London. In 1914, a Home Rule Act was passed but suspended for the duration of World War I. The Protestants in the north opposed home rule because it would leave them in a minority in a Catholic land. Some of the Catholics did not want to wait for the end of the war and wanted complete independence. The rebellion by Catholics began on Easter Monday. The British army quelled the revolt after 8 days' fighting and executed 16 rebel leaders.

Russian Revolution

Growing unrest at the autocratic powers of the tsar had been a feature of Russian life for many years before 1917. By 1917 the huge losses Russia had suffered in the war and the miserable conditions of the soldiers at the front sparked off the February Revolution. Troops mutinied, there were strikes and riots. The tsar abdicated and a provisional government was formed. The new government was moderate in its views, but the Bolsheviks, a radical left-wing party, determined to seize power. Their leader, Vladimir Ilyich Lenin, had been in exile in Switzerland, but the Germans allowed him to travel across Europe in a sealed train, hoping (rightly) he would gain power and take Russia out of the war. On November 6, 1917 the October Revolution took place and Lenin and the Soviets (workers' councils) under Leon Trotsky, seized power. The revolution in November is called the October revolution because the Russians had not adopted the Gregorian Calendar (see page 53). By 1917 the Russian calendar was 13 days behind the rest of the world. The Bolsheviks (radical left wing party soon to change its name to Communist) were in a minority in the Constituent Assembly, so they dispersed it. The new government rapidly centralized control of land and food production and confiscated Church property.

The Rise of the Dictator

The period after the First World War in Europe was one of deep economic depression, and political bitterness, between the forces of the Left – Communists and Socialists – and the forces of the Right – the Fascists and Nazis.

In 1919 on the abdication of Kaiser William, Germany became a republic. But the Weimar Republic, as it was called, was unable to solve the country's economic and social problems or repay the huge reparations (war damages) demanded by the Allies. By the time of the presidential elections in 1932, the German *mark* was worthless and 6 million people were unemployed. In the elections of that year Hitler's National Socialist Party (the Nazis) gained the most seats, though not a majority, and the old President, Field Marshal Paul von Hindenburg, was obliged to appoint as chancellor, Hitler whom he despised. Hitler took office in January 1933 and within a short time he had suppressed all other political parties and begun persecuting the Jews.

In Italy right-wing forces came to power early. The Fascists were the nationalist supporters of Benito Mussolini, a strong leader elected by the middle classes to oppose Bolshevism and Communism. After the Fascists had staged a march on Rome in 1922, King Victor Emmanuel III invited Mussolini to form a government. By 1935 he was at the height of his popularity and power. Mussolini wanted greater power and having invaded Ethiopia in 1935, formed an alliance with Hitler. In 1938 Germany annexed Austria and, following the meeting between Hitler and Mussolini with Chamberlain and Daladier at Munich, Germany annexed the Sudetenland of Czechoslovakia.

A left-wing Republican government was voted into power in Spain early in 1936. It had the support of both Socialists and Communists. It was opposed by the army, the right-wing parties and the Roman Catholic Church. In July, army officers in Spanish Morocco began a rebellion and this soon spread to the mainland. A bitter civil war then followed. This lasted until 1939 when the Fascist rebels (Falangists) captured Madrid, and their leader, General Francisco Franco, became head of state. It was a brutal war with atrocities committed on both sides. Altogether about 600,000 people were killed. The left-wing Republicans were helped by volunteers drawn from more than 50 countries, including the USSR, to form an 'International Brigade'. The Falangists were assisted by the Italians and Germans who were able to try out new weapons and techniques in the war.

Fashionable society at the Lido, Venice enjoying the bright extravagant 1920s before the 'Great Depression', triggered off in October 1929 by the New York stock market 'crash'. The effect was that many banks and businesses closed, and by 1931, 12 million Americans were out of work. The panic spread to Europe and it wasn't until the late 1930s that the world's economies were recovering.

Gandhi and British India

The period between the wars witnessed a growing sense of doubt among the British about their place in India. There had been a sharp increase in Indian nationalism developing out of the Congress movement. To a large extent the movement was centred upon one of the most remarkable men of the century – Mohandas Karamchand Gandhi (1869–1948). He was known as Mahatma or 'great soul'. He dressed in Indian style, wearing only homespun cloth.

Gandhi fought the case for an independent India with illegal acts of disobedience without violence. He frequently used the weapon of 'fasting to death' and was sent to prison on a number of occasions but this only added to his prestige. To the Indian masses he was a saint.

A turning point for Indian independence came in 1919 when a crowd, peacefully taking part in a forbidden political meeting, was fired upon by imperial forces at Amritsar and 379 people, including women and children, were killed. This massacre permanently altered relations, so that even the most determined imperialists began to realize that sooner or later India must achieve its independence.

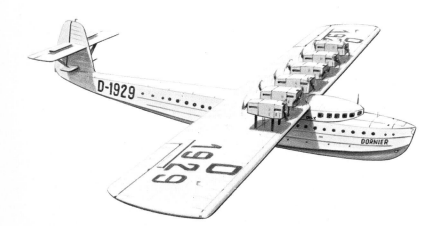

The Dornier DoX super flying boat (1929), which could carry up to 170 persons. The first international airline ran a daily service from London to Paris from 1919. The first round-the-world flight, taking 75 days, was made in 1924 by US Army planes. The 1920s and 1930s saw steady progress in aviation. The American Charles Lindbergh made the first solo transatlantic flight in 1927. Americans began the first transatlantic airmail service in 1939, followed by a passenger service.

EUROPE

1921 Irish Free State established.
Irish Republican Army (IRA) continues opposition.
Greece attacks Turkey and is defeated in 1922.
Treaty of Riga ends Russo-Polish war.
1922 Fascists march on Rome – King Victor Emmanuel asks Benito Mussolini to be prime minister.
USSR established.
Mustafa Kemal deposes the sultan of Turkey.
1923 Adolf Hitler, founder of the National Socialist (Nazi) Party in Germany attempts to overthrow Bavarian government, but is imprisoned.
Turkey proclaims itself a republic – first president Mustafa Kemal (Atatürk).
1923–1930 Virtual dictatorship under Spanish General Primo de Rivera.
1924 First Labour government in Britain under J. Ramsay MacDonald.
Italian fascists murder the Socialist, Giacomo Matteotti.
Death of Lenin – succeeded by Joseph Stalin.
1926 General Strike in Britain.
Portuguese government overthrown by army.
Germany is admitted to the League of Nations.
1930 London naval conference – great powers fail to agree upon naval limitations.
Treaty of Ankara between Greece and Turkey.
1931 Statute of Westminster defines status of British Dominions.
Commonwealth of Nations replaces 'British Empire'.
Financial crisis splits the British Labour government – formation of the Coalition National Government, devaluation and finally Britain abandons the gold standard.
King Alfonso XIII of Spain flees the country – republic is proclaimed.
1932 Portuguese Finance Minister Antonio de Oliveira Salazar, becomes dictator of Portugal.
1933 President Hindenburg of Germany appoints Adolf Hitler chancellor.
Burning of the German *Reichstag* (parliament).
Germany withdraws from League of Nations.
National Socialists (Nazis) begin to eliminate all opposition and gain control in Germany.
Stalin purges the Communist Party in Russia.
Spanish government suppresses Anarchists in Barcelona.
1934 Nazis kill the Austrian chancellor, Dollfuss.
Death of President Hindenburg – Hitler becomes *Führer,* leader of Germany.
1935 Hitler renounces the Treaty of Versailles – declares a policy of rearmament for Germany.
Nuremberg Laws – persecution of Jews begins in Germany.
Restoration of monarchy in Greece
1936 Edward VIII, king of Britain, abdicates to marry Mrs Simpson.
Germany reoccupies Rhineland.
Military revolt by General Francisco Franco against the left-wing Republican government begins the Spanish Civil War.
Italy and Germany support the Fascist Spanish rebels under Franco and use the war to test weapons and men in the field.
USSR sends aid to the Spanish Republicans.
Oct 25: Agreement between Italy and Germany leads to the Rome-Berlin Axis.
1937 Apr 26: German planes bomb Guernica, Spain.
May 28: Neville Chamberlain forms government in Britain and favours a policy of appeasement against Hitler.
1938 Mar 13: Germany invades and annexes Austria.
Sept 29: Munich Pact between Hitler's Germany, Mussolini's Italy, Chamberlain of Britain and Daladier of France. Germany gains Sudetenland in Czechoslovakia.
1939 Jan 26: Franco's nationalists capture Barcelona.
Mar 10: Germany annexes Czechoslovakia.
Apr 1: Madrid surrenders – end of the Spanish Civil War. Franco becomes dictator of Spain.
Apr 7: Italy invades Albania.
Sept 1: Germany invades Poland – beginning of World War II.

ELSEWHERE

A rare colour picture showing the Italian Fascist dictator Benito Mussolini reviewing his troops accompanied by the German High Command in 1938.

1921–1922 Washington Conference to discuss naval armaments – Pacific Treaty between Britain, France, Japan and USA.
1922 Egypt declared independent of British and French influence.
1923 Ethiopia admitted to the League of Nations.
1924 China: Sun Yat-sen establishes government including Communists at Canton.
1925–1926 Africa: Arab uprising in Morocco led by Abd-el-Krim crushed by France and Spain.
1926 Australia: Canberra becomes the federal capital.
1927 Charles Lindbergh (US) makes first solo flight across the Atlantic.
China: Chiang Kai-shek (successor to Sun Yat-sen) purges Communists – sets up government at Nanking.
Civil war follows between Communists and Nationalists.
1929 US stock market collapses leading to worldwide economic depression.
Palestine: First major conflict between Jews and Arabs.
1930 Africa: Ras Tafari crowned as Haile Selassie I of Ethiopia.
1931 Japanese occupy Manchuria.
1932 Canada: Imperial Conference at Ottawa – Britain gives trade preferences to her Commonwealth.
USA: 12 million Americans unemployed.
1932–1935 S. America: Paraguay and Bolivia at war over the Chaco region.
1933 USA: End of Prohibition.
1933–1936 USA: Roosevelt becomes president on campaign to introduce reforms known as the 'New Deal', to bring USA out of the depression.
1934 China: Mao Tse-tung leads Communists northwards on the Long March from Kiangsi – they reach Yennan in 1935.
1935 Africa: Italian forces invade Ethiopia and the League of Nations fails to intervene effectively.
Persia changes name to Iran.
India: Government of India Act passed by British Parliament – sets up provincial councils.
1936 Africa: Italians take Addis Ababa and annex Ethiopia.
1937 Africa: Anglo-Egyptian Treaty – British forces in Egypt are restricted to the Suez Canal zone. Treaty to last for 20 years.
China: Jul 7 – Japanese invade, capture Shanghai and Peking.

1920 AD

1939 AD

THE MODERN WORLD AD 1939–AD 1960

EUROPE

1939 Sept 1: Germany invades Poland.
Sept 3: Britain and France declare war on Germany.
Sept 17: Russia invades Poland.
Sept 29: Nazi-Soviet Pact – Poland partitioned between two powers.
Russo-Finnish war – Finland defeated in Nov 1940.
1940 Apr 9: Germany invades Denmark and Norway.
May 10: Germany invades Belgium, the Netherlands.
May 17: Germany invades France.
May 27: British army evacuated from Dunkirk in France by domestic fleet.
Jun 10: Italy declares war on Britain and France.
Jun 14: Germans occupy Paris, France surrenders.
Jul 10–Oct 31: Battle of Britain – British air victory because Germany fails to concentrate attack on RAF bases – discourages German invasion of Britain.
Oct 28: Italy invades Greece.
1941 Jun 22: Germany invades Russia.
Leningrad besieged by Germans – relieved in January 1944.
Dec: Russian counter-offensive in the Ukraine.
1942 Sept 6: Battle of Stalingrad – Germans defeated.
1943 Sept 3: Italian government surrenders.
1944 Jun 4: Allies enter Rome.
Jun 6: Allies land in Normandy ('D-Day') – German retreat.
Jul 20: Bomb plot to assassinate Hitler fails.
Sept 2: Allies liberate Paris and Brussels.
Oct 3: Warsaw (Poland) rising is crushed by the Germans.
1945 Jan 17: Russians capture Warsaw.
Feb 7: Yalta Conference in Crimea – Churchill, Roosevelt and Stalin discuss post-war settlements.
Mar 7: Allies invade Germany – Dresden flattened by bombs.
Apr 28: Mussolini assassinated by Italian partisans.
Apr 30: Hitler commits suicide.
May 7: Germany surrenders.
May 8: 'VE Day' (victory in Europe).
Potsdam Conference – Allies discuss post-war settlements.
1946 League of Nations formally ended.
Nuremberg trials – Nazi leaders sentenced by the international court for war crimes.
1947 Allied peace treaties signed in Paris with Italy, Romania, Hungary, Bulgaria and Finland.
Marshall Aid – programme of aid for European recovery introduced by the US Secretary of State, George Marshall.
1948 Communist coup in Czechoslovakia.
1948–1949 USSR blockades Berlin – Allies 'airlift' supplies.
1949 North Atlantic Treaty Organization (NATO) is formed as a western defensive alliance.
Germany is divided into the Federal Republic (West) and Democratic Republic (East).
1952 Bonn Convention – Britain, France and the USA end the occupation of West Germany.
Greece and Turkey join NATO.
1953 Death of Stalin – Georgi Malenkov becomes Soviet prime minister.
Marshal Tito becomes president of Yugoslavia.
1954 Growth of demands for *enosis* – the union of Greece and Cyprus – leads to disturbances on the island.
1955 Formation of Warsaw Pact – treaty between East European Communist powers to oppose NATO.
EOKA, Greek Cypriot organization led by Grivas, begins anti-British terrorist activities in Cyprus.
West Germany is admitted to NATO.
1956 Khrushchev, new Soviet prime minister denounces Stalin.
Anti-Russian uprising in Hungary crushed by Soviet forces.
1957 Treaty of Rome establishes the European Economic Community – the EEC or Common Market – (Belgium, France, West Germany, Italy, Luxembourg and Holland).
1958 Charles de Gaulle returns to power as first president of the French Fifth Republic.
1960 Cyprus becomes an independent republic under Archbishop Makarios.

ASIA & THE PACIFIC

1940 Apr 30: Japan joins Axis powers (Germany-Italy).
1941 Dec 7: Japan attacks the US Pacific fleet in Pearl Harbor, Hawaii.
Dec 25: Japan takes Hong Kong.
1942 Jan: Japan captures Manila, Singapore, Rangoon, Mandalay and the Philippines.
1942 Jul 1: USA begins to recapture Pacific islands held by Japan.
1944 Oct 25: Battle of Leyte Gulf – defeat of Japanese navy by USA.
1945 Aug 6: First atomic bomb dropped on Hiroshima, Japan.
Aug 9: Second atomic bomb dropped on Nagasaki, Japan.
Aug 14: Japan surrenders – World War II ends.

1946 Transjordan (Jordan) becomes independent of Great Britain.
1946–1954 Civil War in Indochina between Vietnamese Nationalists under Ho Chi Minh and the French.
1947 Cheribon Agreement between the Dutch and Indonesia leads to the establishment of the United States of Indonesia.
India gains independence – two dominions are created; India (Hindu) and Pakistan (Muslim).
Dispute between India and Pakistan over Kashmir, which is ceded to India.
Burma independent.
Partition of Palestine into Arab and Jewish states is agreed by UN but rejected by Arabs.
1948 State of Israel is declared.
1948–1949 War between Israel and the Arab League.
1948 Assassination of Mahatma Gandhi by a Hindu extremist in India.
Ceylon independent as a dominion in the Commonwealth.
China split by conflict between Communists and Nationalists.
Korea is divided into Republic of Korea (south) and Communist People's Republic (North).
1949 Mao Tse-tung establishes Communist regime throughout China – Nationalist government escapes to Formosa (Taiwan).
France recognises independent Vietnam and Cambodia.
Arab-Israeli peace and the partition of Jerusalem.
USSR recognises the People's Republic of China.
1950–1953 Korean War – North Korea supported by China, South Korea by UN force.
1951 Chinese forces occupy Tibet.
Colombo Plan for economic development of south and south-east Asia comes into effect (the beginning of aid).
1952 China accuses USA of waging germ warfare in Korea.
First national elections in India – Jawaharlal Nehru becomes prime minister.
1953 Hillary and Tenzing, first men to reach the top of Everest, the world's highest mountain.
Treaty of Panmunjon ends Korean War.
French forces occupy Dien Bien Phu, North Vietnam – Viet Minh forces invade Laos.
1954 French are defeated at Dien Bien Phu by Viet Minh.
Geneva Conference: Vietnam is divided – North Vietnam under Ho Chi Minh (Communist) and South Vietnam with the support of the USA and Britain. Beginning of the Vietnam war as the Communists of the north try to take over the south.
Formation of South-East Asia Treaty Organization (SEATO) to prevent the spread of Communism in south-east Asia.
1955 Israel raids Egyptian and Syrian borders.
Baghdad Pact – Turkey, Iraq, Iran, Pakistan and Britain.
Bandung Conference – first meeting of what became the Non-Aligned Movement – 29 Asian and African states attend.
1958 Egypt and Syria form the United Arab Republic (UAR) later joined by Yemen to form the United Arab States.
Abdul Kassem leads military revolt in Iraq – King Faisal II is assassinated and Iraq becomes a republic.
1959 Uprising against the Chinese in Tibet – Dalai Lama flees to India, the revolt is crushed.

The Second World War

World War II began on September 1, 1939 when Germany invaded Poland. When it came to an end with the surrender of Japan on August 14th, 1945, the power balance of the world had been irretrievably changed. The human cost has been estimated at around 50 million dead and 34 million wounded.

The war was fought in four main theatres – Europe, Asia, Africa and at sea. The main cause of the war was Germany, Italy and Japan wanting more territory.

After the fall of Poland – the Russians invaded eastern Poland to provide a buffer between Russia and Germany – there was a lull of some months (the 'phoney' war). Then in a lightning campaign of seven weeks the Germans swept through Europe using their new *blitzkrieg* (lightning war) tactics. Its chief characteristic was wave after wave of air attacks followed by panzer tank divisions. They invaded Denmark and Norway, swept through Belgium and Holland and conquered France. The British army was evacuated from Dunkirk and only because of British air power in the weeks of the 'Battle of Britain' was the danger of German invasion removed.

In 1941 the Germans turned eastwards to invade Yugoslavia and Greece, as well as Russia. They almost reached Moscow before heroic resistance and sub-Arctic weather stopped them – the USSR was too big to fall to *blitzkrieg* tactics.

On December 7, 1941 Japan launched its attack, without warning, on the American fleet at Pearl Harbor, and within five months had conquered huge areas of Asia and was threatening Australia. This brought America into the war against all the Axis powers.

In north Africa the Italians saw their chance to drive the British out, so they joined the war in 1940 on the side of Germany and attempted to invade Egypt. But the British pushed the Italians back. The Germans in 1942 sent forces to north Africa under the brilliant German commander, Rommell, who pushed the British back. Finally at El Alamein in October 1942, the Axis powers were defeated by the Allies under General Montgomery supported by 300 Sherman tanks. Rommel was forced to retreat. But he was caught between Montgomery in the east and an Allied force, under the American General Eisenhower, which had just landed in Morocco. Rommell had no alternative but to flee north Africa. From Africa, the Allies invaded Sicily and mainland Italy. The Italians rejected Mussolini and joined the Allies. Although the Germans put up strong resistance in northern Italy, they had started to retreat.

On the Russian front the German army besieging Stalingrad was destroyed in 1943 and in 1944 the Russians began advancing on Berlin. In the Pacific the Americans had regained the initiative by mid-1942, when they defeated the Japanese fleets at the battles of the Coral Sea and Midway.

In June 1944 a huge Allied army landed on the Normandy beaches. By early 1945 they had pushed the Germans back across the Rhine. Eventually, the Allied army met the advancing Russian army on the River Elbe in the heart of Germany. Hitler committed suicide in his ruined bunker in Berlin on April 30, 1945 and Germany surrendered on May 7. Mussolini was assassinated by Italian partisans on April 28th, 1945. The war against Japan continued until August 1945. Then the first nuclear bombs – atomic bombs as they were called – were dropped on Japan, leading to Japan's surrender.

The battleship HMS *Rodney* with a main armament of nine 40.6cm (16 inch) guns leads the Atlantic fleet. During World War II, aircraft became the main weapon of war. However convoys carrying vital provisions across the Atlantic had to be protected by the Allied navies; their main enemies were German U-boats (submarines). The other great theatre of sea warfare was in the Pacific where the USA defeated Japan in 2 crucial battles.

The Cold War

When in 1947 the Americans offered Marshall aid to help European recovery they included the USSR and the countries of eastern Europe in the offer, but Russia declined. In a famous speech at Fulton, Missouri in 1946, Churchill, then leader of the opposition in Britain, used the phrase 'an iron curtain' which he said had come down across Europe. This speech signified the first recognition by a major statesman of the fact that the world had divided into two camps.

After the war, the four powers – Britain, France, Russia and the USA – could not agree over a settlement for Germany, although they did work out peace terms for the other defeated states. In 1948 in an effort to put pressure on the western nations, the Russians blockaded Berlin which was occupied by the four powers, although deep inside the Russian zone of Germany. The western powers, however, airlifted supplies to west Berlin for more than a year until the blockade was lifted and west Berlin remained part of the Allied settlement. But the pressure precipitated a decision over the rest of Germany. The western powers combined their three occupation zones in 1949 to form what is now the German Federal Republic (West Germany) and Russia turned her zone into the German Democratic Republic (East Germany).

As a result of these antagonisms both sides rearmed. In 1949 the western powers formed the North Atlantic Treaty Organization (NATO), a defensive alliance against Russia in Europe. In 1955 the Communist Bloc formed the Warsaw Pact, its reply to NATO. The Cold War – a term meaning armed hostility and suspicion which does not actually develop into fighting – was at its height through the 1950s. By then China had become united under the Communist Mao Tse-tung and briefly, it seemed, was part of a Soviet-dominated bloc of gigantic proportions.

At the very end of the Eisenhower government in 1960, the possibility of a thaw appeared when Eisenhower was to meet Russia's Khrushchev. But any improvement was delayed because an American spy plane was shot down over Russia.

Young Chinese bandsmen hold up little red books containing the *Thoughts of Chairman Mao*. From the 1920s onward, China was torn by sporadic civil war between the Nationalists, led by Chiang Kai-shek, and the Communists, led by Mao Tse-tung. The Nationalists were ineffective and torn by internal rivalries. They quickly lost popular support, and the Communists won a long series of victories. In 1949 the last Nationalist strongholds were captured, and Chiang Kai-shek fled to Taiwan.
By 1966 Mao Tse-tung felt that Communist party officials were not spending enough time working with the people. He wanted everybody to spend part of each year working like a peasant on the land. He called this the 'Cultural Revolution'. Young people gave great support to Mao's Cultural Revolution but by 1969 the movement had lost momentum and in economic terms it had done much harm. Some countries, particularly the United States, did not recognize the Communist regime for many years.

Man's capacity to kill is hardly new. At the battle of Cannae in 216 BC. 70,000 Romans and Carthaginians were killed in one day by sword and spear. In 1398 Tamburlaine massacred 100,000 Hindus. But the instantaneous effect of nuclear bombs, coupled with the knowledge that the major powers hold enough of them to destroy every important city in the world, is what spawns peace movements such as the Campaign for Nuclear Disarmament in Britain.

End of Empires

The Second World War gave an impetus to nationalism throughout Asia that led to the end of the great European empires. When the British collapsed so ignominiously before the Japanese invaders at Singapore it became impossible to sustain the fiction that Europeans were superior to Asians.

India, Burma and Ceylon all became independent soon after the war. Independence for India in 1947 acted as a spur to nationalists in all the other colonies of all the colonial powers – Indonesia in 1947, Vietnam in 1955, Malaya in 1957.

The astonishing fact is that the British, French and Dutch had managed to control such huge populations for so long. The newly independent powers of Asia had political contributions to make that were very different from those of their former imperial masters. Inevitably many of the new nations were unprepared for self-government, and the old evils of imperialism were often matched with new ones, born of coups, dictatorships, tribal hatreds and corruption.

The State of Israel

The Balfour Declaration of 1917 promised British support for a Jewish state in Palestine (a former part of the now vanished Ottoman or Turkish empire). Jewish entry into Palestine in the years after the war, when the territory was a British mandate (administered by Britain), led to the first major Arab-Jewish clash in 1929. Under Arab pressure Britain had to curb Jewish immigration. When Hitler came to power in 1933 he began a policy of persecuting the German Jews and after the Nuremberg Laws of 1935 more Jews were allowed to emigrate to Palestine.

After the Nazi regime had crumbled, many thousands of European and other Jews emigrated to Palestine. The UN were asked by the British to make a decision on Palestine's future. In 1947 they decided to partition Palestine into a Jewish and an Arab state and make Jerusalem an international city. The Jews accepted the proposal but the Arabs rejected it. On May 14, 1948 the British Mandate over Palestine came to an end, and the Jews proclaimed the state of Israel. On the same day, the neighbouring Arab states of Egypt, Lebanon, Syria and Transjordan attacked the new state of Israel in the first of a series of Arab-Israeli wars. The Arabs were driven back and Israel survived.

The second Arab-Israeli war was fought in 1956 when Israel, with French and British support, attacked Egypt and advanced across the Sinai desert to the Suez Canal. This was part of the wider Suez crisis of that year. As a result, a UN peacekeeping force was stationed on the Gaza Strip (border between Israel and Egypt). But in 1967 it was withdrawn at the insistence of the Egyptian President Nasser. There followed the *Six Day War* in which the Israeli forces captured the West Bank (of the River Jordan), took over the Arab part of Jerusalem, the Gaza Strip and the Sinai Peninsula. Six years later (1973) came the fourth Arab-Israeli war. The *Yom Kippur War* was named after the Jewish festival on the day when Egypt and Syria attacked. This time the fighting was more even and the Arabs made gains and strengthened their position.

In 1977 President Sadat of Egypt and Prime Minister Begin of Israel exchanged visits as part of a peace process between their two countries – the impossible appeared to have happened. Yet throughout this period, the Palestinians, who had left when Israel was formed, remained homeless. Their plight was brought to world attention during the 1970s by the increasingly effective terrorist tactics of an organization fighting on their behalf, the Palestine Liberation Organization (PLO). Their activities were a reminder that if one people, the Jews, had gained a homeland another, the Palestinian Arabs, had lost one. In 1982 there was no solution to the problem in sight.

Vietnam and Korea

In 1945 Korea had been divided into a Communist north, under Russian influence, and a non-Communist south which had American support. In 1950 the Communists attacked the south and overran almost the whole country. South Korea appealed to the United Nations for help and soon an army, mainly American but provided by 15 countries, was fighting the north. It drove the Communists right back to the Chinese border which alarmed China, who sent 150,000 'volunteers' to help the North Koreans. They were successful in pushing back the UN forces to the original frontier between north and south.

In 1954 the French left Vietnam which, like Korea, was divided into a Communist north and a non-Communist south. The Americans believed in the 'domino' theory, that is if one country became Communist so would the country next to it. For the next 20 years the United States supported weak governments in South Vietnam by providing them with money, arms and later, troops.

The Americans sent in more and more of their own troops (over 500,000 by 1968). They began to bomb northern cities and use chemical weapons like napalm against the Vietcong (Vietnamese Communists). In the end the Americans, suffering 500 casualties a week, pulled out of a war they could not win, and in 1975 Saigon, the southern capital, fell to the Vietcong. Vietnam was united as a Communist country, and was soon followed by the neighbouring countries of Laos and Cambodia. This was the United States' biggest defeat in the Cold War.

Refugees flee from the fighting in a Vietnamese town. Refugees have proved an appalling problem from the mid-20th century on, with mass movements of people escaping from battle areas or from hostile regimes. International agencies do all they can to help. Even so, many people spend years in crowded refugee camps.

The Technological Age

The world has made enormous strides in technology since the World War II. Experiments with atomic fission have produced the nuclear bomb, but the peaceful uses for nuclear energy will be of incalculable value in this era of energy shortages. Sooner or later we will almost certainly have used up all the non-renewable sources of energy in the world. Exactly when that might happen varies from fuel to fuel. Perhaps the greatest hope of all lies in mastering the process of nuclear fusion. Uncontrolled fusion has already been achieved in the hydrogen bomb. Scientists now have to achieve it in safe, controlled conditions. The advantages of fusion are considerable. It is clean and safe, and, above all, it will provide unlimited energy for thousands of years.

Space Travel

Perhaps the most exciting technological breakthrough concerns space travel. But space travel could never have happened without computers and other developments made in the field of electronics. Since 1971, with the invention of the silicon chip, computers have become much more sophisticated allowing more complex space missions to be attempted – the Pioneer 10 space probe to Jupiter and returnable space shuttle, to name but two.

The space age began in 1957 when the USSR launched Sputnik I, the first artificial earth satellite. This was soon followed by another satellite. Then the USA launched Explorer I and the two super powers had started a space race. The first manned flight in space occurred in 1961 when the Russians sent up Yuri Gagarin. Then in 1969 the Americans achieved the first landing on the moon. An estimated 600 million television viewers saw Neil Armstrong from Apollo 11 take the first step on the moon.

Space travel has also provided us with a possible solution to Earth's severe problem of overpopulation. Where will people live when the world population reaches 12 billion in 2050, what will they eat?

Life on Mars?

As space ships become more sophisticated, the possibility of colonizing the planets and producing artificial habitats to grow food becomes more real. In many ways, day-to-day life on another planet will be remarkably like day-to-day life on Earth. Indeed, it will have to be, if humans, who are designed to live on Earth, are to survive there at all. Water will have to be imported from Earth, although on Mars ice could be obtained from the polar caps. Food would be grown in huge greenhouses, heated by artificial electric light generated by nuclear power. Many of the planets have their own supplies of raw materials, which would be recycled to avoid waste. It is thought that the USSR may be planning a manned expedition to Mars before the end of the 20th century. Then – who knows?

Satellite Communication

By 1982, there were also hundreds of space satellites circling the earth. They have many purposes such as communications and weather-forecasting. The launching in 1962 of the American Telstar communications satellite meant that live television broadcasts could be instantly exchanged between North America and Europe. Television which is taken for granted by millions of people in many parts of the world represents one of the greatest of all revolutions. The growing revulsion of many young people in the USA against the American involvement in Vietnam, for example, was partly because day after day, they could follow the war on television as it took place.

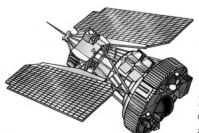

Nimbus weather satellite, one of a series designed to record and transmit details of weather conditions on a world-wide scale.

1960 Civil War follows independence in the Congo as Katanga Province under Moise Tshombe attempts to secede – UN intervention.
1961 Murder of Patrice Lumumba, first prime minister of Congo.
South Africa becomes Republic and withdraws from Commonwealth.
1962 Algeria becomes independent of France after eight years at war.
1963 Organization of African Unity (OAU) is formed by independent African states.
1965 Ian Smith and white Rhodesian minority government make Unilateral Declaration of Independence (UDI) from Britain – British sanctions are applied but fail to halt crisis.
1966 Assassination of South African prime minster, Dr. Verwoerd – succeeded by John Vorster.
Rhodesian whites reject British proposals for a settlement.
1967–1970 Nigerian civil war – Biafra (east of Nigeria) attempts (unsuccessfully) to break away from Nigeria.

1974 Coup in Portugal leads to the withdrawal of Portuguese from Africa – independence for all Portuguese African territories is recognized.
1976 Soweto riots in South Africa.
Kissinger plan for black majority rule in Rhodesia – accepted by whites, rejected by blacks.
1979 Amin flees Uganda in face of invasion by exiled Ugandans supported by Tanzanian army.
Commonwealth Conference in Lusaka leads to Lancaster House Conference in London and a new constitution for Rhodesia – Britain takes control again.
1980 Elections in Rhodesia return Robert Mugabe with absolute majority – becomes the first prime minister of an independent Zimbabwe.

EUROPE & AMERICA

1961 East Germany tightens border – Berlin Wall built.
Russian cosmonaut, Tereshkova, first woman in space.
Nuclear test ban treaty signed by Britain, USA and USSR.
Latin American Free Trade Association (LAFTA) is formed.
Bay of Pigs – abortive invasion of Castro's Cuba by American-backed Cuban exiles.
1962 US-USSR confrontation (the Cuban missile crisis) – President J. F. Kennedy orders a naval blockade of Cuba and demands that the Russians remove their missiles and bombers. Faced with threat of war, Russia's Nikita Khrushchev agrees.
Telstar communications satellite launched – first live TV broadcasts between USA and Europe.
1963 Assassination of US President Kennedy in Dallas – France vetoes British application to join the EEC.
1964 Fighting between Greek and Turkish communities in Cyprus – UN peacekeeping force is sent to the island.
Civil Rights Act becomes law in USA.
Soviet leader Khrushchev succeeded by Alexei Kosygin.
1965 Death of Sir Winston Churchill.
Britain abolishes death penalty for murder.
1966 French president De Gaulle vetoes the second British application to join the EEC.
1967 Military coup in Greece – reactionary regime of 'The Colonels' leads to violent clashes with police – universities and factories are taken over by students and workers.
Soviet troops invade Czechoslovakia to crush liberalism of Alexander Dubcek – Czech leader.
Troops sent to Northern Ireland (Ulster) to assist civil authorities.
French president Charles de Gaulle resigns.
Death of Salazar, Portuguese dictator since 1933.
1968 Student demonstrations in Paris lead to clashes with police.
1968 Assassination of black civil rights leader Martin Luther King in USA.
Assassination of US presidential candidate Robert Kennedy, brother of former president.
1969 American astronauts – Neil Armstrong and 'Buzz' Aldrin – land on moon.
1970 US President Richard Nixon announces the invasion of Cambodia.
1972 Britain assumes direct rule in Ulster.
Britain, Denmark and Republic of Ireland join the EEC.
Greek-Turkish conflict in Cyprus. Turks occupy Nicosia, capital of Cyprus.
Greek military junta in Athens resigns.
1973 US-backed military coup in Chile overthrows Marxist President Salvador Allende, who is killed.
1974 President Nixon is forced to resign over Watergate scandal – he is succeeded by Vice President Gerald Ford.
1975 Spanish dictator Franco dies. Juan Carlos, grandson of last king of Spain, becomes king.
1976 Jimmy Carter wins US Presidential election.
1978 USA establishes diplomatic relations with Communist China, ends those with Taiwan.
1979 53 Americans held hostage by Islamic students in Iran.
First direct elections to the European Parliament are held in the nine EEC countries.
1980 Death of President Tito of Yugoslavia.
Polish Solidarity trade union, led by Lech Walesa, confronts Communist government.
Martial law in Poland – many Solidarity members imprisoned.
Assassination attempt on Pope John Paul II.
1981 Ronald Reagan becomes US president.
US hostages in Iran freed.
Assassination attempt on President Reagan.
1982 Argentina invades Falkland Islands. British taskforce reoccupies the islands.
Full diplomatic relations are established between Britain and the Vatican for the first time since England's 1534 break with Rome.
President Brezhnev of USSR dies.

ASIA

A few silicon chips like these can do the same work as a room-sized computer of twenty years ago.

1962 Border clashes between China and India.
1963 South Vietnamese government overthrown by military coup.
1964 Increased US involvement in Vietnam.
US declares support for South Vietnam against the Communist Viet Cong.
1964–1966 War between Malaysia and Indonesia.
1965 US begins regular bombing raids against North Vietnam.
War between India and Pakistan over Kashmir – UN calls for ceasefire.
First American marines arrive in Vietnam.
1966 End of war between Malaysia and Indonesia.
'Cultural Revolution' in China (to 1968).
1967 Six Day War (June 5–10) between Arabs and Israel.
1968 Vietcong launch the major Tet offensive in Vietnam.
1970 Civil war in Jordan between government troops and Palestine guerrillas.
1971 E. Pakistan breaks away from Pakistan to form new state of Bangladesh following civil war and Indian intervention.
Communist China joins the UN; Taiwan is expelled.
1972 Ceylon becomes Sri Lanka.
1973 USA withdraws troops from Vietnam – peace settlement signed in Paris.
October *(Yom Kippur)* War – Arab states attack Israel, ceasefire after five weeks.
Arab oil-producing states restrict oil supplies, quadruple the price and spark off world economic crisis.
1975 Communist victories in Cambodia – South Vietnam surrender to North Vietnam, end of Vietnam War.

1976 Death of Mao Tse-tung.
1977 President Sadat of Egypt goes to Israel on peace mission – Prime Minister Begin of Israel returns the visit and two countries negotiate.
1978 UN force is sent to Lebanon to police border with Israel.
Vietnamese troops invade Cambodia to support rebels.
1979 A peace treaty is signed between Egypt and Israel in Washington.
Riots and collapse of law and order in Iran – the Shah leaves the country. Exiled religious leader, Ayatollah Khomeini, returns to Iran – Islamic Republic is declared. Many supporters of the Shah are executed.
Russian military forces move into Afghanistan.
1980 War between Iran and Iraq.
1981 President Sadat of Egypt assassinated.
1982 Israel invades Lebanon and advances on Beirut to drive PLO fighters from the country.

1960 AD

1983 AD

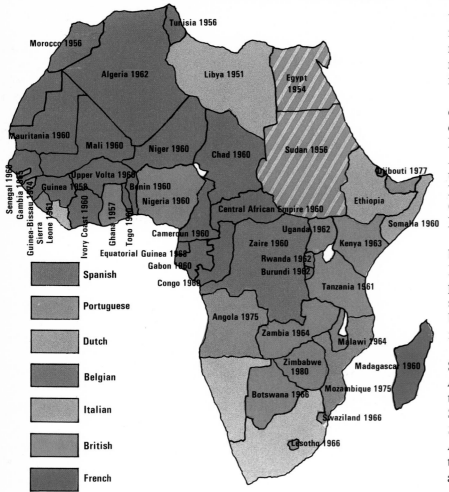

The newly independent African countries, with their dates of independence. The colours show the former colonial powers. Striped areas are those of colonial influence.

African Independence

The African continent of more than 30 million sq km had been carved up between the imperial powers during the 19th century. In 1945, except for South Africa, Ethiopia, Liberia and Egypt, it remained part of those empires.

Africans who had served with the Allied forces abroad then returned home and demanded independence. In Algeria, where there were one million French settlers or *colons*, a bitter war was fought against the French from the early 1950s until de Gaulle withdrew and granted independence in 1962. In Kenya, a rebellion known as Mau Mau lasted from 1952 to 1959 – the cost in lives and money persuaded Britain to grant Kenya independence. A few countries were given independence in the 1950s – Morocco, Tunisia, Libya, Sudan.

Then in 1957 the first black African colony, the Gold Coast, became independent and changed its name to Ghana. Ghana's leader, Kwame Nkrumah, put pressure on the colonial powers to grant independence to other parts of Africa. The year 1960 was outstanding for African independence – seventeen colonies became independent states. During the next few years most of the others also achieved their freedom. Some maintained close relations with the former colonial powers, others adopted more radical anti-western policies. But in almost all cases the new countries had weak economies and were greatly in need of financial assistance (aid) in the period after independence.

Some of the most awkward problems remained to the end. The Portuguese (the first European power to establish colonies in Africa in the 15th century) tried desperately to hold on to their huge territories of Angola and Mozambique. They fought three bitter wars in Africa until the strain upon the Portuguese economy (the poorest in Europe) led to a military coup in Portugal against the Caetano government in 1974. A year later all five Portuguese African territories were independent.

The British self-governing colony of Rhodesia was ruled by a white minority which declared independence from Britain in 1965. Only after fifteen years of international pressure, sanctions and a long guerrilla war was a settlement reached. A general election produced the first black majority government in 1980. The country changed its name to Zimbabwe.

South Africa

A major cause of concern to black Africa has always been the policy of *apartheid* or separate racial development in South Africa. Only one African country has recognized the South African regime. African countries insist that South Africa must change its laws so that blacks and whites are treated on exactly the same basis as each other, which they are not under the apartheid system.

In 1919 South Africa had been given the mandate over the former German colony of South-West Africa. In 1966, however, the UN declared that South Africa was illegally in the territory which was renamed Namibia. Since that date, a guerrilla war has been fought there against the South Africans, but, so far, the South Africans have refused to leave. Although politically weak, the African continent as a whole possesses an estimated 30 per cent of the world's mineral resources.

The signing of the Rhodesia cease-fire agreement in December 1979. From left to right: Lord Carrington (British foreign secretary), Sir Ian Gilmour (his deputy), Joshua Nkomo, and Robert Mugabe who became the first black prime minister in 1980 when the former colony became independent as Zimbabwe, with majority African rule.

An oil rig in the North Sea. These huge latticework structures are towed out of their construction dock on their side. Once in position, they are turned upright and secured on the sea bed. The crew sleep, eat and live here while outside the sea batters the rig. The drills probe thousands of metres into the sea bed searching for oil.

Oil Power

Some of the richest oilfields in the world are to be found in the Gulf, in such Arab states as Saudi Arabia, Bahrain, Iraq, Kuwait and the United Arab Emirates. Others are located in north Africa and South America.

Most of the Arab world was a part of the Turkish empire which broke up after Turkey's defeat in World War I. The Arab states remained weak – some were made mandates of Britain or France. In the 1950s huge new oil discoveries were made and these brought great riches to the area. But the oil industry was controlled by the foreign oil companies rather than the states where the oil was found.

In 1969, King Idris of Libya was overthrown by a military coup which brought a young colonel, Muammar Gadaffi, to power. He soon insisted that his government should take a majority interest in Libya's vast oil resources and his example was copied throughout the Middle East. Then, following the *Yom Kippur War* of 1973 the Arab oil states cut supplies of petroleum to the USA and the Netherlands for supporting Israel, reduced output and supplies to other countries, and quadrupled the price of oil. Oil power had arrived.

Oil prices continued to rise in the following years, and industrial countries, especially, ran up huge international debts to pay for their fuel. This produced a world recession, although this was almost certainly coming in any case. It also led the major oil importing nations to seek alternative sources of energy and the world then experienced the 'energy' crisis. By 1980 Britain and Norway had become self-sufficient in oil as a result of developing the huge resources under the North Sea, while Mexico had also developed new oilfields.

Apart from oil most of the Arab states had few other resources. The sudden huge increase in economic wealth that oil gave these countries in the 1970s was used to launch some major development plans. It also gave a new confidence to the Arab world. When OPEC (the Organization of Petroleum Exporting Countries) meets to make its decisions, it is a focus of world attention.

Popular music boomed throughout the world in the 1960s. The Beatles were the most successful of all pop groups. They achieved world-wide fame. The four members, all British, were Paul McCartney, Ringo Starr, George Harrison and John Lennon. John Lennon was shot dead in New York in December 1980. Between February 1963 and June 1972 their group sales were estimated at 545 million in singles' equivalents.

The World – Today and Yesterday

This map shows the countries of the world in 1983. Surrounding the map is a list of the place names mentioned in the text. The numbers refer to their positions on the map which, on this scale, are approximate.

Greenland

Iceland

Canada

172

United States of America

170

169

174
175
176
177

178

Bermuda

171

Bahamas

Mexico

179

180

Cuba
Haiti
Dominican Rep.
Puerto Rico

Belize
181 Honduras Jamaica
Guatemala
El Salvador Costa Rica
Nicaragua

Trinidad & Tobago
Guyana
Surinam
Guiane

Panama

Venezuela

Colombia

Ecuador

Peru
182

Brazil

Bolivia

Paraguay

Chile

Argentina

Uruguay

183

184

United Kingdom
4
Ireland 5 Netherlands
3 2 Belgium
Lux
10
Switzerl
11
34 35 32
Spain
36
37 33
Portugal
38
39
40

Morocco Algeria

Mauritania

165
Senegal 160 Mali
Gambia 163 164 Upper Volta
Guinea-Bissau
Guinea Nige
Sierra Leone 162
Liberia
Ivory Coast Togo Camer
Ghana Gab

166

Aachen 13
Abu Simbel 143
Acre 86
Actium 45
Addis Ababa 148
Aden 151
Adowa 147
Adrianople 84
Aegospotami 45
Agra 107
Alamo 171
Aleppo 88
Alexandria 138
Almanzer 38
Alsace-Lorraine 9
Altamira 35
Altranstat 19
Angkor 123
Ankara 84
Annam 99
Antioch 76
Anyang 129
Apulia 28
Aquitaine 11
Arbela 89
Arcot 115
Argos 45
Armenia 80
Astrakhan 82
Aswan 143
Athens 46
Augsburg 17
Avignon 12
Babylon 90
Baghdad 90
Balkans 49
Baltic Sea 62
Barcelona 32
Bavaria 17
Belgrade 51
Bengal 111
Berlin 18
Bihar 106
Black Sea 74
Bohemia 19
Bokhara 93
Bologna 24
Bombay 112
Bosnia 50

Budapest 53
Bunker Hill 174
Burgundy 10
Bursa 75
Byzantium 84
Calais 6
Calcutta 110
Canaan 86
Canberra 122
Cannae 28
Canossa 23
Canterbury 2
Canton 125
Cape Horn 184
Cape of Good Hope 168
Cape Verde Islands 165
Caporetto 52
Cappadocia 77
Capua 25
Carthage 42
Caspian Sea 83
Caucasus 73
Cawnpore 105
Cerignola 28
Châlons 9
Charleston 178
Choson 133
Concord 174
Constantinople 84
Cordoba 37

Corinth 45
Coronea 45
Corsica 31
Covadonga 34
Crecy 6
Crimea 72
Cunaxa 90
Cuzco 182
Cyrenaica 144
Damascus 87
Dardanelles 84
Delhi 103
Dessau 19
Diu 109
Dresden 19
Dublin 5
Dunkirk 6
Durban 157

East Anglia 2
East Prussia 59
Elmina 162
Estonia 61
Falkland Islands 183
Fashoda 146
Fatepur Sikri 107
Fayoum 140
Florence 24
Formosa (Taiwan)
Gallipoli 84
Ganges Valley 105
Garigliano 26
Gaul 10
Gdansk 58
Georgia 81
Gettysburg 177
Ghazni 95
Gibraltar 38
Gilboa 86
Giza 139

Granada 37
Hamadan 91
Hamburg 15
Hanoi 124
Hatra 89
Hebrides 4
Herat 96
Herzegovina 50
Hohenlinden 17
Hubertsberg 18
Hudson Bay 172
Hyderabad 113
Idaho 170
Istanbul 84
Jaffa 86
Java 120
Jenne 163
Jericho 86
Jerusalem 86
Judah 86
Jutland 16

84

Kabul 95
Kandahar 97
Kano 161
Karakorum 41
Karlowitz 51
Karnak 142
Kashmir 101
Kazan 68
Khartoum 146
Kiangsi 127
Kiaochow 130
Kiev 69
Kilwa 154
Kimberley 159
Knossos 44
Kossovo Plain 48
Kumbi Saleh 160
Ladysmith 157
Lascaux 10
Latium 25
Latvia 60

Little Big Horn 170
London 1
Lorraine 9
Louisbourg 173
Lübeck 15
Lucknow 105
Lützen 19
Luxor 142
Macedon 47
Madeira Islands 39
Madras 114
Madrid 36
Mafeking 158
Malplaquet 6
Manchuria 136
Mandalay 117
Manila 160
Manzikert 78

Mycenae 45
Mysore 116
Nanking 130
Naples 26
Narbonne 12
Natal 157
Nerchinsk 137
New York 176
Nicaea 79
Nicopolis 48
Nola 26

Normandy 7
Northumbria 3
Novgorod 66
Noyon 6
Nubia 145
Nuremberg 17
Nystat 63
Omdurman 146
Orange Free State 159
Otranto 28
Oudenarde 13
Palermo 27

Punjab 103
Punt 152
Pydna 47
Pylos 45
Qadesh 87
Quiberon 7
Ramillies 13
Rangoon 118
Ravenna 24
Rheims 6
Romagna 24
Rome 25
Roncesvalles 11
Rouen 6
Rossbach 18
Rubicon River 23
Salamis 85
Samarkand 94

San Francisco 169
Saqqara 143
Saratoga 175
Sardinia 30
Savoy 12
Saxony 15
Schleswig-Holstein 15
Sekingahara 135
Sena 155
Serbia 51
Shanghai 130

Shimonoseki 134
Sicily 27
Siena 24
Silesia 54
Sind 98
Smyrna 76
Sofala 156
Solferino 23
Somme River 13
Sparta 45
St Helena 167
St Petersburg 64
Stralsund 56
Stolbovo 65
Sudetenland 55
Sumatra 119
Surat 108
Tangier 40
Tannenberg 58
Tarsus 77
Tehuacan Valley 180

Tenochtitlan 179
Tete 155
Thebes 141
Thermopylae 45
Thrace 47
Timbuktu 164

Tokyo 135
Toledo 36
Tonkin 99
Toulouse 11
Trafalgar 38
Transylvania 71
Trasimene 25
Trebia 23
Tripoli 43
Troy 76
Troyes 8
Tunis 42
Turkestan 92
Tuscany 24
Tyre 87
Ukraine 70
Uruk 90
Utrecht 14
Varna 84
Vasvar 53
Venice 23
Verdun 9
Victoria Falls 153
Vienna 21
Wallachia 49
Warsaw 57
Waterloo 13
Weimar 19
Wittenburg 19
Yalta 72
Yathrib 149
Yennan 131
Ypres 13
Yucatan 181
Zayton 128
Zenta 51
Zorndorf 56

Marathon 45
Marchfeld 21
Marengo 22
Marignano 26
Marne River 8
Mecca 150
Medina 149
Megiddo 86
Meroë 145
Mesopotamia 89, 90
Milan 23
Miletus 76
Milvian Bridge 25
Minorca 33
Modena 23
Mohenjo-Daro 100
Molucca Islands 121
Montenegro 50
Moscow 67
Muhlberg 19
Multra 104

Panipat 102
Paris 8
Parma 23
Pegu 118
Peking 131
Peloponnese 45
Pharsala 47
Phoenice 29
Piedmont 22
Pisa 24
Platea 45
Poltava 69
Port Arthur 132
Potsdam 18
Prague 20
Pretoria 158
Provence 12
Prussia 58

Lepanto 49
Leningrad 64
Leuthen 55
Lexington 174
Limoges 10
Lithuania 59

Who's Who in History

Agricola, Gnaeus Julius (37–93) Roman soldier, governor of Britain 78–84. Carried Roman conquest to the farthest northern point of the empire, when he defeated Caledonians at Mt Graupius somewhere near Aberdeen, in 83.

Alaric (370–410) Leader of the Visigoths, ravaged Thrace to the gates of Constantinople at the end of the 4th century. In 410 Alaric sacked Rome – he died soon after in southern Italy.

Alexander the Great (356–323) Became king of Macedon at 20 and then set out to conquer the world. By 323, his empire stretched from Greece to the River Indus in N.W. India and south to include Egypt – perhaps the world's greatest military commander.

Archimedes (287–212) Greek mathematician and engineer, discovered principles of buoyancy and the lever. Calculated accurate value of pi (ratio of circle's circumference to its diameter). His military defensive devices prolonged the siege of Syracuse by the Romans. He was reputedly killed by a Roman soldier because he would not stop the experiment upon which he was working when the Romans broke into the city.

Atatürk, Kemal (1881–1938) Turkish general and statesman – founder of modern Turkey. Atatürk was a general in the First World War, he overthrew the Sultan and turned Turkey into a republic becoming its president in 1923. Made Turkey secular, forbade the wearing of the fez (hat) and discouraged women using the veil.

Kemal Atatürk (1881-1938) led the movement for reform in his country and was elected first president of the Turkish republic in 1923.

Baber (1483–1530) Mongol descendant of Genghis Khan, he became ruler at Kabul when aged 21. From there set out upon the conquest of northern India to establish the Mughal empire which lasted until the coming of the British to India in the 18th century.

Becket, Thomas à (1118–1170) Friend and Chancellor of Henry II. The king made him Archbishop of Canterbury, but he then quarrelled with the king over the balance of church and state power. He was murdered in Canterbury Cathedral by followers of the king. Subsequently made a saint.

Bede, the Venerable (673–735) English monk and scholar. His *History of the English Church and People* written in medieval Latin is one of the first source books of English history. It was translated into English by King Alfred the Great.

Bismarck, Prince Otto von (1815–1898) Prussian statesman, prime minister of Prussia and then Germany from 1862 to 1890. He is the creator of modern – united Germany. He was known as the 'Iron Chancellor'.

Boadicea (died AD62) Queen of Iceni tribe of Britain, she revolted against the Roman occupation. Only defeated after a major campaign that endangered Roman control of Britain.

Buddha (Siddhartha Gautama) (563–483) Founder of Buddhism, well-born Indian who renounced worldly pleasures and sat under a *bodhi* tree until mysteries of life were unfolded to him.

Burton, Sir Richard (1821–1890) Eccentric British traveller and explorer. One of first Europeans to enter Mecca (Muslim capital) in disguise. Discovered Lake Tanganyika with Speke. Wrote more than 50 books including a famous translation of the *Arabian Nights*.

Caesar, Julius (100–44) Roman statesman and general. Conquered Gaul and wrote his account – De Bello Gallico. Defied orders of the Senate and crossed the River Rubicon with his army to invade Italy and become dictator. Assassinated by his political rivals and in the power struggle that followed Augustus emerged victorious to become first Roman emperor.

Alexander the Great (356-423) from a mosaic found at Pompeii in southern Italy.

Canute (994–1035) Son of Sweyn Forkbeard of Denmark. King of England from 1016 to his death. Strong king who restored order to the country after a period of weakness. The famous story of Canute telling the sea to stop has often been misunderstood. He wished to demonstrate the limit of kingly power to foolish courtiers, who said he could do anything.

Castro, Fidel (1927–) Cuban Marxist, overthrew President Batista (1959) and became prime minister.

Catherine II, the Great (1729–1796) Deposed her mad husband Tsar Peter III of Russia and became empress (1762). Strengthened power of nobility; captured Crimea, Black Sea coast and much of Poland.

Charles V (1500–1558) Holy Roman emperor from 1519. King of Spain as Charles I from 1516. Ruled over more of Europe than any other Habsburg. Abdicated 1556.

Charles Martel (688–741) The Hammer. Frankish ruler of Austrasia (715–741). Halted Muslim advance into western Europe at battle of Tours (732).

Cheops (c 2600 BC) He had the Great Pyramid built – the largest stone monument the world has seen. It contains 2,300,000 blocks of stone with an average weight of two-and-a-half tons each.

Chiang Kai-shek (1888–1975) Chinese Nationalist leader who succeeded Sun Yat-sen in 1925 as leader of the Kuomintang (Nationalist Party). He and his followers were forced from China by the victorious communists under Mao Tse-tung in 1949. He established a Nationalist government on Formosa (Taiwan).

Churchill, Winston S. (1874–1965) British soldier, statesman and author. First Lord of Admiralty 1911–1915 and 1939–1940, Chancellor of Exchequer 1924–1929. Britain's war time prime minister from 1940–1945 and again from 1951–1955. Also a writer – he won the Nobel prize for literature in 1953.

Prince Otto von Bismarck (1815-1898) became chief minister of Prussia in 1826 and by clever scheming united the German states in a new German empire.

Cleopatra VII (69–30) Macedonian queen of Egypt from 51 to 30 BC. Caesar supported her against a rival claimant to the throne. She became his lover and bore him a son. After his death she became the lover and later wife of Marcus Antonius. Attempted but failed to captivate Augustus and in 30 BC committed suicide. Her great beauty is almost certainly a later exaggeration but she used her attractions to keep her throne.

Clive, Robert (1725–1774) British soldier who did much to bring India under British control in the 18th century. Governor of Bengal (1764–1767). On his return to England he was censured for misgovernment and corruption and said that in retrospect he was astonished at his own moderation. Committed suicide.

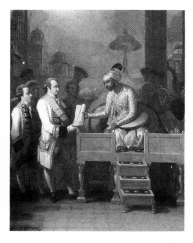

Robert Clive (1725-1774) of the East India Company is granted permission to collect revenues by the Mughal emperor.

Columbus, Christopher (1451–1506) Genoese navigator who discovered Cuba (the New World) in 1492. Made four trips to New World but never realized he had found a new continent. Died in poverty.

Confucius (K'ung Fu-tzu) (c551–479) Chinese philosopher who preached absolute justice and moderation. The *Analects* are his collected sayings. Confucianism has been the greatest influence upon Chinese thinking.

Cook, James (1728–1779) British navigator. First person to sail south of Antarctic Circle. Explored Pacific, charting coasts of New Zealand and Australia. Died in a scuffle in Hawaii.

Cortes, Hernando (1485–1547) Greatest Spanish *Conquistadore* – who conquered Mexico (the Aztecs) in 1519–1521 with a mere 550 men. He ruled as governor until 1530.

Cromwell, Oliver (1599–1658) Leader of the Roundhead (Parliamentary) faction in the civil war in England. Brilliant soldier and great statesman. Had Charles I executed and ruled as Lord Protector of England (1653–1658).

Cyrus (600–529) King of Persia and founder of the Persian empire. He overthrew Croesus and conquered Babylon, freeing the Jews from captivity there.

Danton, Georges Jacques (1759–1794) Lawyer and revolutionary who became a leader in the French Revolution of 1789. He helped organize the Reign of Terror and was himself guillotined by Robespierre.

Darwin, Charles Robert (1809–1882) English naturalist whose major work, *The Origin of Species,* proposed the theory of evolution by natural selection. This was utterly opposed to the ideas of the Church and caused major controversy.

Davy, Sir Humphry (1778–1829) English chemist who was also an important inventor, best remembered for his miners' (Davy) lamp. Using electrolysis he isolated potassium, sodium, barium, strontium and magnesium. Proved chlorine to be an element.

De Gaulle, Charles (1890–1970) French general and statesman. Only French soldier who successfully withstood the German panzer tank tactics of 1940. After the fall of France in 1940 he organized the Free French movement from London. President of France from 1945–1946 and during the important period from 1956–1969, with a new constitution (the Fifth Republic). Granted full independence to France's African colonies in 1960 and ended the war in Algeria in 1962. Retired from politics.

Drake, Sir Francis (1543–1596) English adventurer, plundered Spanish settlements in America. Sailed round the world in 1577–1580. Burned a Spanish fleet at Cadiz in 1587 and helped to defeat Spanish Armada in 1588. He died in the West Indies.

Francis Drake (1543-1596), the Elizabethan seaman, was known to the Spaniards as 'El Draque' – the Dragon.

Edward, the Black Prince (1330–1376) Son of Edward III, he 'won his spurs' at the Battle of Crecy . Regarded as the greatest knight of his age. He died a year before his father and his son became king of England as Richard II.

Einstein, Albert (1879–1955) German-born theoretical physicist, made greatest scientific advances since Newton over 200 years earlier. In 1905 used quantum theory to explain photoelectric effect, produced famous $E=mc^2$ equation relating mass to energy, explained Browning movement thus confirming atomic theory of matter, and expounded special theory of relativity. Published general theory of relativity in 1916 (replaced Newton's gravitational theory) and unified field theory in 1929. Became Swiss citizen 1901, American 1940 (as a Jew could not work in Germany in 1930s). Reluctantly persuaded President Roosevelt to begin atomic research 1939. Fought for world peace. Nobel physics prize 1921.

Albert Einstein (1879-1955) whose special theory of relativity superseded Newton's gravitational laws.

Ericsson, Lief (CAD 970–?) Viking explorer who crossed the northern Atlantic about 1000 to found the colonies of 'Woodland' and 'Vinland' – possibly Newfoundland and Maryland.

Eugène of Savoy, Prince (1663–1736) Austrian general, born in France, who with Marlborough won many victories against the French in the War of Spanish Succession. Napoleon considered him to be one of the greatest generals of all time.

Ford, Henry (1863–1947) American car manufacturer who pioneered methods of mass production to make cheap cars.

Fox, Charles James (1749–1806) British politician, arch opponent of George III, rival to Pitt. One of few British parliamentarians to support the French Revolution.

Franklin, Benjamin (1706–1790) American statesman and scientist and one of the founding fathers of the USA. He invented bifocal glasses and the lightning conductor.

Frederick II, the Great (1712–1786) King of Prussia from 1740, brilliant general. Fought Empress Maria Theresa in War of Austrian Succession. Skilled flautist.

Freud, Sigmund (1856–1939) Austrian psychiatrist whose theories of the conscious and subconscious mind and infantile sexuality have had a major influence upon modern psychiatry.

Gandhi, Mohandas Karamchand (1869–1948) Indian Lawyer, ascetic, and Hindu spiritual leader; worked for independence from Britain, largely by non-violent civil disobedience; jailed several times; assassinated by Hindu fanatic because he preached peace with Muslims. Known as *Mahatma*, great soul.

Frederick the Great (1712-1786) was nicknamed the 'Soldier King'. His army was a very efficient fighting machine. He introduced light, horsedrawn guns which could be moved from place to place during the course of a battle.

Garibaldi, Giuseppe (1807–1882) Italian patriot who played a major part in the struggle to bring about the unification of Italy (1861). His most famous feat was the conquest of the kingdom of the Two Sicilies in 1860 with 1000 men (Redshirts). Twice tried to conquer Rome (1862, 1867). Fought for France (1870–1871). Member of Italian parliament (1874).

Gladstone, William Ewart (1809–1898) British Liberal statesman who was four times prime minister of Britain. Failed in several attempts to persuade Parliament to agree to Home Rule for Ireland. When, as an old man in 1894, he went to resign, Queen Victoria, who disliked him, kept him standing throughout the interview.

Goebbels, Joseph Paul (1897–1945) Chief of propaganda in Nazi Germany. He perfected a number of propaganda techniques. Close friend of Hitler, committed suicide.

Hammurabi the Great (1800 BC) Sixth king of the first Babylonian dynasty, he conquered all Mesopotamia. He was a great builder and his code of laws was not surpassed until Roman times.

Hannibal (247–183) Greatest of Carthaginian soldiers and statesmen. Crossed the Alps (with elephants) to invade Italy, where he defeated the Romans in many battles. He was, himself, defeated at Zama in 202 by the Romans and was later exiled. He committed suicide so as not to fall into Roman hands.

Harun-al-Raschid (?–AD809) Caliph of Baghdad from 786–809, he was one of the greatest and most splendid of the Abbasid rulers made famous through the pages of the *Arabian Nights*.

Herodotus (c484–424) Greek traveller and writer, called the 'Father of History'. Recorded customs, manners and traditions of peoples in places he visited. It was Herodotus who described Egypt as 'The Gift of the Nile'.

Homer (c850 BC) Traditionally a Greek poet, author of the *Iliad* and the *Odyssey*, though nothing certain is known of him.

Ivan IV, the Terrible (1530–1584) First tsar of all Russia. Became ruler 1533, assumed personal power 1546. Vicious and cruel, had many people murdered and tortured. Developed religious mania, murdered eldest son, repented and became a monk on his death bed.

Joan of Arc (Jeanne d'Arc) (1412–1431) The peasant girl who 'heard voices' and led the French armies against the English in the Hundred Years' War. She was burnt as a witch by the English.

Johnson, Samuel (1709–1784) English writer and debater who was renowned as a wit. He produced his Dictionary in 1755. One of the most famous biographies was Boswell's *Life of Johnson*.

Justinian I (483–565) Last great Roman emperor, he became emperor of the eastern empire in 526 at Constantinople, and reconquered much of the old western empire (Italy) which was then in the hands of the barbarians.

Kenyatta, Jomo (c1883–1978) Kenyan nationalist leader who spent much of his life campaigning for Kenyan independence from British rule. His book *Facing Mount Kenya* was a landmark in African nationalism. He became the first prime minister and then president of an independent Kenya (1963). He died in office in 1978.

Kitchener, Horatio Herbert (1850–1916) Governor-general Sudan, recapturing Khartoum from Muslim fanatics. British soldier who won the battle of Omdurman in 1898. Became c-in-c in South Africa during the Boer War (1900) and was secretary of state for war in 1914. His features became famous on the first World War poster 'Your Country Needs You'. Drowned when ship hit mine.

Lawrence, Thomas Edward (1888–1935) British archaeologist soldier and author who helped to organize the Arab revolt against Turkey in Arabia in 1917. Became famous (and lionized) as Lawrence of Arabia. Wrote *Seven Pillars of Wisdom* and *The Mint*.

Lenin, Vladimir (1870–1924) Russian revolutiontary who was exiled from Russia from 1895–1917. He founded the Bolshevik (later the Communist) party. Allowed across Germany in a sealed train after the February Revolution, he then led the October Revolution. Fell ill and lost control of government in 1922. Succeeded by Stalin in 1924.

Leo the Great (?–AD461) First great pope who obtained from the Emperor Valentinian III an edict to the effect that papal decisions had the force of law. He was traditionally credited with stopping Attila the Hun's westward advance.

Livingstone, David (1813–1873) Scottish missionary and explorer of Africa who became a hero to Victorian England. After crossing the Kalahari Desert and travelling down the River Zambesi, he sought sources of Congo and Nile rivers. Feared lost, he was found by Stanley. In a famous speech to Cambridge undergraduates he called upon them to go out as missionaries to Africa and a generation was to follow his advice. Died still exploring.

Loyola, St Ignatius (1491–1556) Basque nobleman, soldier and theologian. After being wounded in battle, experienced religious conversion that led to his founding Society of Jesus (Jesuits).

Mao Tse-tung (1893–1976) Chinese Communist leader who defeated the Nationalists, under Chiang Kai-shek, in 1949 to rule all China. His revolutionary method was constantly to upset the Chinese establishment and after his death the Maoist notion of continuous cultural revolution was rejected.

Maria Theresa (1717–1780) Austrian empress of Holy Roman empire from 1740. Defended her right to the throne in the War of Austrian Succession, 1740–1748. Her husband, Francis of Lorraine, was recognized as emperor in 1748.

Marx, Karl (1818–1883) German Jewish philospher who in his writings laid the foundations of Communism. In 1848 (with Engels) he published the Communist Manifesto. His doctrine in *Das Kapital* (1867) revolutionized political thinking.

More, Sir Thomas (1478–1535) English lawyer and statesman who was made chancellor by Henry VIII. His *Utopia* describes an ideal society. He refused to recognize the king as head of the Church and was executed for treason. Declared a saint in 1935.

Nasser, Gamal Abdel (1918–1970) Egyptian revolutionary and army officer. Helped depose King Farouk (1952). While president from 1956 tried to modernize country. Nationalized Suez Canal.

Nehru, Jawahalal (1889–1964) Indian statesman who played a leading part in the nationalist struggle to gain independence from Britain. Prime minister of India from 1947–1964. He was one of the founders of the political movement known as Non-Alignment.

Nelson, Horatio (1758–1805) British naval hero, lost eye and arm in battle. Destroyed French fleet at Battle of Nile (1798), won Battle of Copenhagen (1801), destroyed another French fleet at Trafalgar (1805), dying in moment of victory. Created viscount, 1801. Liaison with Emma, Lady Hamilton, a public scandal.

Nero (37–68) Roman emperor from 54 to 68. Rebuilt city after the great fire and was wrongly depicted by later Christian writers as playing the lyre while Rome burnt. He led a dissolute private life and committed suicide in 68 when the army revolted.

Nightingale, Florence (1820–1910) English reformer, became nurse. Against great opposition she organized nursing reforms during

Benjamin Franklin (1706-1790) showed the electrical nature of lightning by flying a kite in a thunderstorm and drawing sparks from a key tied to the lower end of its string.

the Crimean War when she became known as the 'Lady with the Lamp'. Her system of sanitary barrack hospitals was to be adopted worldwide.

Nkrumah, Kwame (1909–1972) Gold Coast nationalist, he founded the Convention People's Party and became the country's first prime minister at independence and then its first president when Ghana became a republic in 1960. He was ousted in a coup in 1966 and died in exile in Guinea. He was the author of several books the most important of which was *I Speak of Freedom*.

Park, Mungo (1771–1806) Scottish explorer who twice went to west Africa in search of the source of the Niger. In 1806, while travelling down the Niger, he was drowned at Bussa.

Pasteur, Louis (1822–1895) French chemist, established bacteriology as science – devised method of gentle heating (pasteurization) to kill micro-organisms in wine and beer. Showed air to contain spores of living organisms. Proposed germ theory of disease. Developed inoculation of animals against anthrax and rabies.

Pericles (495–429) Greatest Athenian of its 'golden age', he led Athens from 460 to 430 and was responsible for making Athens the 'most beautiful city in the world'. He died in 429 of the plague. Known as the 'father of democracy'.

Mahatma Gandhi (1869-1948) led a non-violent campaign to free India from British rule.

Pizarro, Francisco (1474–1541) One of the greatest of the Spanish *Conquistadores,* he conquered the Inca empire of Peru in 1528 with only 180 men. Assassinated.

Plato (427–347) Greek philosopher who was a pupil of Socrates and teacher of Aristotle. Enshrined his philosophy in his *Dialogues*. Platonism, stressing idea of the good rather than material appearances, has had a profound influence upon philosophy.

Polo, Marco (1254–1324) Venetian merchant who travelled to the court of the great Mongol Emperor Kublai Khan in Cathay (China). Returned to Venice in 1295, after 24-year absence, a wealthy man. Described journeys in *Travels* which astonished Europe of his day.

Ptolemy I Sotor (?–283BC) Half-brother to Alexander the Great and one of his most trusted generals. Ptolemy took Egypt as his 'share' of Alexander's empire when Alexander died and founded the Ptolemaic line of pharaohs which lasted until the time of Julius Caesar.

Raleigh, Sir Walter (1552–1618) English soldier and courtier who established the first colony of Virginia and introduced the habit of smoking to England. Explored Guiana region of South America and was executed by James I after failing to find gold.

Rhodes, Cecil John (1853–1902) British statesman. As a young man went out to South Africa for his health. He made a fortune in diamonds, became prime minister of Cape colony and created Rhodesia between 1890 and 1895. His dream was a Cape to Cairo railway through British-controlled territory in Africa. Disgraced over Jameson Raid in Transvaal (1896).

Richelieu, Cardinal Armand Jean du Plessis (1585–1642) French statesman who became the first minister of Louis XIII from 1624–1642 and virtually ruled France. He curbed the old nobility, broke the independent power of the Huguenots and extended France's boundaries and power in Europe.

Robespierre, Maximilien (1758–1794) Leader of the Jacobins in the French Revolution, became the most important figure in the 'Reign of Terror'. Almost a dictator for a time, he himself was denounced and guillotined.

Roosevelt, Franklin Delano (1884–1945) Four times president of the USA, he was responsible for the New Deal in the 1930s to help end the Great Depression. He led his country through the Second World War until his death in 1945. He was a polio victim and spent his last years in a wheelchair.

Savonarola, Girolamo (1452–1498) Italian priest who denounced the corruption of Florentine society, led a rebellion against Pope Alexander VI. Captured and executed for sedition and heresy.

Shaka (1787–1828) He became king of the Zulus in 1818 and devised new military strategy and new weapons, creating a standing Zulu army of *impis* (regiments). His military conquests caused a dispersal of his people that had widespread effects throughout southern Africa.

Shakespeare, William (1564–1616) England's greatest dramatist, whose plays and poetry have had a profound effect upon the English language and have been translated into most languages in the world.

Smuts, Jan Christian (1870–1950) Boer general in the Boer War of 1899–1902, he was twice prime minister of South Africa and a supporter of the connection with Britain.

Stuart, Charles Edward (1720–1788) Known as the 'Young Pretender' to the British crown. Son of James Edward Stuart and grandson of King James II. Led the unsuccessful 1745 invasion of Scotland in an attempt to bring about a Jacobite rebellion against the Hanoverian dynasty. Defeated at Culloden (1746), lived rest of his life in exile.

Sun Yat-sen (1866–1925) Chinese revolutionary who overthrew the Manchu dynasty and turned China into a republic. He was president of China from 1921 to his death.

Tamerlane (1336–1405) Name means Timur the Lame. He created a huge Mongol empire from Turkey to India and north to Moscow. A brilliant soldier, he was feared for his ruthlessness.

Toussaint L'Ouverture, Pierre Dominique (1743–1803) Haitian liberator, born of African slave parents, became leader of French republican rebels. Gained control of island and ruled well until overthrown by French military intervention (1802).

Trotsky, Leon (Lev Davidovich Bronstein; 1879–1940) Russian revolutionary. Minister under Lenin (1917). Organized Red Army in civil war of 1918–1921. Opposed Stalin – exiled 1929. Assassinated by a Stalin agent in Mexico.

Victor Emmanuel II (1820–1878) King of Sardinia. Leader in war against Austria and struggle for unification of Italy. First king of Italy (from 1861) guided by Cavour, his chief minister.

Walpole, Sir Robert (1676–1745) Britain's first and one of her longest serving prime ministers (1721–1742). His general motto was 'let sleeping dogs lie'.

Wesley, John (1703–1791) English evangelist who rode thousands of miles in England on preaching tours. He was the founder of the Methodist Church.

Wilberforce, William (1759–1833) English reformer and evangelist who spent his life campaigning to end the slave trade and slavery. Achieved it in 1833.

Zoroaster (Zarathustra; c660BC) Persian who founded the religion of Zoroastrianism – said to have written its sacred book, *Avesta*.

William Shakespeare (1564-1616) and the Globe Theatre at which many of his plays were first produced. He is acknowledged to be the greatest playwright of the English language. Much of his life is still the subject of speculation.

Glossary of Politics

Annex To take possession of a territory, especially against the wishes of the territory concerned.

Apartheid Policy of separate development for different races as practised in South Africa since 1949. It has been universally denounced and is the reason why African states will not enter into diplomatic relations with South Africa.

Capitalism Production of goods for profit. The term has come to be associated with the policies of the western nations which predominantly pursue economic policies of free enterprise.

Civil Rights Freedoms that members of any community should enjoy. They include freedom from imprisonment without trial and the right to participate in political choices. Demands for civil rights in the USA by American blacks led to the Civil Rights Bill of 1964. Demands for civil rights in Northern Ireland by Roman Catholics led to the troubles and confrontations which has forced Britain to station troops in the province since 1969.

Cold War Description of the political confrontation between the western countries and the communist countries.

Colony Country that recognizes some form of direct rule from a mother country.

Common Markets Groups of countries banded together for trade and economic co-operation.

Arab Common Market (ACM) Formed in 1965, it comprises Egypt, Iraq, Jordan and Syria.

Central American Common Market (CACM) Formed in 1960, it comprises Costa Rica, El Salvador, Guatemala, Honduras and Nicaragua.

Council for Mutual Economic Assistance (COMECON) Formed by the Communist states of East Europe and the USSR in 1949 – Albania, Bulgaria, Czechoslovakia, Hungary, Poland, Romania and the USSR. Albania later left the organization but East Germany, Mongolia and Cuba joined it.

European Economic Community (EEC) The 1957 Treaty of Rome brought the EEC into existence at the beginning of 1958. It then consisted of six members – Belgium, France, West Germany, Italy, Luxembourg and the Netherlands – they were known as 'The Six'. In 1973 Britain, Denmark and Ireland joined. Greece joined in 1981. In 1982 both Portugal and Spain were negotiating for membership. It has proved the most effective of the world's common markets perhaps because it contains four of the world's major economies – Britain, France, West Germany and Italy. The Treaty of Rome envisages that in the long run the countries of the Common Market will also become united politically. In 1979, the first steps towards political unity were taken when the Nine held the first direct elections to the European parliament.

At a mass rally – Adolf Hitler (1889-1945) who ruled Nazi Germany as a supreme dictator from 1933 until 1945.

European Free Trade Association (EFTA) Formed in 1960 on British initiative when Britain opposed the EEC and wanted to see a looser organization which was concerned with trade only, rather than politics, as was the EEC. The original members were Austria, Britain, Denmark, Norway, Portugal, Sweden and Switzerland. Iceland joined in 1970. Britain and Denmark left in 1973 when they joined the EEC. Finland is an associate member.

Latin American Free trade Association (LAFTA) Founded in 1961 by the Treaty of Montevideo, it comprises ten countries – Argentina, Brazil, Chile, Colombia, Ecuador, Mexico, Paraguay, Peru, Uruguay and Venezuela.

Commonwealth of Nations Free association of 48 independent countries which have in common their former membership of the British empire. Most British colonies on achieving independence elected to remain associated with each other through their membership of the Commonwealth. The British monarch is recognized as the head of the Commonwealth (although there is no reason why the head of state of another member country should not be recognized in this capacity). There is a *Commonwealth Secretariat* in London and the Secretary-General is appointed for a five-year term. The heads of government of the Commonwealth meet about once every 18 months. These meetings are the main decision-making occasions for the association. There are about 240 Commonwealth bodies which deal with a wide range of problems from education to law and aid.

Communists Members of a political party which believes that all property and means of production should belong to the State.

Confederation Alliance between states.

Constitution Rules (written or unwritten) by which a state is governed.

Coup d'état Referred to as a coup – swift overthrow of government by illegal, and often violent, means.

Democracy Rule by the people. Usually this means that an entire adult population elects a government for fixed periods.

Dictatorship Form of one-man rule in which a single individual wields effective power, although (in many cases) he may go through the form of consulting an assembly. A dictatorship may also be wielded by a small group often called a *junta* or *praesidium*, a council of state.

Dominion Self-governing territory. A dominion within the British empire was a self-governing territory that recognized the supremacy of the British crown.

Fascism Political theory that believes that the rights of the individuals should take second place to the interests of the state.

Franchise Right to vote.

Imperialism Control exercised over other countries or territories which are ruled as colonies by the imperial power.

Liberal Any political movement that favours freedom from central control and is against privilege.

Mandated Territory Region which the League of Nations decided should be administered by one of the 'great powers' following the Great War.

Nationalism Determination of groups who have various factors in common – for example, language, religion, history, geographic area – to run their own affairs as a state or nation. Nationalism was the pressure that forced the European imperial powers to relinquish their empires in the period 1945 to 1970.

North Atlantic Treaty Organisation (NATO) Formed at the height of the Cold War in 1949 by the western nations, NATO is a defensive military alliance whose principal object is to prevent possible Russian expansion into Europe. The Supreme Commander of NATO is always an American. There are 15 members: Belgium, Canada, Denmark, France, West Germany, Greece, Iceland, Italy, Luxembourg, Netherlands, Norway, Portugal, Turkey, United Kingdom and United States.

Neutrality Refusing to take sides in a war. Sweden and Switzerland in Europe have long mantained a policy of neutrality.

Non-Alignment Relatively new policy pioneered in the 1950s by leaders such as Nehru of India and Tito of Yugoslavia. It was the response of weak countries to the Cold War. The Non-Aligned states are mainly countries of Africa or Asia who insisted that they were not obliged to 'line up with' either the western or eastern blocs.

Above: The flags of the nine Common Market countries in 1973.

Right: A soldier in a United Nations peace-keeping force. Such forces patrol strife-torn areas, observing and acting rather as police but not fighting for either side. Although it has not succeeded in its aim of preventing all wars, it has helped to stop several.

Organization of African Unity (OAU) In 1963 African leaders feared that the continent was in danger of being split between rival groups. All the then independent African countries met in Addis Ababa to create the OAU. The OAU holds an annual meeting of heads of state in a different African capital each time (the headquarters of the organization are in Addis Ababa) and the head of state of the host country becomes the chairman for the year. There is an OAU secretariat with an appointed secretary-general and a number of subsidiary bodies which deal with economic and other matters. The OAU has always opposed apartheid in South Africa and has refused to allow that country to join the organization. In 1980, following the admission of newly independent Zimbabwe, the OAU had 50 members.

Organization of Petrol Exporting Countries (OPEC) Formed in 1960 but only became prominent after the *Yom Kippur War* of 1973 when its members quadrupled the price of their oil exports. There are 13 member countries and the basis of membership must be that a significant proportion of total export earnings come from oil. Thus huge producers of oil such as the USA or the USSR who consume most of it themselves would not be allowed to join OPEC. OPEC's main object is to keep the price of petroleum products high for the benefit of its members, who produce them.

Protectorate Weak territory which is given protection by a stronger one.

Racialism Persecution or belittlement of people of a different race, which often takes the form of denying groups in a particular community full political or social rights.

Religion Estimated world membership of the main religions is given in millions and can only be approximate.
Christians – 1000 million. Of these 585 million are Roman Catholics, 90 million are Eastern Orthodox and 325 million are Protestants. *Jews* – 15 million. *Muslims* – 500 million (possibly the fastest growing religion at the present time. *Shintoists* – 60 million. *Taoists* – 30 million. *Confucians* – 300 million. *Buddhists* – 200 million. *Hindus* – 500 million.

Reparations Compensation demanded by victors for damage resulting from war.

Secede To make a formal withdrawal from membership.

Third World Term applied to countries that insist upon being Non-Aligned (see above) and often to the nations of the 'developing world' that are heavily dependent upon economic assistance from the more advanced economies.

United Nations Britain, China, the USSR and the USA agreed to

create an international body as soon as World War II came to an end. At San Francisco in 1945 the United Nations Organization was formally established, based in New York. When Zimbabwe joined the UN in 1980 this brought the membership of the world body up to 149.

The General Assembly consists of all the members, who each have a single vote for or against a proposal (resolution) put by one of the members. The work is done by committees of which there are six: Political Security; Economic and Financial; Social, Humanitarian and Cultural; Decolonization; Administrative and Budgetary; Legal.

The Security Council consists of 15 members. Five are permanent – China, France, the UK, the USA and the USSR – and they have a veto (the right to stop a resolution being passed, whatever the voting). The other ten members are elected on a two-year term. Each member has a single vote. The Security Council is primarily concerned with the maintenance of peace.

The Economic and Social Council carries out many of the general functions of the UN. The *Trusteeship Council* administers Trust Territories (although the most important of these, Namibia, is at present administered by South Africa against the wishes of the UN). The *International Court of Justice* has 15 judges elected by the UN and meets at the Hague.

The Secretariat is responsible for the running of the UN, and is headed by the Secretary-General and an international staff. There are a number of agencies concerned with international problems such as health, agriculture, labour or finance. The most important of these bodies are: the *International Labour Organization (ILO)* in Geneva, the *Food and Agricultural Organization (FAO)* in Rome, the *United Nations Educational, Scientific and Cultural Organization (UNESCO)* in Paris and the *World Health Organization (WHO)* in Geneva. There are three organizations concerned with finance: the *International Bank for Reconstruction and Development (IBRD)* – better known as the *World Bank* which has become the world's largest aid agency, the *International Monetary Fund (IMF)*, and the *International Development Agency (IDA)*. They each have their headquarters in Washington.

Warsaw Pact Communists answer to the Western alliance (NATO), in the form of a defence treaty between its members. There are seven members: Bulgaria, Czechoslavakia, East Germany, Hungary, Poland, Romania and the USSR.

Zionism Move to establish a Jewish state in Palestine (achieved in 1948) and the subsequent organized campaign among Jews and their supporters to maintain the new state of Israel.

Index

93

TSARS OF RUSSIA

The last tsar of Russia, Nicholas II (1894-1917) with his family.

Ivan III the Great	1462–1505
Basil III	1505–1533
Ivan IV the Terrible	1533–1584
Fëdor I	1584–1598
Boris Godunov	1598–1605
Fëdor II	1605
Demetrius	1605–1606
Basil (IV) Shuiski	1606–1610
[Interregnum, 1610–1613]	
Michael Romanov	1613–1645
Alexis	1645–1676
Fëdor III	1676–1682
Ivan V and Peter the Great	1682–1689
Peter the Great (alone)	1689–1725
Catherine I	1725–1727
Peter II	1727–1730
Anna	1730–1740
Ivan VI	1740–1741
Elizabeth	1741–1762
Peter III	1762
Catherine II the Great	1762–1796
Paul I	1796–1801
Alexander I	1801–1825
Nicholas I	1825–1855
Alexander II	1855–1881
Alexander III	1881–1894
Nicholas II	1894–1917

[Revolution; Alexander Kerenski, Socialist leader, provisional head, Aug.–Nov. 1917]

Tsar Peter the Great (1672-1725).

BRITISH RULERS

Oliver Cromwell ruled the Commonwealth (1649-1660) after the execution of Charles I.

Rulers of England (to 1603)
Saxons

Egbert	827–839
Ethelwulf	839–858
Ethelbald	858–860
Ethelbert	860–865
Ethelred I	865–871
Alfred the Great	871–899
Edward the Elder	899–924
Athelstan	924–939
Edmund	939–946
Edred	946–955
Edwy	955–959
Edgar	959–975
Edward the Martyr	975–978
Ethelred II the Unready	978–1016
Edmund Ironside	1016

Danes

Canute	1016–1035
Harold I Harefoot	1035–1040
Hardicanute	1040–1042

Saxons

Edward the Confessor	1042–1066
Harold II	1066

House of Normandy

William I the Conqueror	1066–1087
William II	1087–1100
Henry I	1100–1135
Stephen	1135–1154

House of Plantagenet

Henry II	1154–1189
Richard I	1189–1199
John	1199–1216
Henry III	1216–1272
Edward I	1272–1307
Edward II	1307–1327
Edward III	1327–1377
Richard II	1377–1399

House of Lancaster

Henry IV	1399–1413
Henry V	1413–1422
Henry VI	1422–1461

House of York

Edward IV	1461–1483
Edward V	1483
Richard III	1483–1485

House of Tudor

Henry VII	1485–1509
Henry VIII	1509–1547
Edward VI	1547–1553
Mary I	1553–1558
Elizabeth I	1558–1603

Rulers of Scotland (to 1603)

Malcolm II	1005–1034
Duncan I	1034–1040
Macbeth	1040–1057
Malcolm III Canmore	1058–1093
Donald Bane	1093–1094
Duncan II	1094
Donald Bane (restored)	1094–1097
Edgar	1097–1107
Alexander I	1107–1124
David I	1124–1153
Malcolm IV	1153–1165
William the Lion	1165–1214
Alexander II	1214–1249
Alexander III	1249–1286
Margaret of Norway	1286–1290
Interregnum	1290–1292
John Balliol	1292–1296
Interregnum	1296–1306
Robert I (Bruce)	1306–1329
David II	1329–1371

House of Stuart

Robert II	1371–1390
Robert III	1390–1406
James I	1406–1437
James II	1437–1460
James III	1460–1488
James IV	1488–1513
James V	1513–1542
Mary	1542–1567
James VI	1567–1625

Became James I of England in 1603.

Rulers of Britain
House of Stuart

James I	1603–1625
Charles I	1625–1649
Commonwealth	1649–1660

House of Stuart (restored)

Charles II	1660–1685
James II	1685–1688
William III jointly	1689–1702
Mary II	1689–1694
Anne	1702–1714

House of Hanover

George I	1714–1727
George II	1727–1760
George III	1760–1820
George IV	1820–1830
William IV	1830–1837
Victoria	1837–1901

House of Saxe-Coburg

Edward VII	1901–1910

House of Windsor

George V	1910–1936
Edward VIII	1936
George VI	1936–1952
Elizabeth II	1952

Queen Victoria (1837-1901) at the age of 20.

BRITISH PRIME MINISTERS

W=Whig, T=Tory, Cln=Coalition, P=Peelite, L=Liberal,
C=Conservative, Lab=Labour

Sir Robert Walpole (W)	1721–42
Earl of Wilmington (W)	1742–43
Henry Pelham (W)	1743–54
Duke of Newcastle (W)	1754–56
Duke of Devonshire (W)	1756–57
Duke of Newcastle (W)	1757–62
Earl of Bute (T)	1762–63
George Grenville (W)	1763–65
Marquess of Rockingham (W)	1765–66
Earl of Chatham (W)	1766–67
Duke of Grafton (W)	1767–70
Lord North (T)	1770–82
Marquess of Rockingham (W)	1782
Earl of Shelburne (W)	1782–83
Duke of Portland (Cln)	1783
William Pitt (T)	1783–1801
Henry Addington (T)	1801–04
William Pitt (T)	1804–06
Lord Grenville (W)	1806–07
Duke of Portland (T)	1807–09
Spencer Perceval (T)	1809–12
Earl of Liverpool (T)	1812–27
George Canning (T)	1827
Viscount Goderich (T)	1827–28
Duke of Wellington (T)	1828–30

Arthur Wellesley, Duke of Wellington (prime minister 1828-1830).

Earl Grey (W)	1830–34
Viscount Melbourne (W)	1834
Sir Robert Peel (T)	1834–35
Viscount Melbourne (W)	1835–41
Sir Robert Peel (T)	1841–46
Lord John Russell (W)	1846–52
Earl of Derby (T)	1852
Earl of Aberdeen (P)	1852–55
Viscount Palmerston (L)	1855–58
Earl of Derby (C)	1858–59
Viscount Palmerston (L)	1859–65
Earl Russell (L)	1865–66
Earl of Derby (C)	1866–68
Benjamin Disraeli (C)	1868
William Gladstone (L)	1868–74
Benjamin Disraeli (C)	1874–80
William Gladstone (L)	1880–85
Marquess of Salisbury (C)	1885–86
William Gladstone (L)	1886
Marquess of Salisbury (C)	1886–92
William Gladstone (L)	1892–94
Earl of Rosebery (L)	1894–95
Marquess of Salisbury (C)	1895–1902
Arthur Balfour (C)	1902–05
Sir Henry Campbell-Bannerman (L)	1905–08
Herbert Asquith (L)	1908–15
Herbert Asquith (Cln)	1915–16
David Lloyd-George (Cln)	1916–22
Andrew Bonar Law (C)	1922–23
Stanley Baldwin (C)	1923–24
James Ramsay Macdonald (Lab)	1924
Stanley Baldwin (C)	1924–29
James Ramsay MacDonald (Lab)	1929–31
James Ramsay MacDonald (Cln)	1931–35
Stanley Baldwin (Cln)	1935–37
Neville Chamberlain (Cln)	1937–40
Winston Churchill (Cln)	1940–45
Winston Churchill (Cln)	1945
Clement Attlee (Lab)	1945–51
Sir Winston Churchill (C)	1951–55
Sir Anthony Eden (C)	1955–57
Harold Macmillan (C)	1957–63
Sir Alec Douglas-Home (C)	1963–64
Harold Wilson (Lab)	1964–70
Edward Heath (C)	1970–74
Harold Wilson (Lab)	1974–76
James Callaghan (Lab)	1976–79
Margaret Thatcher (C)	1979–

AMERICAN PRESIDENTS

F=Federalist; DR=Democratic-Republican;
D=Democratic; W=Whig; R=Republican; U=Union
* Died in office; †Assassinated in office

		Term
1	George Washington (F)	1789–1797
2	John Adams (F)	1797–1801
3	Thomas Jefferson (DR)	1801–1809
4	James Madison (DR)	1809–1817
5	James Monroe (DR)	1817–1825
6	John Quincy Adams (DR)	1825–1829
7	Andrew Jackson (D)	1829–1837
8	Martin Van Buren (D)	1837–1841
9	William H Harrison* (W)	1841
10	John Tyler (W)	1841–1845
11	James K Polk (D)	1845–1849
12	Zachary Taylor* (W)	1849–1850
13	Millard Fillmore (W)	1850–1853
14	Franklin Pierce (D)	1853–1857
15	James Buchanan (D)	1857–1861
16	Abraham Lincoln† (R)	1861–1865
17	Andrew Johnson (U)	1865–1869
18	Ulysses S Grant (R)	1869–1877
19	Rutherford B Hayes (R)	1877–1881
20	James A Garfield† (R)	1881
21	Chester A Arthur (R)	1881–1885
22	Grover Cleveland (D)	1885–1889
23	Benjamin Harrison (R)	1889–1893
24	Grover Cleveland (D)	1893–1897
25	William McKinley† (R)	1897–1901
26	Theodore Roosevelt (R)	1901–1909
27	William H Taft (R)	1909–1913
28	Woodrow Wilson (D)	1913–1921
29	Warren G Harding* (R)	1921–1923
30	Calvin Coolidge (R)	1923–1929
31	Herbert C Hoover (R)	1929–1933
32	Franklin D Roosevelt* (D)	1933–1945
33	Harry S Truman (D)	1945–1953
34	Dwight D Eisenhower (R)	1953–1961
35	John F Kennedy† (D)	1961–1963
36	Lyndon B Johnson (D)	1963–1969
37	Richard M Nixon (R)	1969–1974
38	Gerald R Ford (R)	1974–1977
39	Jimmy Carter (D)	1977–1981
40	Ronald Reagan (R)	1981–

RULERS OF FRANCE

King Louis XIV of France, *Le Grand Monarque.*

CAPETIAN LINE

Hugh Capet	987–996
Robert II, the Pious	996–1031
Henri I	1031–1060
Philip I	1060–1108
Louis VI, the Fat	1108–1137
Louis VII, the Young	1137–1180
Philip II Augustus	1180–1223
Louis VIII	1223–1226
Louis IX, Saint Louis	1226–1270
Philip III, the Bold	1270–1285
Philip IV, the Fair	1285–1314
Louis X	1314–1316
John I	1316
Philip V	1316–1322
Charles IV	1322–1328

HOUSE OF VALOIS

Philip VI	1328–1350
John II	1350–1364
Charles V	1364–1380
Charles VI	1380–1422
Charles VII	1422–1461

Louis XI	1461–1483
Charles VIII	1483–1498
Louis XII	1498–1515
François I	1515–1547
Henri II	1547–1559
François II	1559–1560
Charles IX	1560–1574
Henri III	1574–1589

HOUSE OF BOURBON

Henri IV	1589–1610
Louis XIII	1610–1643
Louis XIV	1643–1715
Louis XV	1715–1774
Louis XVI	1774–1792
The First Republic	1792–1804
Napoleon I (Emperor)	1804–1814
Louis XVIII	1814–1824
Charles X	1824–1830
Louis Philippe	1830–1848
The Second Republic	1848–1852
Napoleon III (Emperor)	1852–1870

909
Arn

Arnold, Guy
Datelines of world
history

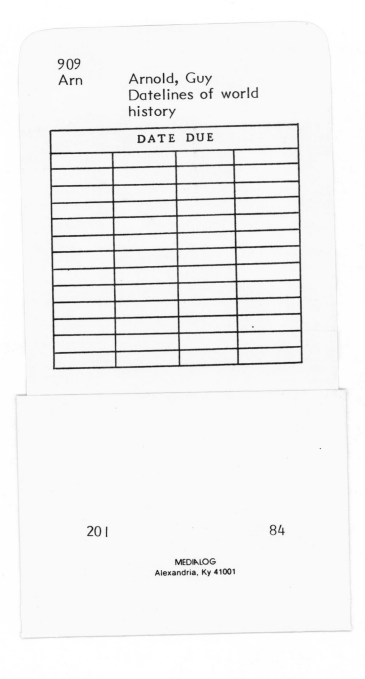

DATE DUE			

201   84

MEDIALOG
Alexandria, Ky 41001